A History of
London's Prisons

TRUE CRIME FROM WHARNCLIFFE

Foul Deeds and Suspicious Deaths Series

OTHER TRUE CRIME BOOKS FROM WHARNCLIFFE

Please contact us via any of the methods below for more information
or a catalogue
WHARNCLIFFE BOOKS
47 Church Street, Barnsley, South Yorkshire, S70 2AS
Tel: 01226 734555 • 734222 • Fax: 01226 734438
email: enquiries@pen-and-sword.co.uk
website: www.wharncliffebooks.co.uk

A HISTORY OF LONDON'S PRISONS

GEOFFREY HOWSE

This book is dedicated to Sister Julia Keane
of Nightingale Ward, Whittington Hospital,
Highgate Hill, London,
for her kindness and compassion

First Published in Great Britain in 2012 by
Wharncliffe Books
an imprint of
Pen and Sword Books Ltd.
47 Church Street
Barnsley
South Yorkshire
S70 2AS

Copyright © Geoffrey Howse 2012

ISBN: 978-1-84563-134-5

Typeset in 11/13pt Plantin by Concept, Huddersfield.

Printed and bound in England by
CPI Group (UK) Ltd, Croydon, CR0 4YY

Pen & Sword Books Ltd incorporates the Imprints of Pen &
Sword Aviation, Pen & Sword Family History, Pen & Sword
Maritime, Pen & Sword Military, Pen & Sword Discovery,
Wharncliffe Local History, Wharncliffe True Crime,
Wharncliffe Transport, Pen & Sword Select, Pen & Sword
Military Classics, Leo Cooper, The Praetorian Press,
Remember When, Seaforth Publishing and
Frontline Publishing.

For a complete list of Pen & Sword titles please contact PEN
& SWORD BOOKS LIMITED
47 Church Street
Barnsley
South Yorkshire
S70 2BR
England
E-mail: enquiries@pen-and-sword.co.uk
Website: www.pen-and-sword.co.uk

Contents

Introduction

It will probably come as no surprise for the reader to learn that London has contained more prisons than any other English city. It has, after all for centuries, been the seat of government and the largest city in the land. In addition to giving historical information concerning London's various penal institutions, I have also endeavoured to give an insight to some of the individuals who found themselves wrapped up within the complexities and intricacies of English law, through the centuries, since the reign of William the Conqueror. In general terms I have covered the area which we today know as London, including, the City of London, the City of Westminster, parts of the County of Middlesex and the area on the south bank of the River Thames, the County of Surrey; for all of which London's prisons were built and grew to serve.

In the Middle Ages, judicial power was vested not only in the king's authority but also extended to the bishops and lords. More often than not each had his own personal place of detention within a palace or castle. In London, however, these powers extended to elected officials who administered their own justice in virtually all cases excepting those involving the gravest of treasons. For both the common and general populace some degree of law and order was established during the reign of Edward 1 (1272–1307) when his majesty instituted the watch, to patrol the streets at night and keep the peace.

The highest in the land were protected by their own retainers who in turn were offered some degree of security in varying degrees down the ranks of the hierarchical structure that existed then; and until at least the 1920s. The watch gradually expanded to safeguard London's interests but it was not until Charles II's reign (1660–85) that this force had a considerable impact on the stability of day-to-day life for the ordinary citizens of London, as well as the highly born. Watchmen took on a more significant role and began to wear a distinctive uniform of greatcoats and leather helmets, they carried lanterns and were protected by bludgeons; they also carried rattles to use in alarm situations. The watch, fortified by local constables, remained London's only major contribution to the protection of the man-in-the-street until the Metropolitan Police Force was established in 1829.

During early times, London had two sheriffs. A Sheriff or 'Shire Reeve' was a county justice, in effect the local representative of the king's law. In 1132, it was granted that London should have two sheriffs, one for London and one for Middlesex, although both posts were in fact held within the City of London itself. The office of sheriff remains important to this day and in London predates that of mayor, which did not become part of London's political and judicial structure until 1192.

Up until well into the nineteenth century, with few exceptions, prisons were not generally intended to hold people for extended periods of time (except in the case of debtors, until 1869). Many criminals were imprisoned whilst awaiting their trials and if found guilty, were generally hanged, shortly afterwards, often for relatively minor offences. Indeed, up until the early years of Victoria's reign (1837–1901) there were no fewer the 204 capital offences. During the eighteenth and nineteenth centuries some prisoners were fortunate, being spared the noose and transported to the colonies instead. There were many debtors incarcerated within several of London's prisons along with their families, many children being born and raised there. In other European countries imprisonment for debt was limited to one year, but in England debtors were imprisoned until their creditors were satisfied. When the Fleet Prison closed in 1842, some debtors had been imprisoned there for as many as thirty years. Prior to the Bankruptcy Act of 1869 which abolished debtors' prisons, both men and women were routinely imprisoned for debt at the whim of their creditors, sometimes for comparatively small amounts and often for decades. With this act imprisonment for debt was finally outlawed in England, except in cases of fraud or refusal to pay. After more than two centuries of lobbying governments, penal reformers have gradually chiselled away at some of the more gruesome aspects of imprisonment. During the twentieth century the concept of imprisonment changed dramatically, with the emphasis placed on the reform and rehabilitation of offenders, a concept which has continued to be developed and modified in the present century.

Acknowledgements

Iris Ackroyd (1925–2012), Victoria Ackroyd, Keith Atack, Vera Atack, Zak Azzouz, Michael Barber, Susan Barber, Peter Beard, Ann Becouarn, Professor John Betteridge, Christine Boyce, Norma Braddick, Fred Calcott, Margaret Calcott, Sister S Choi, Robert A Dale, Kathleen Dale, Chantelle Daniels, Tobie Daniels, Iris J Deller, Joanna C Murray Deller, Ricky S Deller, Tracy P Deller, Emma Duke, Professor Nick Finer, Kristin Finney, Paulette Finney, James Friend, Carol Gardner, Jean Gardner, Alice Gazet, Chris Gill, John Goldfinch, Leo Gonzales, Frederick Griffiths, Leroy Griffith, Rosina Gusterson, Geraldine Healy, Ann Howse, Doreen Howse, Joy Howse, Kathleen Howse, Claire Hunte, Dr Hidayat Hussain, Nishat Hussain, Mr Andrew Jenkinson, Charles Keane, Eamon Keane, Andrew R D Lane, Heather Law, Kevin McGovern, Susan McGovern, Raymond Mellor Jones, Grace L McHenry, Brendan E McNally, Hannah McNally, Jenny McNally, Victoria McNally, Marc Murray, Eleanor Nelder, Stanley Nelder, Anthony Richards, Aydan Sener, Ian Senior, Aishwarya Tara Sethi, Kristina Suberg Sethi, Vichel Sethi, Sofia Sibari, Andre Spence, Christian Spence, Kai Spence, Annie Souter, Debbie Teape, Bob Toh, Breda Toh, Sylvia Toh, Adam R Walker, Anna Walker, Arthur O Walker, Christine Walker, Darren J Walker, David Walker, Emma C Walker Ivan P Walker, Jenny Walker, Paula L Walker, Polly Walker, Suki B Walker, Thomas Walker, Dave Webster, Terry Webster, Clifford Willoughby, Margaret Willoughby, Professor D J Withers; also the staff of the British Library, the staff of the Guildhall Library, the staff of the Metropolitan Archive and the staff of The National Archive at Kew. In addition I am grateful to John D Murray, who has assisted me over many years; and finally, not forgetting my ever-faithful walking companion, Coco.

CHAPTER 1

The Tower of London

The original function of the Tower of London, built for William I (William the Conqueror) and completed in 1097, was to act as a power base for the king within the City of London itself. As well as being a royal palace and serving many other purposes such as housing the Royal Mint and the Crown Jewels, and a garrison, it has also served as a prison and place of execution. The Keep, which became known as the White Tower in the thirteenth century (following its outer walls being painted white), contained dungeons and cells constructed beneath and on its upper floors; as well as in various towers within the precincts and around the outer walls. Each of these towers have been used as prisons at some time during their existence.

The first recorded prisoner in the Tower was Ranulf Flambard, Bishop of Durham, imprisoned in 1101. The Tower has held many notable prisoners over more than 900 years. Six hundred Jews were imprisoned in the Tower by Edward I in 1278, allegedly for being falsely charged with coin-clipping. Two-hundred and sixty were executed and many others died in the Tower dungeons.

Royal prisoners, of which there have been many through the centuries, were usually lodged in considerable style and comfort whilst incarcerated in the Tower. John Baliol, King of the Scots, was imprisoned there in 1296; and in 1356, having been captured during the Battle of Poitiers, King John II of France spent three years in the Tower, until a ransom was paid. The deposed King Henry VI was imprisoned on an upper floor in the Wakefield Tower in 1465. He was restored to the throne in 1470, by the Earl of Warwick, recaptured by Edward IV and murdered in the Wakefield Tower on 21 May 1471. George, Duke of Clarence, a younger brother of Edward IV, was imprisoned in the tower for plotting against his brother, the king, in 1478. By tradition, he was murdered later that year by being drowned in a 'butt of Malmsey'. On Edward IV's death in 1483, his two young sons, Edward V and the Duke of York, were held in the Garden Tower (some years later named the 'Bloody Tower'). Their uncle, the Duke of Gloucester, became Protector and was subsequently proclaimed Richard III. His nephews mysteriously disappeared and were generally believed to have been murdered. The question by whom were the little princes in the Tower murdered, has been a matter of considerable speculation down the centuries. Two of Henry VIII's wives were imprisoned and executed in the Tower. Henry's second wife, Anne Boleyn, was beheaded on Tower Green on 19 May 1536 by a specially imported swordsman from France; and Henry's fifth wife, Katherine Howard, suffered a similar fate by a headsman yielding the customary axe, also on Tower Green, on 13 February 1542. Lady Jane Grey (sometimes referred to as the 'Nine Day Queen'), was held in the Lieutenant's House and her husband, Lord Guildford Dudley, in the Beauchamp Tower, prior to their executions on 12 February 1554. Princess Elizabeth (later Elizabeth I), daughter of Henry VIII and Queen Anne Boleyn were imprisoned in the Tower in 1554, suspected of complicity in plots to usurp her half-sister, Queen Mary I. James Scott Duke of Monmouth (illegitimate son of Charles II and Lucy Walters) was imprisoned in the Tower prior to his execution on Tower Hill on 15 July 1685. Monmouth, having expressed the opinion to his executioner Jack Ketch (or John Catch, after whom London's subsequent executioners were commonly known) that the axe was not sharp enough, suffered a truly horrible end. Ketch swung the axe through the air and dealt Monmouth a blow that caused him only superficial harm. As the duke's head moved under the blow, he gave Ketch a look of disdain. Two more blows of the axe followed but the Duke's head was still attached to his body. Five blows of the axe could not do the job, and finally the duke's head was removed only after the last sinews were cut through with a knife. Curiously, the dead Duke's head was stitched back on his body, not just for his dignified burial under the altar in the church of St Peter Ad Vincula (St Peter in Chains), within the precincts of the Tower (where Henry VIII's two executed queens were also buried), but to be dressed in his finery and his lifeless body posed as if the duke were still alive, to have his portrait painted.

Sir Thomas Overbury (1581–1613), poet and statesman, was the victim of the greatest scandal of James I's court. He was the son of a Gloucestershire landowner. Overbury served as Secretary of State under the Earl of Shrewsbury, who sent him travelling to the Low Countries. Tall, good looking and extremely vain, Overbury possessed a literary talent. His influence increased after he became a friend of Robert Carr, a page to the Earl of Dunbar, whom he met in 1601. They came to London together, and Carr attracted the eye of the king who made him his favourite and created him firstly Viscount Rochester and after Overbury's death, Earl of Southampton. Carr's homosexual relationship with James I is well documented. Some commentators suggest that a homosexual triangle existed between Overbury, Carr and the king. Overbury returned some influence over the far less astute Lord Rochester, who turned to him as a friend and confidante and it was said by many at court that 'Rochester ruled James and Overbury ruled Rochester'. In 1611, Lord Rochester fell in love with the young Countess of Essex, Frances Howard. Her marriage was unconsummated and she wished to obtain a divorce and marry Rochester. Overbury took a dislike to her and was concerned that his influence might be usurped by the powerful Howard family. Overbury enraged the lovers with his opposition to their union and, with the help of the Earl of Northampton, was imprisoned in the Tower on the dubious charge of refusing to go as an ambassador to Russia, as this was contrary to the king's wishes. Frances Howard, it was said by some, dabbled in black magic. Using her influence, through the agency of Sir Gervaise Helwyss, who saw to it that one of her servants, Richard Weston, was employed as Overbury's personal gaoler; he with the assistance of a physician's widow named Anne Turner, and a city apothecary, James Franklin, poisoned Overbury in a slow and ghastly manner, with copper vitriol. Sir Thomas Overbury died in September 1613. Two years passed before the truth came to light. Meanwhile, the lovers had married and Rochester had been created Earl of Southampton. A dying young man who had worked in the Tower spilled the beans and confessed to his part in the poisoning and implicated the others involved. Sir Gervaise Helwyss, Anne Turner, Richard Weston and James Franklin were convicted of murder in November 1615 but not before they had implicated Lord and Lady Somerset. The Somersets were tried before the House of Lords, found guilty and condemned to death. However, the king pardoned them and they were confined in the Tower until 1621.

Sir Walter Raleigh

Sir Walter Raleigh (1552–1618). Courtier, navigator and writer, became a principal favourite of Elizabeth I. He was imprisoned in 1592, for having the audacity to marry one of her Maids of Honour, Bess Throckmorton. Raleigh spent his confinement lodging with his cousin, the Master of the Ordnance, in the Brick Tower, while Bess was given separate accommodation within the Tower but was not permitted to communicate with her husband. The newlyweds spent several weeks incarcerated in the Tower, until the queen's anger subsided and they were set free. When James I succeeded Elizabeth to the throne, Raleigh's enemies turned the king against him, resulting in him being found guilty of treason on spurious charges in 1603 and sentenced to death. The death sentence was commuted to life imprisonment and he remained in the Tower, living in some style with his family and servants. During his imprisonment, among several other works, he wrote his *History of the World* (1614). In 1616 Raleigh made an expedition to the Orinoco in search of a gold mine. The expedition was a failure and on his return to England his death sentence was revoked and he was beheaded on 29 October 1618.

Thomas Wentworth, Earl of Strafford

One of the Tower's most tragic prisoners, executed for political expediency, rather than for being guilty of any offence, was the highly gifted and charismatic statesman Thomas Wentworth, Earl of Strafford (1593–1641), known to history as the Great Earl of Strafford.

Lord Strafford had risen to a position of great eminence and power and had latterly served as Lord Lieutenant of Ireland. He had also becomes Charles I's principal and most trusted adviser, a position which had singled him out as the main target for the king's enemies. Strafford was arguably the most able and gifted statesman of the day, and the king relied heavily on his judgement. With Strafford at his side, Charles I had a greater chance of achieving his aims and of stamping his authority on those who were rallying against him. Those who hoped to restrict the king's authority knew that without Strafford at his side His Majesty would be much easier to deal with. With that end in sight Strafford's enemies impeached him on nine general and twenty-eight specific charges; and he was committed to the Tower on 25 November 1640, having being moved there from the Houses of Parliament by coach.

When Lord Strafford first entered the Tower he occupied the king's apartments, and was allowed the use of the 'royal stuffs'. Strafford commented in a letter to the Earl of Ormonde shortly after his incarceration in the Tower:

I thank God I see nothing capital in their charge, nor any other thing which I am not able to answer as an honest man.

Within a short time of his arrival, His Lordship was moved to write to his wife:

All will be done against me that art and malice can devise ... Yet I am in great inward quietness and a strong belief that God will deliver me out of all these troubles. The more I look into my case, the more hope I have and sure if there be any honour and justice left my life will not be in danger. Therefore hold up your heart, look to the children and your house, let me have your prayers ...

If the scales of justice had been fairly and correctly calibrated Lord Strafford need have indeed had no worries about his deliverance from all his troubles, but as C E Wade, biographer of Strafford's implacable enemy, Pym, commented, 'Strafford had yet to learn what "honour and justice" meant to the hounds of Puritanism in full cry and whipped in by John Pym.'

Strafford's incarceration in the king's apartments irked his enemies in the Commons, so early in December the Lieutenant of the Tower was summoned to Westminster. The Scottish divine and historical writer Robert Baillie (1602–62), himself vehemently opposed to Strafford, wrote in his journal:

... our good kind countriman, the Lieutenant of the Tower, Sir William Balfour, was sent for by the Lower House, and enjoyned to keep his prisoner straite; so he has now got the liberty of 3 rooms, in the outmost of which is a guard.

As well as being confined to three rooms, the other restriction imposed on Lord Strafford's freedom did not appear to cause him too much discomfort. Two guards were placed around the clock in the outer of Strafford's three rooms. His door was locked at night and he was allowed to take exercise only under close supervision. Unperturbed, Lord Strafford promptly ordered new liveries for his servants, selected his seat in the Tower Chapel, and inspected the recently fashioned silver mounted headman's axe without embarrassment or trepidation.

At seven o'clock on Monday 22 March 1641, Strafford came down to Traitor's Gate with Sir William Balfour and took his place in the barge that was to convey him to Westminster. A procession of seven barges propelled by fifty pairs of oars left the Tower on route to the quay at Westminster. On arrival there Strafford walked between a double row of 200 picked men of the London bands to Westminster Hall, where his trial was to begin that morning. The usual formality of carrying the axe before the prisoner was dispensed with, for as Black Rod pointed out to Sir William Balfour, not only had the king expressly forbidden this grim bit of pageantry but that it was against precedent unless the accused was already an attainted traitor. Strafford acted as his own defence, and conducted the entire proceedings with great skill. His powers of reasoning, intellectual prowess, considerable knowledge of legal matters and fine oratory skills were all put to the test, and his defence was masterly. There was nothing treasonable in the charges against him, although it was on a charge of high treason that his enemies wished to see him brought down. He stood his ground and by 10 April it was clear that a guilty verdict could not be brought. However, his enemies were not satisfied. Conventional means had failed to bring him down but there was another course and Strafford's enemies were determined to take it. Irrespective of any evidence of commission of a crime, an individual could be found guilty by Act of Parliament. Known as an Act of Attainder, it was a procedure seldom adopted to bring down a minister of the Crown and had not been used for 240 years. So long as the Attainder was endorsed by the king an individual could be automatically found guilty of any charge mentioned on the document itself. As the Parliamentarians crowded out of Westminster Hall, one of them, Sir Arthur Hazelrig, a friend and associate of John Pym, was carrying in his pocket a scroll that contained the substance of the charges against Strafford, already in the form of a Bill of Attainder. Chillingly, it included the charge of high treason.

The king wrote to Strafford on 23 April, two days after the Attainder had been passed in the House of Commons:

Strafford,

The misfortune that is fallen upon you by the strange mistaking and conjecture of these Times being such that I must lay by the thought of employing you hereafter in my affairs; yet I cannot satisfy myself in Honour or Conscience, without assuring you (now in the midst of your troubles) that, upon the word of a King, you shall not suffer in Life, Honour or Fortune: This is but Justice and therefore a very mean reward from a Maister to so faithful and able a Servant as you have showed yourself to be; yet it is as much as I conceive the present times will permit, though none shall hinder me from being – Yr. constant faithful friend, CHARLES R.

The bill received its first reading in the House of Lords on 26 April and was read again on 27 April. Riots, threats, abuse and general social unrest stirred up by the Puritans were the order of the day, as

Pym and his cronies strived to bring about Strafford's end. Timidity prevailed in the Lords. The whole bench of bishops took it upon themselves to decide they were disqualified from voting. On 8 May, the bill was finally put to the vote. Only forty-eight of the 147 peers entitled to vote took their seats. The Bill of Attainder was passed by thirty-seven votes to eleven. Now only the King stood in its way and His Majesty had repeatedly stated throughout the proceedings that he would refuse to sign it. However, Pym had contrived to bring pressure from every quarter and on Sunday 9 May the mob stormed Whitehall Palace and threats were made against the lives of the queen and other members of the royal family. The Constable of the Tower, Lord Newport, declared he would have his prisoner killed if the king refused to sign Strafford's Attainder. At nine o'clock in the evening the king yielded. With tears in his eyes he told the Council that next morning he would affix his signature to the death warrant, before adding, 'If my own person only were in danger I would gladly venture it to save Lord Strafford's life; but seeing my wife, children, and all my kingdom are concerned in it, I am forced to give way unto it.'

Late on that same Sunday, Sir Dudley Carleton arrived at the Tower to convey the news to Strafford. At first Strafford looked at Sir Dudley in disbelief that he was the herald of death and asked him to repeat the message. Having paused for a few moments Strafford arose from his chair, and standing up, lifted his eyes to heaven, and, placing his right hand over his heart, said, 'Put not your trust in Princes, nor in the sons of men, for in them there is no salvation.' Now all was over and Strafford's enervating life quickened towards its last crescendo. The Act of Attainder provided that as a traitor he should be hanged, drawn and quartered. However, Strafford's death was all his enemies wanted and no one talked of enforcing the law to its full brutal extent. Even his enemies, it seems, possessed some scruples and were content to see him beheaded.

On Wednesday 12 May 1641, a crowd estimated to comprise 200,000 souls, gathered on and in the vicinity of Tower Hill. Special stands were hurriedly erected to afford the assembly a better view of the scaffold. During the proceedings a terrible accident occurred when one of the stands collapsed and sixteen people were killed and large numbers seriously injured. At eleven o'clock, Sir William Balfour came to see if the prisoner was ready. Dressed in black, as was his custom, the prisoner, Thomas Wentworth, was calmly waiting with his two chaplains. Balfour, afraid that the mob would tear Wentworth to pieces, advised him to send for his coach. Wentworth declined, saying, 'No. I would sooner look death in the face and I hope the people too; I care not how I die whether by the hand of the executioner or by the madness and fury of the people; if that may give them better content it is all one to me.' As the prisoner and the execution party of officials and friends walked to Tower Hill, they passed the window of Wentworth's fellow-prisoner Archbishop Laud, his friend and ally, who was shortly to suffer a similar fate. Wentworth knelt down and said 'Your prayers and your blessing.' Laud held out his hand, but was overcome with grief and fainted. As Wentworth continued on his journey he called out 'Farewell my Lord; God protect your innocency.'

As the party made their way through the gates, a narrow pathway cleared. Wentworth was saluted by some people in the crowd and he walked with dignity, hat in hand, acknowledging the courtesies extended to him. Some commented afterwards that he walked like a great general marching to victory. On the scaffold he made several speeches. He addressed the crowd, asking them, when the times changed, to judge him by his actions. Some more speeches followed until in due course Wentworth took off his doublet and said 'I thank God I am no more afraid of death, nor haunted with any discouragements arising from my fears, but do as cheerfully put off my doublet at this time as ever I did when I went to bed.' Putting on a white cap, he asked, 'Where is the man that shall do this last office?' The executioner, Richard Brandon, stepped forward to ask his forgiveness, and Wentworth replied, 'I forgive you and all the world.' After refusing a blindfold with the words 'Nay, for I will see it done,' he knelt in prayer for a few moments with the Bishop of Armagh on one side and the minister on the other. After first trying out the block, he finally laid his head down for the last time, and Brandon severed it from his body with a single stroke. The dripping head was held up by Brandon with the words, 'God save the King.' Horseman rode out from all four corners of the scaffold to be first to spread the news, calling out 'His head is off! His head is off!' Sometime during the afternoon Strafford's head and body were washed, embalmed and prepared for their coffin and amid great secrecy spirited out of the Tower and transported to his estate at Wentworth in Yorkshire, where they were buried in the family chapel within Holy Trinity Church.

Other Notable Tower Prisoners
William Laud, Archbishop of Canterbury, was in fact imprisoned in the tower from 1641, until his execution on Tower Hill on 10 January 1645.

The notorious Judge Jeffreys (George Jeffreys (1648–89), Lord Chief Justice was imprisoned in the Tower in 1688, at his own request, for fear of being lynched by the mob. Ill and believed to be suffering from cancer, his health deteriorated rapidly and he died there on 18 April 1689, having spent his last weeks unable to eat hardly anything other than poached eggs.

Many of the leaders of the Jacobite Rebellion of 1745, were held in the Tower prior to their execution on Tower Hill, including Simon Fraser (12th Baron Lovat).

Lord Lovat was eighty years old when he was executed on Tower Hill on 9 April 1747. A similar tragedy occurred at his execution to that of Lord Strafford's in 1641. A stand collapsed killing twenty spectators. Lord Lovat had the dubious honour of being the last nobleman to be beheaded on Tower Hill.

Arthur Thistlewood and the ringleaders of the Cato Street Conspiracy were imprisoned in the Tower as State prisoners in 1820 (see pages 56–8).

Sir Roger Casement was imprisoned in the Tower in 1916, prior to his trial for treason and subsequent execution at Pentonville, as was William Joyce ('Lord Haw Haw'), in 1945, awaiting execution for treason.

Adolph Hitler's deputy, Rudolph Hess, was held in the Tower, on Winston Churchill's orders, in May 1941, when Churchill instructed that Hess was to be treated in a 'dignified manner'.

Among the last prisoners to be held in the Tower were the notorious gangster brothers, the Kray Twins. Ronald and Reginald Kray were serving in the Royal Fusiliers during their National Service. Being absent without leave, they were spotted by a policeman, whom they assaulted as he attempted to arrest them. They were subsequently imprisoned in the Tower, before being taken to a military prison.

CHAPTER 2

Newgate

There is very little evidence to tell us what the original prison at Newgate was actually like. It is known that Newgate was formed out of one of the western gates of the City of London, being part and parcel of the city's Roman London Wall fortifications and its original main function was that of defence. Various accounts suggest that Newgate was rebuilt or formed out of a gate known as Chamberlain's Gate, so called because the Lord Chamberlain's Court once held sway in nearby Old Bailey. Opinions differ concerning the origins of the 'New Gate' itself. However, whatever its actual origins might have been, its name seems to indicate it was either a modified previous gate, a gate built as a replacement for one that had been demolished, or possibly even a completely new gate formed out of a gap created in the Roman London Wall. In many places elsewhere throughout England, the use of the word gate does not in actuality mean a gate or gateway to anything in particular, as more often than not the use of the word gate has its origins in the Danish word '*gata*', which simply means street. London's gates, however, have since time immemorial been actual gates.

Prison accommodation was first provided at Newgate in 1188, on the orders of Henry II, and as was the general practice at that time and throughout the medieval period, the prison was above the gate itself or in the gate-house, or indeed, both. Records during the reign of King John (1199–1216) mention Newgate as a gaol or prison for felons and trespassers.

In 1218, John's son and successor, Henry III (reigned 1216–72), commanded the sheriffs of London to repair Newgate, giving an undertaking to reimburse them for their outlay from his own exchequer; a fact that has given rise to the belief that Newgate was at this time under the direct control of the king.

Only passing references to Newgate in early times exist. Ancient chroniclers indicate Newgate was for centuries a densely-crowded, noisome, dark, pestiferous den, perpetually ravaged by deadly diseases.

Operated as a prison for the City of London and Middlesex, Newgate fell under the auspices of the Sheriffs who appointed the Keeper of the Prison (usually offered to the highest bidder for the office, as like London's other gaols, Newgate was run by the keeper for profit). It was common practice for keepers and the gaolers under them to abuse, ill-treat and even torture prisoners, as well as robbing them of their money and possessions.

During Edward I's reign (1272–1307), when there was little security in London's streets for life or property, particularly during the hours of darkness, a brother of Earl Ferrers was slain. The king, on hearing this, swore that he 'would be avenged on the citizens'. Records show that in the city 'an hundred or more in company of young and old to make nightly invasions upon the houses of the wealthy, to the intent to rob them, and if they found any man stirring in the city they would presently murder him, insomuch that when night was come no man durst adventure to walk in the streets'. Matters grew worse until 'a party of citizens young and wealthy, not mere rogues' attacked the storehouse of a certain rich man and broke through the wall. However, 'the good man of the house' was prepared for such an eventuality and, suspecting an attack was imminent, lay in wait for them 'in a corner' and saw they were led by one Andrew Bucquinte, who 'carried a burning brand in one hand and a pot of coals in the other, which he essayed to kindle with the brand'. Upon this the master, 'crying "Thieves!" rushed at Bucquinte and smote off his right hand.' Excepting Bucquinte, the other members of the marauding mob fled the scene. Next morning Bucquinte was taken before the king's justice, Richard de Lucy, whereupon the thief turned informer, and 'appeached [sic] his confedarates [sic], of whom many were taken and many were fled'. One of those apprehended was a citizen 'of great countenance, credit, and wealth, named John Senex, or John the Old, who, when he could not acquit himself by the water dome, offered the king 500 marks for his acquittal, but the king commanded that he should be hanged, which was done, and the city became quieter'.

Newgate was used to incarcerate persons of high rank long before the Tower of London was used for that purpose. During the reign of Edward II (1307–27), the Chancellor, Robert de Baldock, to whom many of the miseries then afflicting the kingdom were attributed, was dragged to Newgate by an angry mob, 'but the unmerciful treatment he had met with on the way occasioned him to die there within a few days in great torment from the blows which had been inflicted on him'. In 1414, the Keeper of Newgate, as well as sixty-four inmates, died of plague.

In 1423 Newgate was rebuilt under the terms of the will of the former Lord Mayor, Sir Richard Whittington (*c.* 1358–1423), English merchant, city alderman and sheriff; and thrice Lord Mayor of London (1397–9, 1406–7 and 1419–20). This new prison stood five storeys high and included among its facilities a dining room for the prisoners. It was a curiously ornamental prison, decorated with crenulated towers and statues, with a wide central arch for vehicles and a smaller flanking entrance for foot passengers. Newgate gradually expanded to incorporate adjoining buildings. The practice of abusing and robbing prisoners continued and in 1449, the keeper, one William Arnold, was himself imprisoned for raping a female prisoner.

In 1457, Sir Thomas Percie and Lord Egremont are recorded as being inmates at Newgate. In 1539, during the reign of Henry VIII (1509–47), ten friars of the Charterhouse were sent to Newgate for refusing to sign the Oath of Supremecy. Nine died of gaol fever and filth, the tenth, William Horn, was transferred to the Tower, where he was kept for three years until his execution at Tyburn. Later that century many other Catholic and Protestant martyrs were incarcerated at Newgate.

Towards the end of the fifteenth century, one of England's finest dramatists who was also a convicted murderer, found himself imprisoned within Newgate's walls. Red-headed Ben Jonson (1572–1637), the posthumous son of a clergyman, was educated at Westminster School and for a brief period worked in his stepfather's trade as a bricklayer. He joined the Army and served in Flanders, returning to England in 1592. In 1594 he married Anne Lewis and about 1597 joined a theatrical company owned by Philip Henslowe as actor and playwright. In September 1598, Jonson's play *Every Man in his Humour* was being successfully performed at the Curtain Theatre in Shoreditch. On 22 September, Jonson fought a duel in the fields near the theatre with an important actor in the Admiral's Company, Gabriel Spencer. Spencer possessed a vicious and ungovernable temper and less than two years before had quarrelled with a goldsmith's son in Shoreditch. When the boy picked up a candlestick and threatened to throw it at Spencer, the latter lunged at him with a sword still sheathed in its scabbard, which pierced his head just above the right eye. The boy died three days later. Exactly what the quarrel was between Jonson and Spencer is not known, as the report of the coroner's inquest is missing. Jonson was injured in the arm by Spencer's rapier but he managed to run in under Spencer's guard and pierce his side, which

killed the actor instantly. Jonson was taken before the nearest Justice
of the Peace and imprisoned in Newgate charged with murder, an
offence for which bail could not be granted. Fortunately for Jonson,
he was to spend a shorter time at Newgate than his previous stay in
prison at the Marshalsea, where he had been imprisoned in 1597 for
collaborating and acting in Tom Nashe's play *The Isle of Dogs,* which
the Privy Council regarded as being seditious and highly slanderous.
He appeared before the next sessions on 6 October in the open air
court held in the street called Old Bailey that ran by the prison
(in years gone by trials had been held in Newgate itself but the fear of
the judges and officials catching gaol fever resulted in trials being held
in the open air). The jury having considered Jonson's case decided
that:

> The aforesaid Benjamin Johnson [sic] feloniously and willfully
> [sic] slew and killed the aforesaid Gabriel Spencer at Shoreditch
> aforesaid.

Jonson promptly pleaded *benefit of clergy* as soon as the verdict had
been handed down.

Benefit of clergy was a medieval privilege originally applied to the
exemption of christian clerics from secular courts and it extended only
to the commission of felonies. In the process of time a much wider
comprehensive criterion was established. Benefit of clergy could be
claimed by anyone who could read a passage from the Bible. In some
cases even those who were unable to read could satisfy the criterion if
they were taught by a literate person to memorise a passage, and in
doing so could automatically claim benefit of clergy. Benefit of clergy
had its origins in Psalm 51:

> Have mercy upon me, O God, after thy great goodness: according
> unto the multitude of thy tender mercies blot out my transgressions.

Henry VII decreed that non-clergymen could only claim benefit
of clergy once. In 1512 he further restricted benefit of clergy by
removing certain offences as being 'unclergyable'. In 1547, the
privilege of claiming benefit of clergy more than once was extended
to peers of the realm. The ecclesiastical courts lost their jurisdiction
over all criminal matters in 1576 and under statute law were either,
discharged, branded on the thumb or sentenced to one year's imprisonment. With the decrease in capital offences in all but the most serious

cases, benefit of clergy was abolished in 1827, it being deemed to be no longer necessary.

The bishop's representative present in court gave Johnson a psalter. Jonson was allowed to choose his own passage for what was commonly known as the 'neck verse'. In accordance with ancient tradition, the judge asked if he had read it like a clerk, '*Legit ut clericus?*'; the reply came from the bishop's representative, '*Legit.*' With those words the shadow of the hangman's noose at Tyburn had been lifted. To ensure that he could not plead benefit of clergy a second time he was immediately branded with a letter M on the base of the left thumb and, after paying the jailer's fees, Jonson was allowed to leave prison.

Newgate was badly damaged in the Great Fire of London, which raged for three days in September 1666, destroying 13,200 homes, ninety-three churches, St Paul's Cathedral and thousands of other buildings in its wake. Some of Newgate's buildings were soon back in service but a massive rebuilding programme was undertaken, the work not being entirely completed until 1672. As building work continued, Newgate remained a place of imprisonment and in 1669, Stephen Eaton, George Roades and Sarah Swift, found themselves within its walls.

The Reverend John Talbot had been chaplain to a regiment in Portugal before he returned to London, where he preached for three months at St Alphage in the Wall. He then became curate at Laindon in Essex, where he was involved in a lawsuit with several parishioners, on account of which he returned to London. A group of friends became acquainted with this curate and believing him to be a man of fortune decided to waylay, rob and murder him. On Friday night, 2 July 1669, Talbot was followed to Gray's Inn by Stephen Eaton, a confectioner, George Roades, a broker, Henry Pritchard, a tailor and Sarah Swift, who might reasonably be described as an opportunist; and according to Talbot, at least two others, who remain unknown. The clergyman felt ill at ease at being followed, for what purpose he had no idea. He spent some time writing letters and after taking a little refreshment, assuming the danger to be over, took the back way home, through Old Street and over the fields to Shoreditch. It was at about eleven o'clock that he was seized by his pursuers, who began to pick his pockets. They took about twenty shillings and also his knife with which they attempted to kill him by cutting his throat. They first cut out a piece of flesh from his throat without touching the windpipe, then stabbed him so deep that the point almost reached his lungs.

However, they did not sever any nerves, which would have prevented him speaking; and having stripped him of his coat and doublet, fled the scene. Talbot was given assistance by some nearby brickmakers and the Watch at Shoreditch was summoned. He received medical attention from a surgeon, Mr Litchfield, and it appeared he might recover. Other physicians also attended him free of charge. Four of the culprits were quickly apprehended and identified by Talbot and taken to Newgate. The Reverend John Talbot died on Monday 11 July, as a result of the injuries he received in the attack, after a violent fit of coughing seized him and broke his jugular vein. The four culprits were tried at the next sessions at the Old Bailey, where they were all found guilty of murder and sentenced to death. Henry Pritchard received a pardon upon some favourable circumstances that were produced. On Wednesday 14 July 1669, Stephen Eaton, George Roades and Sara Swift were taken in a cart from Newgate to the dreaded triple tree at Tyburn, where they were hanged. The two men confessed but Sarah Swift remained obstinate to the last.

In 1670, Newgate played host to one of its most celebrated prisoners. Although others might legitimately lay claim to greater notoriety or even infamy, there was certainly one who can lay claim to being the most dashing of his genre. One January night in 1670, Claude Duval (or Du Vall), that most glamorous of gentlemen of the road, as some would have it, more commonly known as highwaymen, was arrested in the Hole-in-the-Wall public house (now The Marquis of Granby). The pub was established in 1638, on the corner of Chandos Place and Bedfordbury, a narrow thoroughfare, running south to north and sandwiched between the Strand and New Row, Covent Garden. Unwisely, Duval had ventured back to England, where he had taken refuge when things became too hot for him. There was still a price on his head, and when he reached London, brimming with over-confidence, he let his guard slip. Prone to heavy indulgence in wine, women and song, on the night of his arrest, he became outrageously drunk and completely incapacitated, which was fortunate for the bailiff and his men who arrested him, for as well as three pistols in his pocket, one of which could shoot twice, he had an 'excellent sword' by his side. One commentator wrote about Duval's armed expertise:

> ... which, managed by such a hand and heart, must without a doubt, have done wonders ... I have heard it attested by those

that knew how good a marksman he was, and his excellent way of fencing, that had he been sober, it was impossible he could have killed less than ten.

Born at Domfront in Normandy in 1643, the son of a miller, Claude Duval went to Rouen, when he was fourteen and found work with a group of exiled English royalists. He came to England at the Restoration in the service of the third Duke of Richmond, as a footman, and he developed a good command of English. However, he did not remain a footman for long. Duval had developed a taste for fine clothes and high living. Following daring robberies in Highgate, Islington and Holloway, and one exploit which led to a road being named Duval Lane, Hampstead (now Platt's Lane), his name soon became synonymous with highway robbery. He sometimes worked with a gang but many of his legendary exploits seemed to have occurred largely when he was working alone. Regarded as a true knight of the road, he was certainly most charming, to both male and female victims. He dressed fashionably, sometimes flamboyantly so, was courteous in both speech and manner and it was said that his Gallic flourish made him particularly attractive to the ladies. Despite his charms, like many other more ruthless highwaymen, Duval was not averse to relieving his victims of large sums of money, jewels and trinkets, whenever the opportunity presented itself, although he concluded the proceedings in his own inimitable way, which endeared him to some of his victims. Duval was also a highly dextrous cardsharp and won considerable sums by 'slipping a card'. It was said of him at gaming he was so expert that few men in his age were able to compete with him. No man living could slip a card more dextrously than he, nor better understood the advantages that could be taken of an adversary; yet to appearance, no man played fairer.

In 1668, Duval's name headed a list of highwaymen mentioned in a Royal Proclamation, which offered £20 for his capture. Duval's charming manners and good looks are reputed to have given him many amorous conquests, ranging from serving girls to respectable widows; and sometimes whores and often ladies of high rank. Following his arrest he was taken to Newgate, tried, convicted and sentenced to death. During his incarceration he was visited by many noble ladies. Despite their pleas for clemency, at the express command of the king, Duval was not pardoned.

Claude Duval was twenty-seven years old when he was executed at Tyburn on Friday 21 January 1670 and was accompanied to the scaffold by many ladies of high rank, who wore masks to disguise their identities. In *Tyburn Tree Its History and Annals*, a work which draws on many old documents, Alfred Marks records:

> After he had hanged a convenient time, he was cut down, and, by persons well dressed, carried into a mourning coach, and so conveyed to the Tangier-tavern in St. Giles, where he lay in state all that night, the room hung with black cloth, the hearse covered with escutcheons, eight wax-tapers burning, and as many tall gentlemen with long black cloakes [sic] attending; mum was the word, great silence expected from all that visited, for fear of disturbing this sleeping lion. And this ceremony had lasted much longer, had not one of the judges (whose name I must not mention here, lest he should incur the displeasure of the ladies) sent to disturb the pageantry.

Dr William Pope, who wrote the biography, *Memoirs of Monsieur Du Vall*, in 1670 (from which most of what has since been written about Duval seems to derive), claimed that Duval left behind a 'dying confession' that he had intended to read at Tyburn, but changed his mind.

Duval was given a fine funeral at St Paul's church, Covent Garden and according to popular legend, was buried in the chancel and a white marble stone laid over the site of his tomb. It bore his family's arms, under which was engraved the epitaph:

> *Here lies Duval: reader, if male thou art,*
> *Look to thy purse: if female, to thy heart.*
> *Much havoc hath he made of both: for all.*
> *Men he made stand, and women he made fall.*
> *The second Conqueror of the Norman race,*
> *Knights to his arms die yield, and ladies to his face.*
> *Old Tyburn's glory, England's bravest thief:*
> *Duval, the ladies' joy: Duval, the ladies' grief.*

Like other monuments to those who were buried within St Paul's church, Covent Garden during the seventeenth and most of the eighteenth century, that of Claude Duval was probably destroyed in the fire that wreaked havoc in the church in 1795. However, despite the tradition that Duval was buried there, there is no reference in the burial records at St Paul's to not verify this. Today, at 39 Bedfordbury, close to the place of Duval's arrest, stands a block of flats named Duval Court.

Twelve years after Duval had breathed his last, three individuals of foreign birth rocked London society by a particularly violent act, instigated at the behest of another foreigner, Count Coningsmark, they were Vratz, Stern and Barosky.

Captain Christopher Vratz (some accounts spell the name Urats, others Vrats) was born in Pomerania (a small kingdom adjoining Poland) and although of good birth was a man of little fortune. He became a highwayman and once held up the King of Poland, during the Seige of Vienna, robbing him and his attendants of many diamonds and a considerable quantity of gold. He also committed robberies in Hungary after which time he bought himself a commission in the Emperor of Germany's service, where he became acquainted with the Swedish Count Coningsmark, with whom he came over to England. The Count having been thwarted in his advances to a certain Lady Ogle by one Thomas Thynn, Esquire, decided nothing would satisfy him but the death of his rival. The count allegedly requested thirty-eight-year-old Vratz to carry out the killing. Captain Vratz enlisted the assistance of John Stern, a lieutenant, who was the illegitimate son of a Swedish baron, afterwards made a count and George Barosky, who was Polish. A little after eight o'clock on the night of Sunday 12 February 1681, Thomas Thynn, having visited the Countess of Northumberland and only shortly before been accompanied by the Duke of Monmouth, was riding in his coach up to St James's Street, when Barosky fired a blunderbuss at him. Five bullets tore into his guts, wounded his liver, stomach and gall bladder and broke one of his ribs, of which wounds he died. Vratz, Stern and Barosky were arrested the next day by Sir John Raresby and brought before Justice Bridgman, who committed them to Newgate. Count Coningsmark attempted to leave the country but was found at Gravesend disguised and about to board a ship for Sweden. He was brought back to London and taken before the king and counsel but confessed nothing to either being privy to or concerned in the murder. Vratz, Stern and Barosky were tried at the Old Bailey on Tuesday 28 February before Lord Chief Justice Pemberton. All three were found guilty of murder. Count Coningsmark was acquitted as not being an accessory by the same jury. Vratz, Stern and Barosky were hanged in Pall Mall on Friday 10 March 1682. Barosky was afterwards hung in chains near Mile End at the express command of King Charles II. The diarist, John Evelyn wrote:

March 24 1682. – I went to see the corpse of that obstinate creature Colonel [sic] Vrats [sic], the king permitting that his body should be transported to his own country, he being of a good family, and one of the first embalmed by a particular art, invented by one William Russell, a coffin-maker, which preserved the body without disbowelling [sic] or to appearance using any bituminous matter. The flesh was florid, soft, and full, as if the person were only sleeping. He had now been dead near fifteen days, and lay exposed in a very rich coffin lined with lead, too magnificent for so daring and horrid a murderer.

Another of Newgate's inmates was Tom Kelsey. Born in Leather Lane, Holborn, Tom Kelsey in early childhood went to live in Wales where his mother had inherited a small estate. Aged fourteen, he returned to London to seek his fortune and fell in with bad company, mostly thieves, and within a short time Tom was as bold and dextrous as the best of them. He became involved in some daring robberies but before he had reached the age of sixteen had been condemned to be hanged for stealing a large quantity of silver and £40 from a grocer in the Strand. He got off on account of his youth and at the intervention of his aged father, who upon hearing of his son's sentence, came up to London and procured a full pardon on the day before the appointed execution by enlisting the help of some powerful friends. Tom was apprenticed to a weaver in the hope that he would mend his ways but he simply took to tutoring other young would-be thieves, one of his more promising pupils soon being hanged. Tom robbed the Earl of Feversham's lodgings and got away with £200 worth of silver plate. He also robbed Lady Grace Pierpont and disposed of his ill-gotten gains to a Jew in Amsterdam. He then robbed the Jew and sold the booty to another Jew in Rotterdam, after which he returned to England. Not long afterwards, he was caught breaking into a house in Cheapside. He was sent to Newgate where he was given no hope of ever being released. He resolved to do all mischief he could there. This culminated in him stabbing one of the turnkeys, a Mr Goodman, in the belly. He instantly died and his murderer was convicted at the Old Bailey. Tom Kelsey was hanged on Friday 13 June 1690 on an especially erected gibbet, close to the prison in Newgate Street, 'being no more than twenty years of age. As a terror to the other prisoners who were then in confinement, his body was suffered to hang on the gibbet the space of three hours.'

As the seventeenth century turned into the eighteenth, yet another murder became part of the Chronicles of Newgate. All three murderers in the case were born in Holland. In 1700, Michael Van Berghens and his wife, Catherine ran a public house in East Smithfield. Apart from their bar staff, the Van Berghens were attended by a servant, Geraldius Dromelius. One evening a gentleman named Oliver Norris was drinking in the Van Berghens' house from about eight o'clock in the evening until after eleven. He became extremely intoxicated and asked a maid servant to procure a coach to take him to his lodgings at an inn in Aldgate. No coach could be found, so Norris set off home on foot. On finding his purse was missing he returned to the Van Berghens and accused them of stealing it. Dromelius joined in as tempers became severely heated and Mr Van Berghens seized a poker and struck Norris on the head, fracturing his skull. Dromelius stabbed Norris in several parts of the body, while Mrs Van Berghen looked on. She then helped the two men to strip Norris of his hat, wig, and waistcoat, after which the body was carried to a nearby ditch which drained into the River Thames. While the Van Bergens cleaned up the blood Dromelius took the clothes in a hamper to dispose of at Rotherhithe, where he took lodgings on anticipation of securing a passage to Holland at the first opportunity. The next morning, the body of Oliver Norris was found at low tide. Someone had seen Van Berghens and Dromelius near the spot the night before. A search was made at the Van Berghens but apart from a few bloodstains, little else was found. Suspicion was aroused when the Van Berghens could give no satisfactory explanation for Dromelius having left their service. The maid servant provided crucial evidence against them when she said her mistress had told her to tell Mr Norris that she could not find a coach for him. Dromelius was taken into custody at Rotherhithe and all three were taken to Newgate and tried at the next Old Bailey sessions. They were executed near the Hartshorn Brewhouse, East Smithfield, on 10 July 1700. The bodies of Michael Van Bergens and Geraldius Dromelius were afterwards hanged in chains between Bow and Mile End. Catherine Van Burgens was buried.

In November 1700, Sir Andrew Slanning was in the company of John Cowland and several other gentlemen at the Theatre Royal, Drury Lane, when he arranged an assignation with a willing 'orange-woman'. She accompanied Sir Andrew and the other gentlemen from the theatre as soon as the play was over. When Mr Cowland put his arm around the woman's neck, Sir Andrew asked him not to do that, as she was his wife. Mr Cowland knowing otherwise wanted the woman for himself and began to quarrel. Swords were drawn but were soon put up again. The party then went to the Rose Tavern, where Captain Waggett attempted to reconcile the two men. As they were going upstairs to take a glass of wine. Cowland drew his sword and stabbed Sir Andrew in the back. Sir Andrew called out: 'Murder!' One of Lord Warwick's servants disarmed Cowland, whose sword was smeared with Sir Andrew's blood to a depth of five inches. Cowland was taken as he tried to flee the scene. Sir Andrew was dead within minutes. Incarcerated in Newgate, John Cowland was tried at the Old Bailey on 5 December and executed at Tyburn on 20 December 1700.

German-born Herman Strodtman came to London in 1694 along with a school friend, Peter Wolter, to be apprenticed to city firm Stein & Dorien. They lodged together and were diligent in their work. In 1701, after Wolter's sister made an advantageous marriage, he assumed an air of superiority over Strodtman which he resented. Such was the rift between the two former friends that they began to fight. Wolter struck Strodtman twice, once in the counting-house, another time in the kitchen before the servant-girls. Dislike turned to hatred and Strodtman resolved to murder Wolter. He first tried to poison him by mixing mercury with some white powder Wolter used as a remedy for scurvy, but Wolter had ceased to use the powder at that particular time. Matters came to a head over the Easter period. One night while Wolter was asleep, Strodtman entered the room and hit him on the head. He then stabbed him several times before finishing him off by suffocating him with a pillow. He stole some money, about £8 in cash, from the counting-house and was apprehended when he tried to cash a bill for £20 from his employers at a bankers in Lombard Street. He was taken to Newgate and tried at the Old Bailey in the second sessions following. He died full of contrition, penitence and hope. As he was hanged at Tyburn on 17 June 1701, it was remarked that he kept his hand up for a considerable time after the cart was driven away.

On 2 August 1707, William Elby, along with an unknown accomplice, broke into the house of James Barry at Fulham, intending to burgle it. Mr Barry heard a noise in the house sometime after midnight and went to investigate along with his wife and servant Nicholas Hatfield. They found a window had been broken open and saw two men outside. As Mr and Mrs Barry ran upstairs to arm themselves, Hatfield, on stepping into the kitchen, was met by Elby, who drove him into the pantry and stabbed him in the breast. He died twelve hours later. During the scuffle the other thief had fired a pistol that had wounded Elby in the leg, which led to him being quickly apprehended as he tried to flee. The accomplice got clean away. Elby was imprisoned at Newgate and tried at the Old Bailey sessions. As he received sentence of death, Elby called out: 'God damn you all!' He was hanged at Fulham on 13 September 1707.

Twenty-three-year-old Will Lowther (also see page 86), born in Whitehaven, Cumbria, had spent ten years at sea, latterly as master on a collier given to him by his father, which traded between Newcastle and London. He was seduced by the seedier elements of London's docks and took to robbing ships as they lay at anchor. He also indulged in petty thieving elsewhere in the capital, whenever the opportunity arose. He struck up a friendship with another thief, Dick Keele, with whom he was apprehended in the act of stealing and incarcerated in Clerkenwell Bridewell. There, they caused a riot, during which Edward Perry, a servant to Mr Boreman, the keeper, was killed. Moved to Newgate, Lowther and Keele were found guilty of murder at the Old Bailey and hanged on Clerkenwell Green on 23 December 1713.

Notable inmates of old Newgate

Johnson and Housden, 1714
Butcher William Johnson moved from his native Northampton to open a shop at Newport Market, which was not the success he had hoped for. He made several other business speculations before going to Gibraltar and, having made a little money there, returned to England and promptly spent it. He then took to highway robbery. Apprehended at one such robbery, he was convicted and pardoned. His accomplice in crime, Jane Housden, who had been convicted of coining, was also pardoned. In 1714, Jane found herself charged with the same offence and incarcerated in Newgate. At her trial at the Old Bailey, just as she was being brought down to the bar, Johnson called to see her. On being told by Mr Spurling, the head turnkey, that he could not speak to her until the trial was over, Johnson drew a pistol and shot Spurling dead on the spot, all the time being encouraged by Jane Housden, in the presence of the Court. The judges were of the opinion that it was unnecessary to continue with the trial for Housden's coining and ordered both parties to be immediately tried for murder. Both were duly convicted and sentenced to death. They were hanged on 19 September 1714. Johnson's body was hanged in chains at Holloway, between Islington and Highgate.

The Marquis De Paleotti, 1718
The Marquis De Paleotti was an Italian nobleman born at Bologna, who came over to England following the Peace of Utrecht, after serving in the Imperial Army. He led an extravagant lifestyle and spent

a good deal of his time at the gaming tables, running up debts for considerable sums. After spending his own money, he was constantly bailed out of trouble by his wealthy widowed sister, the Duchess of Shrewsbury. She grew tired of his constant requests for money and eventually refused to support his gambling. The marquis habitually sent his servant out to borrow money for him but as his debts increased the task of procuring funds for his master was an onerous one and one day the servant declined to go, at which point the marquis drew his sword and killed him. The marquis was immediately arrested and committed to Newgate. On being tried at the next sessions, his sister having little interest or few acquaintances in England, no efforts were made to save him from the gallows. De Paleotti was hanged at Tyburn on 17 March 1718.

John Price, 1718

John Price was born in Soho in about 1677. His father, a soldier, was killed in Tangier in 1684. As a boy Price was apprenticed to a rag merchant but after two years ran away and eventually served in the navy in various men-of-war for the next eighteen years. Shortly after his discharge in 1714, through the contacts of his wife, Betty, employed at Newgate in the capacity of a run-around (procuring goods and services from those prisoners who could afford to pay), he secured the position of hangman of London and the County of Middlesex, worth at that time about £40 a year. This was increased by gratuities and other perks.

Price rejoiced in the usual soubriquet of 'Jack Ketch'. However, despite this relatively large income, was a heavy drinker and he spent his money faster than it came in and soon ran up debts. One day in 1715, John Price was passing through Holborn, carrying the clothes of three criminals he had just hanged, when he was arrested for a debt of 7s 6d. He managed to avoid imprisonment by handing over to the bailiffs all the ready money he had on his person and the three suits of clothes, which settled the debt. However, he was arrested a short time later for two further debts. As he did not have the means to pay the debts this time he was committed to the Marshalsea Prison for debt and his position passed to William Marvell, a former blacksmith. This was unfortunate for Price as the post of common hangman was shortly due to prove more lucrative following the 1715 rebellion. Price remained in the Marshalsea Prison until 1718, where he enjoyed the privilege known as the liberty of the Marshalsea, which enabled him to leave the confines of the prison during the day but he was required to return at night. However, he and another prisoner decided to break this parole and absconded.

Not long afterwards, on Sunday 13 March 1718, a great many citizens were making merry and stalls were set up in the fields just outside Moorgate. That evening Price was walking across Bunhill Fields in a state of intoxication when he came across Elizabeth White, an old woman who sold cakes and gingerbread in the streets, who had set up her stall there. Intending to both rob and rape her, he set upon the woman, who resisted the attack, which angered him. He beat her savagely and two passers-by who came to investigate the noise found him 'busy about her' with her 'coats up to her belly and streams of blood issuing out of her eyes and mouth'. They apprehended Price and left the victim alone and senseless, while they took him to the watch-house in Old Street, where a constable detained him. When the old lady was attended to she was found to have a badly bruised scalp, one eye knocked out of its socket by Price's cudgel, some teeth knocked out, a bruised throat, a broken arm and a lacerated womb. Price was arrested on a charge of murder as he was taking a prisoner to be executed at Tyburn – or so the popular story goes.

He was incarcerated in Newgate Gaol to await trial, which took place at the Old Bailey sessions of 23–26 April. He pleaded not guilty and claimed that as he crossed Bunhill Fields on the night in question, he 'found something lying in his way'. He kicked it and found that it was a woman. He said he lifted her up but found that she was unable to stand and it was while he was doing this that he was apprehended. The jury did not believe him and he was found guilty of murder and sentenced to death. He was to be hanged on a temporary scaffold near the place of the murder, and afterwards his body was to be gibbeted. During the time he awaited his execution in the condemned cell, Price attended chapel in Newgate, more often than not in a drunken state, he being allowed to drink spirits, which he did to excess. The Reverend Paul Lorrain found that in drink Price was 'insensible of his misery . . . and unapprehensive of his future state'. In *The Original Weekly Journal* of 7–14 June 1718, it was reported:

A little girl who used to carry victuals to John Price the hangman in Newgate, has declared that a few days before his execution, he had carnal knowledge of her body in the said [gaol].

John Price was hanged at Bunhill Fields on Saturday 31 May 1718. Before his demise, carried out by an executioner named Banks, who had succeeded William Marvell, Price finally confessed his guilt. He told the spectators that they should take warning from his untimely end. After the execution that same day his body was suspended in chains at Stonebridge, near Holloway.

William Hawksworth, 1723

William Hawksworth was a soldier in the Foot Guards. While Hawksworth was marching to relieve the guard in St James's Park, a man named Ransom, in company with a woman, jostled him and called out: 'What a stir is here about King George's soldiers!' Hawksworth broke rank and struck the woman on the face. Ransom called him a puppy and demanded to know why he had hit her, at which point Hawksworth knocked Ransom down with his musket and injured him so badly that he fractured his skull. Hawksworth's fellow soldiers marched on. A crowd gathered round and Hawksworth slipped away to join his company. A surgeon was called to attend Mr Ransom, who concluded he was so badly injured he had no hope of recovery. When Ransom died a few hours later, a witness went to the Savoy and picked out Hawksworth who was promptly arrested and committed to Newgate. Although his colonel testified to his excellent character, Hawksworth was convicted of murder and sentenced to death. Shortly before his execution at Tyburn on 17 June 1723, Hawksworth made a speech to the crowd in which he advised them to keep a strict guard over their passion. He advised his fellow soldiers to submit with patience to the indignities that might be offered, and trust to the goodness of God to recompense their sufferings.

Jack Sheppard, 1724

Newgate incarcerated its fair share of folk heroes over the centuries but Jack Sheppard was the one to which there were arguably more myths and legends attached than any other. John (Jack) Sheppard was born in Spitalfields in 1702, the son of a carpenter, who died when Jack and his brother, Thomas, were young. Some years later Jack was apprenticed to a carpenter in Wych Street, and after he had found his feet, he began frequenting the Black Lion, a tavern situated in nearby Drury Lane. There he fell in with a group of prostitutes, becoming closely associated with two of them, Poll Maggot and Elizabeth Lyon, more commonly known as Edgworth Bess. By then he had completed four years of his apprenticeship. He continued working as a carpenter, but encouraged and tutored by Poll and Edgworth Bess, Sheppard began stealing from houses where he worked, as well as burgling others whenever the opportunity arose. His exploits led him to quarrel with his master, leading to one last incident where Jack attacked him and absconded. Jack found work as a jobbing carpenter elsewhere, enabling him to pilfer from those who engaged his services. He also fell in with one of Jonathan Wild's gangs. When Edgworth Bess was arrested and incarcerated in St Giles' Round House for stealing from one of her clients, Sheppard went to see her there, was refused entry by the Beadle, whom he knocked down and incapacitated, then gave Bess her liberty. Together they carried out a series of robberies along with Jack's brother, Thomas. However, when Thomas was arrested for attempting to sell some of the stolen goods, he was taken to Newgate, where he implicated Jack and Bess. Jack was found, arrested and himself placed in St Giles' Round House, where he soon made a daring escape through the roof. Standing 5ft 4in tall, Jack Sheppard was a strong and agile individual.

Other exploits in the company of Edgworth Bess got Jack into hot water, and once they escaped together from Clerkenwell New Prison. The company Jack Sheppard kept and committed burglaries and robberies with ultimately led to his downfall. His brother, Thomas, was convicted of burglary and transported, as were several of Jack's associates. As the legend of Jack Sheppard gained momentum so did the determination of the authorities to bring him to justice. Sheppard was betrayed by one of his accomplices, William Field, who wanted to keep their ill-gotten gains for himself. He informed Jonathan Wild, who having arrested Edgworth Bess, extracted information containing Sheppard's whereabouts from her and captured him.

Sheppard was tried at the Old Bailey sessions in August 1724, for burglary. William Field and Jonathan Wild gave evidence against him. He was found guilty and sentenced to death. He was held in the condemned cell along with nine others awaiting execution. Being something of a celebrity to some and to others a curiosity, he received many visitors, not at all unusual for condemned or high profile prisoners at Newgate. On 30 August, during a visit by Poll Maggot and Edgworth Bess, Sheppard made a daring escape from the condemned hold, having firstly partly dividing a spike in a hatch at the top of the door, facilitated by tools passed to him by his visitors and unnoticed by his gaolers. Sheppard finished the job and removed the spike, created a space sufficient for his slender frame to be pulled through by Poll and Bess. Although it is not known for certain, it was generally believed that Jack made his first escape from Newgate dressed in women's clothes. He made his way northwards to Finchley, where he hid in an alehouse. However, he was betrayed and his hiding place being quickly discovered, soon found himself back in Newgate. For greater security, having been placed in a strongroom, known as

The Castle, which was situated on the third floor above the arched gate of Newgate, Sheppard was handcuffed and chained to the floor with heavy irons. Greater precautions were taken to ensure that no tools were passed to him but on 15 October, the ingenious Jack, with the aid of a nail, was able to unlock the padlock which secured his chains to the floor and free himself from the handcuffs. He managed to break his way into the room above the Castle, known as the Red Room, from where he gained access to the chapel, escaped onto the roof and made his descent to the ground using twisted blankets. He eventually made his way to Drury Lane where he broke into a pawnbroker's and kitted himself in the finery of a gentleman.

Far to cock-sure for his own good, Sheppard hung around the vicinity of Newgate and during the days that followed took great delight in listening to tales of his exploits and escapes as related in the taverns, inns and ale houses that proliferated the district. It was in one such ale house that he was recognised and apprehended. Returned to Newgate, Sheppard found himself being given no chance of affecting a further escape, he being loaded with irons weighing 300 pounds. There he was visited by a curious public who paid the gaolers enormous sums for the privilege of seeing him.

Sheppard was just twenty-three when he was hanged at Tyburn on 16 November 1724. As he was being cut down a riot broke out and his body was seized by the crowd to prevent it being dissected by surgeons. It was spirited away to Long Acre, Covent Garden, where it rested in a tavern, the Barlow Mow, before it was buried in the churchyard of St Martin's in the Fields. Edgworth Bess was eventually captured, tried, and given a sentence of fourteen-years' transportation.

Catherine Hayes, 1726

Catherine Hayes was born Catherine Hall, of poor parents, at Birmingham in 1690. In 1705, when she was fifteen, she met some army officers and for a while became their collective mistress, until they moved on. Catherine then became maid to a Warwickshire farmer, named Hayes, he had a son named John, aged twenty-one, who was a carpenter. John fell in love with her and before long they married. After six years they moved to London, where John thrived in business, becoming a successful coal merchant, pawnbroker and moneylender. He traded from premises in Tyburn Road (today's Oxford Street). In a little over ten years, he had made enough money to enable him to sell his shop and take lodgings nearby. Catherine made her industrious husband's life miserable and once boasted to neighbours that she would think it no sin to murder him than to kill a dog. She said that her husband was miserly and mean, which if it were true, was at odds with her own desire for luxury.

At the beginning of 1725, a young man named Thomas Billings called at the Hayes' lodgings. He was a tailor by trade and Catherine told her husband he was an old friend and John Hayes allowed Billings to stay with them. When John Hayes ventured out of London on business, his wife took Billings into her bed. While the husband was away, the lovers took advantage of his absence by throwing parties and being frivolous with money. When John Hayes returned, he gave his wife a beating. Billings remained in residence apparently blameless of any indescretions in the eyes of his unsuspecting host. Not long after, another young 'friend' of Catherine's turned up on the door-step. His name was Thomas Wood. Wood also shared her favours whenever the opportunity allowed. She offered him a share in her husband's estate, should she become a widow, which amounted to the then very large sum of £1,500, and persuaded him to help her kill him.

On 1 March 1725, when Wood called at the Hayes's lodgings, he found John and Catherine Hayes in high spirits with Thomas Billings, indulging in a drinking session. Wood joined in with the party and a challenge was issued by the boastful Mr Wood that he could consume more wine than Hayes and still remain sober. As Hayes drank his seventh bottle, he collapsed on the floor. A few minutes passed before he came round and staggered into the adjoining bedroom. Shortly afterwards, Billings went into the room and, finding Hayes face down on the bed, dealt him a violent blow with a coal hatchet, which fractured his skull. As Hayes stirred he was dealt two more blows which finished him off. It was now necessary to dispose of the body.

Notwithstanding the butchery that followed, the bedding was already drenched and the walls and ceiling of the bedchamber spattered with blood. Catherine apparently remained cool and calm. She suggested that in order to avoid identification, her husband's head should be cut off and disposed of separately. The head was placed over a bucket to catch the blood, while the neck was sawn through. The two men balked at the idea of Catherine's to boil the head to remove the flesh. While preparations were being made to dispose of the blood, which was poured down various sinks, Catherine put on a convenient performance calling out goodbye to her husband as if he was going on a journey, in the hope she would be heard by the neighbours, which of course, she was.

Wood and Billings took the severed head out of the house in a bucket concealed beneath Billings' coat, they walked on past Westminster to Horseferry wharf (where the present Horseferry Road meets Lambeth Bridge). There they went to the end of the dock and threw the head in the river and the bucket after it. At daybreak, nightwatchman Robinson saw the bucket and head floating near the shore, from where they were retrieved. Meanwhile, Billings and Wood made their way back to Catherine, expecting the head to have floated away on the next tide. They discussed how to dispose of the body. Catherine had procured a wooden box but it was not large enough for the headless corpse to be placed in it intact. They cut off the arms, then the legs at the thighs and somehow managed to fit all the pieces into the box, which at nine o'clock that night they took out of the house wrapped in a blanket and threw the package into a pond, where it sunk.

Meanwhile, the severed head had been handed over to parish officers. It was washed to remove the blood and mud from the face and hair was combed. It was then attached to a pole and placed in the churchyard of St Margaret's, Westminster for several days, in the hope that someone would recognise it. Eventually, someone did. During the next few days, when enquiries were made of Catherine as to the whereabouts of her husband, her inventive mind came up with the ridiculous story that he had killed a man and absconded. The body parts were found in the pond in Marylebone and as Catherine received more and more visitors enquiring after her husband, the net closed in. As it had been established that Billings and Wood were with Hayes the last time he was seen alive, when a warrant was issued for the arrest of the murderers, their names were included on it.

When Catherine asked if she could see the head that had been displayed in St Margaret's churchyard, Mr Justice Lambert went with her to the barber-surgeon, Mr Westbrook, who was looking after it. When Catherine was shown the head, she took the glass in which the head was preserved and called out: 'It is my dear husband's head!' Catherine's performance knew no bounds. She shed tears as she embraced the container and, as the head was lifted out of the spirit, she kissed it rapturously and begged to be given a lock of its hair. As the barber-surgeon remarked that she had already had enough of her husband's blood, Catherine swooned away.

Wood was arrested and on hearing that the body had been found in the pond, confessed his part in the crime. Catherine obstinately refused to admit her guilt. She was an object of curiosity at Newgate, where she told varying accounts of events to the many visitors she received. Eventually, she admitted that she had wanted to get rid of her husband and had persuaded Billings and Wood to help her. At the trial she pleaded to be exempted from the penalty of petty treason on the grounds that she had not struck the fatal blow herself. A verdict of petty treason, considered more serious than murder, was established when any person out of malice took away the life of someone to whom he or she owed special obedience. For instance, a wife murdering her husband, or a servant killing his or her master, or an ecclesiastic his superior. A wife's accomplices in the murder of a husband, as in this particular case, would not be guilty of petty treason However, Catherine's plea was disregarded and she was told the law must take its course. Thomas Billings and Thomas Wood were condemned to death by hanging and afterwards to be hanged in chains. However, Wood was ailing fast in Newgate. He cheated the hangman and died of fever, on 4 May, in the condemned cell. Although the ages of Wood and Billings were not recorded, they were believed to have been both teenagers.

On 9 May 1726, Thomas Billings was hanged at Tyburn and later his body was suspended in chains a little over a hundred yards from the gallows and not far from the pond where John Hayes' body had been disposed of at Tyburn, that same day. When Catherine had finished her devotions, in pursuance of her sentence, an iron chain was put round her body, with which she was fixed to a stake near the gallows. Faggots were then placed around her and the executioner lit the fire. On these occasions, when women were burned for petty treason, it was customary to strangle them, by means of a rope round the neck and pulled by the executioner, so they were dead before the flames reached the body. But Catherine was literally burned alive, as the executioner, Richard Arnet, let go of the rope sooner than usual, in consequence of the flames reaching his hands. The fire burned fiercely around her, and the spectators watched her pushing away the faggots, while she 'rent the air with her cries and lamentations'. Other faggots were instantly thrown on her; but she survived amidst the flames for a considerable time, and her body was not perfectly reduced to ashes until three hours later.

Richard Savage, 1727
In December 1727, Richard Savage (1697–1743) English poet, satirist and intimate friend of Dr Samuel Johnson, found himself on trial for his life, charged with murder, following a quarrel in a West End coffee house. Savage was the illegitimate son of the Countess of

Macclesfield, the result of a love affair with Captain Richard Savage, afterwards Earl Rivers.

On the evening of Monday 20 November 1727, Savage was in the company of two friends, William Merchant and James Gregory. All three men were the worse for drink when they entered Robinson's Coffee House, near Charing Cross. They forced their way into a room where a private party was just splitting up and began to quarrel with the departing guests. Merchant entered first and kicked over a table, whereupon angry words were exchanged and Savage and Gregory drew their swords. Savage was subject to fits of blind rage, particularly when drunk and on this occasion it seems he lost his head altogether. Mr Nuttal asked them to put them up, but they refused to do so. In the ensuing fight, Savage came up against James Sinclair, made several thrusts at his opponent and ran him through the belly. Sinclair fell, calling out as he did so: 'I am a dead man, and was stabbed cowardly.'

Someone put out the candles and in the darkness one of the maids received a cut to the head while trying to prevent Savage and Merchant fleeing the building. They did manage to escape but were quickly apprehended in a dark court nearby. Gregory was held in the coffee house, where he was arrested. James Sinclair died the next morning but not before identifying Savage as his assailant. The deceased was attended by a clergyman and Sinclair told him he had been stabbed before he had time to draw his sword. Savage later said he had drawn his sword in self-defence. Savage, Merchant and Gregory were taken by soldiers and lodged in St Martin's Round-house, and in the morning were carried before a magistrate who committed them to the Gatehouse, but following the death of James Sinclair, they were sent to Newgate. Arraigned before Sir Francis Page, notorious for his severity and commonly known as the 'hanging judge', their trial took place on Thursday 7 December, in the Old Bailey and lasted eight hours. In his summing-up, the judge instructed the jury that if the prisoners had acted without provocation, they were all three guilty of murder. He rejected the plea of hot blood and dismissed the character witnesses' evidence as irrelevant. In his summing up, Sir Francis Page said:

Gentlemen of the jury, you are to consider that Mr. Savage is a very great man, a much greater man than you or I, gentlemen of the jury; that he wears very fine clothes, much finer than you or I, gentlemen of the jury; that he has abundance of money in his pocket, much more money than you or I, gentlemen of the jury;

but, gentlemen of the jury, is it not a very hard case, gentlemen of the jury, that Mr. Savage should therefore kill you or me, gentlemen of the jury?

The jury found Savage and Gregory guilty of murder, and Merchant, who had been unarmed, guilty of manslaughter. When Gergory and Savage were brought into court for sentencing, Savage, on being given an opportunity to address the court, made a plea for clemency. But his plea did nothing to soften the sentence as both he and Gregory were sentenced to die. In Newgate, as Savage awaited his execution, loaded with chains weighing fifty pounds, he wrote to his friend, the actor Robert Wilks, asking him to seek help from Mrs Oldfield. (Anne Oldfield 1683–1730, the celebrated actress, who had rendered financial help to Savage, partly because of her admiration for him and partly because he had been left nothing in his father's will, whereas Savage's father, Earl Rivers left her £500.)

Mrs Oldfield, who had many admirers at Court and in the higher echelons of society, meant that many doors were open to her. She secured an interview with Sir Robert Walpole, First Lord of the Treasury. She spoke of Savage's many attributes, his talent, his unfair trial, the lack of premeditation and at the end of the interview, Sir Robert promised to do his best. Mrs Oldfield secured the help of Lady Hertford, patroness of literature, who used her influence also. Savage was released with a free pardon, after he had already ordered a suit of clothes for the scaffold. The pardon for both Savage and Gregory was ordered on 6 January 1728 and both were released on bail on 20 January. The pardon passed the seals on 1 February, thereafter Savage and Gregory could not plead His Majesty's pardon in court until the last day of the following sessions during the first week in March, when their bail was discharged. William Merchant, although convicted of manslaughter, claimed Benefit of Clergy and got off with a branding in the thumb.

Major John Oneby, 1727

Major John Oneby was a distinguished officer from the Duke of Marlborough's campaigns. Noted as a swaggerer and a bully, he had gained a reputation as a duellist, and had twice killed rivals in Bruges and Jamaica. Following the signing of the treaties of the Peace of Utrecht in April and July 1713, the major was placed on half pay. To supplement his reduced income he turned to gambling, at which he became a professional.

The quick-tempered major was said to have been seldom without dice or cards in his pocket. His regular gambling partners knew only too well that it was unwise to pick a quarrel with him. One night in 1727, Major Oneby fell out over a bet with a Mr Gower in the Castle Tavern, Drury Lane. He threw a decanter at Gower, who returned the compliment by throwing a glass back at him. Swords were drawn but after the intercession of their fellow gamblers were put up again. Mr Gower was keen to make peace with Oneby but the major was not of the same frame of mind and swore to 'have his blood', a threat that was clearly heard by all present. When the party broke up, Major Oneby called Mr Gower into a private room and shut the door. Swords could be heard clashing and a waiter broke open the door. As the assembled company rushed in, the major, with his sword in his right hand, was holding Mr Gower up with his left. Gower's sword was laying on the floor and a bloodstain, ever increasing in size, marked his waistcoat. When someone called out: 'You have killed him!' The major replied: 'No, I might have done it if I would, but I have only frightened him.'

The wound in Mr Gower's abdomen proved to be more serious than the major believed and he died the next day, which resulted in Major Oneby's incarceration in Newgate. At his trial at the Old Bailey a month later, the jury could not agree on the measure of his guilt. This resulted in a special verdict requiring further consultation with the judge and eleven other judges debating the issue. The major was remanded in Newgate until his case could be heard. Major Oneby was confident that a verdict of manslaughter would be brought but when over two years later his case was finally heard, eleven of the judges decided against him. He was found guilty of murder and sentenced to death. Two days before the major was due to be executed, his servant Philip discovered him in his cell bleeding profusely from a deep gash to the wrist. He died before a surgeon could attend him.

Sarah Malcolm, 1733

Twenty-two-year-old Sarah Malcolm was born in County Durham into a good family. Her father having spent the family money, Sarah moved to London, where she worked for a time at the Black Horse in Boswell Court, Temple Bar, a public house frequented by criminals; and she fell into bad company. She then secured the position of laundress at some chambers in the Temple. There, at Tanfield Court, where Sarah also worked, lived Mrs Lydia Duncomb, variously described as being somewhere between sixty and eighty years old, a wealthy lady who was looked after by two servants, Elizabeth Harrison aged sixty and Anne Price aged seventeen. Sarah decided to rob the old lady and in the process of stripping the chambers of everything of value she could lay her hands on, she murdered Mrs Duncomb and her servants. Mrs Duncomb and the older servant were strangled. The servant girl's throat was slit. A silver tankard was found in Sarah's possession, its handle smeared with blood. She was committed to Newgate, where a considerable number of gold and silver coins were found secreted in her clothing. At her trial at the Old Bailey on Friday 23 February 1733, she tried to blame others for the murders. The jury did not believe her. She was hanged by John Hooper at Temple Gate near Fetter Lane on Wednesday 7 March 1733, on Newgate's portable scaffold. Parish records show that Sarah Malcolm was buried in St Sepulchre's churchyard on 10 March.

William Duell, 1740

Possibly one might consider William Duell to be one of Newgate's more fortunate inmates. Having been incarcerated in Newgate he was hanged at Tyburn on 24 November 1740, for the ill treatment and murder of Sarah Griffin, of Acton. After being executed, along with convicted burglars and felons Thomas Clock, William Meers, Margery Stanton and Eleanor Munoman, Duell's body was taken down and removed to Surgeons' Hall to be anatomised. His body was stripped and washed by servants. One of them noticed signs of life. The hanged man's breathing gradually increased in strength. A surgeon was summoned and he took several ounces of blood from Duell, who soon recovered his senses. Within two hours he was able to sit up in a chair and was well enough that evening to be taken back to Newgate. Sentence of death was commuted to transportation.

John Thrift, 1750

John Thrift, described as being illiterate, nervous and hotheaded, was appointed hangman in 1735, when he is believed to have carried out thirteen hangings on 10 March. Following the rebellion of the Young Pretender in 1745, as well as hanging a great many soldiers at Tyburn and elsewhere, he beheaded several noblemen on Tower Hill, including the last to be executed there, the eighty-year-old Lord Lovat, on 9 April 1747.

Thrift lived for many years in Coal Yard (present-day Stukeley Street, Covent Garden). On 11 March 1750, in the aftermath of the rebellion, when Jack Ketch (the name by which all London hangmen had been popularly known since about 1678), was an even less popular figure, David Farris, his wife and child, and two companions, Timothy Garvey and Patrick Farrel, passed Thrift's house. Thrift overheard some uncomplimentary remarks about Jack Ketch. He armed himself with a hanger (a short broad sword), rushed out of the door and chased them off. They crossed Drury Lane and entered Short's Gardens, where an altercation took place, and all the while Jacobite slogans were being chanted, by an ever increasing mob. David Farris was subsequently found wounded, stabbed by Thrift's hanger. Farris was carried to the house of Henry Fielding (magistrate and novelist), before whom he and his wife accused Thrift of inflicting the wounds. Thrift himself went to see Fielding the following day to ask for a warrant to be issued against Farris for violent assault. Fielding refused, saying he had already issued a warrant regarding the matter and could not issue cross-warrants. Farris died of his injuries on 19 March, Thrift was charged with murder and incarcerated in Newgate, where the thought of Jack Ketch being hanged by his own noose seemed to please the inmates considerably.

Thrift was tried at the Old Bailey on 27 April. Although he maintained that the hanger had been taken from him by one Enoch Stock, who had then slain Farris, Stock admitted that having been knocked senseless in the brawl he could neither confirm nor deny this. Thrift was found guilty of murder and sentenced to death. At the intervention of the city fathers, who had no intention of condoning mob rule and certainly not at the expense of condoning Jacobitism, his sentence was firstly reduced to fourteen years' transportation, then within a matter of days he was granted a free pardon, after which he resumed his post as hangman, which he held until his death on 5 May 1752. He was buried at St Paul's Church, Covent Garden.

Patrick McCarty, 1760

A Marshalsea writ having been issued against Patrick McCarty, a court officer, William Talbot was instructed to execute the warrant. He met McCarty near Drury Lane and accompanied him into the King's Head at the corner of Prince's Street. Apparently without any harsh words being passed between the two men, McCarty pulled out a knife and stabbed William Talbot through the heart and immediately ran off. He was captured by a soldier in Vere Street, Clare Market and taken before magistrate Sir John Fielding, who committed him to Newgate, where he was compelled to linger until his trial at the next Old Bailey sessions. McCarty was found guilty of murder and hanged at the bottom of Bow Street, Covent Garden on 24 October 1760.

Good fortune did not smile upon McCarty, for had his execution not been scheduled for 24 October but merely a day later, he would have been reprieved under the general amnesty and pardon to criminals that followed the death in the early hours of the next morning of King George II, which according to ancient custom, his successor decreed.

Theodore Gardelle, 1761

Theodore Gardelle (also see page 88), the Swiss miniaturist painter, was brought to Newgate in 1761 following having twice attempted to commit suicide at Clerkenwell New Prison. This occurred after his arrest and incarceration there for the murder of his landlady, Mrs King. His two suicide attempts involved, firstly taking forty drops of opium, which didn't work; and secondly by swallowing twelve halfpennies, hoping the verdigris would kill him. It only resulted in severe stomach pains. It was for greater security, that he was removed to Newgate and closely watched. Gardelle was subsequently hanged at the junction of Panton Street and Haymarket, close to the scene of the murder.

Daniel Blake, 1762

In the summer of 1762, twenty-year-old Daniel Blake, the son of a butcher at Bunwell, in the county of Norfolk, came to London to seek employment as a gentleman's servant. He had a fondness for loose women and spent what money he had in low company. Blake obtained a position with Lord Dacre and had been in his lordship's employment for about ten weeks when in order to provide him with the means to satisfy his insatiable lust for carnal pleasures, he committed murder and robbery.

At the dead of night he entered the room of John Marcott, Lord Dacre's butler and repeatedly struck him on the head with a poker. He then slit his throat from ear to ear and, after removing twenty guineas from Marcott's breeches, returned to his room. On the day after the murder Blake discharged several small debts. Under questioning, Blake broke down and confessed his guilt. He was taken before Sir John Fielding who committed him to Newgate. Blake was tried at the next sessions at the Old Bailey and hanged at Tyburn on 28 February 1763.

Elizabeth Brownrigg, 1767

Elizabeth Brownrigg, wife of James Brownrigg, a plumber by trade, by whom she had sixteen children, after having lived the first seven years of married life in Greenwich, moved to Fleur de Lys Court, Fleet Street. She practised midwifery and became an overseer at the workhouse of St Dunstan-in-the-West. Mary Mitchell, a poor girl from Whitefriars was apprenticed as a servant to Mrs Brownrigg in 1765; likewise, Mary Jones, a child of the Foundling Hospital, was also placed with her; she also had other apprentices and increased her income by allowing pregnant women to 'lie-in' at her home. Brownrigg treated her apprentices cruelly, keeping them at near starvation levels and whipping them mercilessly. Mary Jones managed to escape one night and returned to the Foundling Hospital, where she was examined by the surgeon. The governors directed their solicitor to write to James Brownrigg threatening prosecution if he could give no proper reason for this ill treatment. The letter was ignored but fortunately Mary Jones was discharged from her apprenticeship.

Mary Mitchell, having been with the Brownriggs for a year, also resolved to quit their service but she was prevented from escaping by the Brownriggs' younger son and her ill treatment increased. The elder son, John, directed Mary to put up a half-tester bedstead, which she was unable to do so he beat her savagely and continued with the beating until he had exhausted himself. Mrs Brownrigg would sometimes seize Mary by the cheeks and pull them so violently that blood gushed from her eye sockets. Mary was often tied to a chain suspended from the ceiling and beaten and sometimes chained by the neck in the cellar and given only bread and water to eat.

On the morning of 13 July, Mrs Brownrigg went into the kitchen and made Mary Clifford strip naked, and, although she was already bruised and sore, whipped her so violently that blood streamed down her body. Mary was then made to wash herself in a tub of cold water. While she was doing so Mrs Brownrigg struck her on the shoulders with the butt end of her whip. Mrs Brownrigg treated Mary Clifford five times similarly that same day. The parish authorities being made aware of this ill treatment saw to it that James Brownrigg was arrested but Elizabeth and her son escaped. The girls were taken to St Bartholomew's Hospital, where Mary Clifford died of her injuries within a few days. Mrs Brownrigg and her son moved address several times before they went to lodge with Mr Dunbar, who kept a chandler's shop in Wandsworth. Mr Dunbar read a newspaper report on 15 August which so clearly described his lodgers that he was certain they were the wanted murderers. He brought a constable to the house and mother and son were arrested and taken to Newgate.

James and Elizabeth Brownrigg and their son John, were indicted for the murder of Mary Clifford at the next Old Bailey sessions. After a trial lasting eleven hours Elizabeth Brownrigg was found guilty of murder and sentenced to death. Her husband and son were acquitted of murder but were detained and charged with various misdemeanours for which they each received six months' imprisonment. Elizabeth Brownrigg was hanged at Tyburn on 14 September 1767. Afterwards her body was taken to Surgeons' Hall, dissected and anatomised, and there her skeleton was later exhibited.

The Metyards, 1768

Sarah Metyard and Sarah Morgan Metyard, her daughter, were milliners, in Bruton Street, Hanover Square. In 1758, the Metyards had five parish apprentice girls in their service, from different work-houses, among whom were Anne Naylor and her sister. Anne was a sickly girl and unable to carry out her tasks as quickly as the other girls. This caused the Metyards to ill-treat her and after a while she absconded. Being brought back she was locked in an upper room and allowed only a little bread and water each day. Anne tried to escape again but was brought back by the daughter and forced onto the bed; and while the mother held her down the daughter beat her with a broom handle. She was left in that position for three days. The other girls were called to work in an adjoining room in order that they might be deterred from disobedience. Having been given neither food nor water for three days and two nights Anne was weak and unable to walk. On the fourth day her speech failed and within hours she died. Anne was still tied to the door. The other girls were greatly alarmed and called out: 'Miss Sally! Miss Sally! Nanny does not move.' She then proceeded to beat the dead girl on the head with the heel of her shoe. Mother and daughter tried to administer some hartshorn drops. They ordered the other girls downstairs and took the body to the garret.

Afterwards the Metyards told the girls that Nanny had been in a fit but was perfectly recovered. As a further act of subterfuge they took plates of food upstairs to Nanny for the next few days. Four days after the murder the body was locked in a box and the door of the room open. They told one of the girls to go and fetch Nanny for her dinner and to tell her if she behaved well in the future she would be allowed to join the other girls. As Nanny was not to be found a search of the house was organised at the end of which the Metyards said Nanny had run away.

When Anne's little sister said she didn't think she had run away as many of her possessions were still in her room, the Metyards killed her and disposed of her body. As for Anne's body, it remained in the locked box in the garret. The stench became so overpowering that the Metyards realised the body must be disposed of. On Christmas Day 1764, they cut it into pieces. The head and trunk were tied in one piece of cloth, the limbs in another, with the exception of one hand, which had a missing finger, amputated some time previously. After the girls had gone to bed Mrs Metyard put the hand into the fire. The two bundles were disposed of by a grate leading to the common sewer at Chick Lane. At about midnight some body parts were discovered by a watchman who fetched a constable. Mr Umfreville, the coroner, concluded that that the body parts must have been taken from a churchyard for the use of some surgeon.

For four years the murders remained undiscovered. As the daughter grew to maturity she took to arguing with her mother who was also mistreating her. After one particularly savage beating, she threatened to kill herself and to give information against her mother as a murderer. Eventually the overseers of Tottenham parish got to hear about the murders of the Naylor sisters and mother and daughter were committed to the Gatehouse. They were later transferred to Newgate, tried at the Old Bailey and hanged at Tyburn on Monday 19 July 1768. The mother was in a state of high anxiety when she was put in the cart and remained laying down throughout the entire journey to Tyburn; and was completely insensible as she was hanged. The daughter wept throughout the journey to the scaffold. After hanging for an hour, the Metyards' bodies were taken by hearse to Surgeons' Hall and exposed to the curious eyes of the public, before being dissected.

Building began on a new gaol in 1770, at the top end of the street known as Old Bailey. Designed by George Dance the Younger, it was not fully completed until 1780, although the old Newgate was demolished in 1777.

Peter Conway and Michael Richardson, 1770
Peter Conway and Michael Richardson were two would-be robbers, who during their first attempt at robbery committed murder. On Saturday 26 May 1770, Conway and Richardson purchased a pair of pistols. The next day they went to Whitechapel where they drank until dusk. They then ventured out into the streets and stopped a gentleman's servant but having no money they allowed him to pass. Earlier that afternoon, Mr Venables, a butcher, had been walking with his friend, Mr Rogers, a carpenter, who were returning through

Whitechapel to the city. Both men had the appearance of being well-
to-do and they were held up by Conway, Richardson and another
man named Fox. The two men resisted and were immediately shot
dead by Conway and Richardson. The murderers took no booty
with them and all three villains headed off towards Stepney, then to
Ratcliffe Highway and on to Wapping, where they robbed a man of
eighteen shillings and a watch. Conway and Richardson were soon
apprehended as a result of the pewter shot they used, traced to Robert
Dun's shop near Ratcliffe Highway; and through Conway's attempt
at pawning the watch in Jermyn Street, after descriptions of the watch
and culprits had been circulated. Witnesses were able to identify
them as the murderers and Sir John Fielding committed them both to
Newgate. They were tried at the next sessions at the Old Bailey and
hanged at Tyburn on 19 July 1770. Afterwards their bodies were put
in chains and hung on a gibbet on Bow Common, where it was said
more than 50,000 people visited the spot within the first five days.

The Weils, Lazurus and Porter, 1771

Mrs Hutchings was the widow of a farmer. She had three children,
two boys and a girl. Her late husband had left her well provided for
and she lived in the farmhouse in King's Road, Chelsea, attended by
servants. John Slow and William Stone who worked as labourers on
the farm also lived there.

On Saturday evening, just as the Jewish Sabbath had ended, a
gang of Jews assembled in Chelsea Fields. At about 10 o'clock they
went to the Hutchings' farmhouse and demanded admittance. The
household had retired with the exception of Mrs Hutchings and her
two female servants. On being asked what was their business the gang
rushed in and threatened the women with death if they resisted. Mrs
Hutchings' petticoats were tied over her head and the servant girls
were tied back to back. While the remainder of the gang stood guard
five of the villains proceeded to ransack the house. When they came
across the rooms occupied by the sleeping labourers it was decided
they must be murdered. Levi Weil aimed a blow at William Stone's
chest, which only stunned him. Slow woke up and a pistol was
instantly fired at him. He exclaimed: 'Lord have mercy on me! I am
murdered!'

Still alive, Slow was dragged to the head of the stairs while the gang
proceeded to ransack the rest of the house. Stone, having recovered
his senses, made his escape through a window onto the roof. The
thieves took all the plate they could find and threatened to kill

Mrs Hutchings if she did not reveal where she kept her money. She gave them her watch and purse containing £65, after which the gang fled. Mrs Hutchings, having freed the girls, found Slow, who told her he was dying. He died the following afternoon.

This daring raid by a gang of Jews caused a great deal of ill feeling against the whole Jewish people for a considerable time. Fortunately appeasement came in part after some of the gang were apprehended and brought to justice following one of their number, a German Jew named Isaacs, being tempted by the prospect of a reward. It was revealed that the gang consisted of eight Jews headed by Levi Weil, a physician, who had studied at the University of Leyden. On coming to London, Dr Weil did not practice medicine for long. He decided that robbery was a much more profitable occupation to follow and formed a gang of thieves consisting of poor Jews brought over from Amsterdam. Dr Weil sent his men out during the daytime to look for houses that might provide rich pickings; the gang would go back some time later and attack them at night.

Six Jewish men were brought up at the sessions held at the Old Bailey in December 1771, being tried on Friday 6 December. Dr Levi Weil, Marcus Hartagh, Jacob Lazarus, Solomon Porter and Lazarus Harry were indicted for the robbery at Mrs Hutchings' farm and for the murder of John Slow. Dr Weil, Asher Weil, Jacob Lazarus and Solomon Porter were found guilty as charged, but Marcus Hartagh and Lazarus Harry were acquitted, for want of evidence. A rabbi attended the four condemned men in the press-yard at Newgate but declined to accompany them to the place of execution. Having prayed together and sung a Hebrew hymn on the scaffold they were hanged at Tyburn on Monday 9 December 1771.

Reverend James Hackman, 1779

One of London's most famous meeting places, the piazza of Covent Garden, was the scene of arguably the most notorious West End murder in the last quarter of the eighteenth century. It was also notable for the swiftness of justice which followed the tragic event. Martha Reay (or Ray), mistress of the Earl of Sandwich, was shot by Reverend James Hackman, as she left the theatre on 7 April 1779.

Miss Martha Reay was born at Leicester Fields, Hertfordshire in 1742, the daughter of a staymaker, and at the age of fourteen was placed as an apprentice with Mrs Silver, of St George's Court, St John's Lane, Clerkenwell, to be instructed in the business of a mantua-maker (maker of gowns). Attractive and highly accomplished, with a pleasant singing voice, Martha, in 1761, at the age of nineteen, caught the eye of the Earl of Sandwich (John Montagu, the 4th Earl, 1718–92, First Lord of the Admiralty), who took her as his mistress. Lord Sandwich had married in 1741 but Lady Sandwich's state of mental health had declined since the birth of their fifth child in 1751; and in 1755 the couple had parted forever. Her condition gradually declined until she was eventually formally declared insane by the Court of Chancery and made a ward of court. Lord Sandwich settled down to life with Martha. Martha and her children were referred to as Lord Sandwich's 'London family' and there was peace and harmony within the household.

There was to be a blight on this happy relationship. It came in the form of a young man named James Hackman. Hackman was born in Gosport, Hampshire, of very respectable parents, who at the age of nineteen purchased for him a commission in the 68th Regiment of Foot. Soon after he obtained his commission he was quartered at Huntingdon, where he was in charge of a recruiting party. He was invited by Lord Sandwich to his nearby country seat, Hinchbroke, where he first met Martha Reay, who was under Lord Sandwich's protection. Hackman fell desperately in love with Miss Reay and she, flattered by the young man's attentions, did little to discourage his advances. Hackman took holy orders and was appointed to a parish in Norfolk in 1768. When in London, he would often attend the theatre and concerts with Martha and Lord Sandwich and the relationship between Martha and the amorous clergyman grew stronger. Hackman had every intention of marrying her. However, considering Martha's position in life, the mistress of a peer of the realm, with five illegitimate children, it was doubtful Hackman could really have secured a living, had they married.

By the beginning of 1779, Martha and Lord Sandwich had lived together, very happily, for over eighteen years and she had borne him nine children, five of which had survived. In March 1779, Martha decided to end the relationship with Hackman. On 7 April 1779, Hackman dined with his sister and brother-in-law, who was also his first cousin. The couple had married only five weeks previously. He left them promising he would return for supper. That evening Lord Sandwich was working late at the Admiralty. Hackman, on seeing his lordship's coach with Martha Raey inside, concluded, quite correctly, that Miss Reay was going out to the opera, and would probably call on Signora Galli, at her lodgings in the Haymarket (Catherina Galli was a retired *prima donna*, who amongst other fine singers had given Martha lessons. It was said that Martha Raey possessed a singing voice that could have earned her a high income, had she chosen a career on the stage). Hackman followed the two ladies into the theatre and there observed a gentleman talking to Miss Raey, who was later discovered to be Lord Coleraine. Hackman was seized with a fit of jealousy and at that moment decided to end his own life.

He left the theatre, went to his lodgings in Duke's Court, St Martin's Lane and returned a little while later with a brace of loaded pistols, intending to kill himself in Martha's presence. When questioned later why he had a brace of pistols, he replied that if one misfired on himself, he meant to use the other. When the play was over Martha, in the company of Signora Galli and Lord Coleraine, entered the lobby of the theatre, and it was there that Hackman first attempted to shoot himself, but the thickness of the crowd prevented him. He pursued Martha to the door of her coach. It was not until he beheld Martha's face that he thought of killing her at that instant. He took a pistol from each pocket and discharged the pistol in his right hand first, immediately afterwards he discharged this in his left hand at himself. Martha was shot through the head. She, upon lifting her hand to her face, fell and died on the spot. Only slightly wounded, Hackman beat his head with the pistol and called out: 'Kill me! Kill me!' Martha was carried to the Shakespeare Tavern and Hackman with her. Her lifeless body was taken to a separate room within the tavern while Hackman's wounds were dressed in another. Hackman freely gave his name and was shortly afterwards taken before the magistrate, Sir John Fielding (the celebrated blind magistrate, half-brother of lawyer and novelist Henry Fielding), who committed him to Tothill Fields, Bridewell.

The Reverend James Hackman was transferred to Newgate Gaol. During his incarceration he remained calm and composed and it is said that he spoke of the name and memory of Martha Reay with the highest rapture. On the morning of his trial at the Old Bailey sessions, before Mr Justice Blackstone, Hackman ate a hearty breakfast in Newgate, with his brother-in-law and two of his friends in attendance. He was found guilty of murder and sentenced to death. Following the verdict Lord Sandwich wrote to Hackman:

17th April 1779

To MR HACKMAN IN NEWGATE

If the murder of Miss —— wishes to live, the man he has most injured will use all his interest to procure life.

Hackman sent an immediate reply:

The Condemned Cell in Newgate

17th April 1779.

The murderer of her whom he preferred, far preferred to life, respects the hand from which he has just received such an offer as he neither desires nor deserves. His wishes are for death, not life. One wish he has. Could he be pardoned in this world by the man he has most injured – oh, my lord, when I meet her in another world enable me to tell her (if departed spirits are not ignorant of earthly things) that you forgive us both, that you will be a father to her dear infants!

J. H.

There was to be no reprieve or pardon for the Reverend James Hackman. Justice was swift, for there were only twelve days between the murder and the murderer's dissection. On 19 April 1779, James Hackman was hanged by Edward Dennis at Tyburn, and life, having at last been pronounced extinct, much as he had wished, his body was left hanging for the customary one hour, before being taken to Surgeons' Hall for dissection. Martha Reay was taken back to her native Hertfordshire, where she lies buried in Elstree.

In 1780, the same year Dance's Newgate was completed, the prison was extensively damaged by fire during the Gordon Riots. Rioters broke into the gaol by attacking the gates with crowbars, in order to release three fellow rioters who had been imprisoned there. Rebuilding of the damaged gaol went ahead with the original design being modified.

In 1783, the site of London's gallows were moved from Tyburn to Newgate, where executions took place in the open space outside the Debtors' Door, in the Old Bailey. Lord George Gordon was a younger son of the Duke of Gordon, a vociferous opponent against what were considered to be 'Popish leanings' by some members of the government, whose followers had wreaked havoc at Newgate some thirteen years previously. He had been convicted of libel in 1787 and 1788, and was now incarcerated in Newgate, where he died of gaol fever in 1793.

Notable New Newgate Inmates

Maria Theresa Phipoe, 1797
Maria Theresa Phipoe, also known to some by the name of Mary Benson, was powerfully built and of masculine behaviour and disposition. In 1795, she attempted to kill John Cortois after having tied him

up and, under threats of violence procured a promissory note for £2,000 from him. He managed to escape as she tried to stab him, sustaining severe cuts to his hands and fingers as he fended her off. For this crime, due to a point of law being raised, having been found guilty of assault on 23 May 1795, Phipoe was committed to twelve months in Newgate. Within months of her release she murdered Mary Cox, by stabbing her five times in the throat and in several other parts of the body, at the latter's home in Garden Street, in the parish of St George's-in-the-East. She had sold the woman a gold watch and other articles for which she had paid £11, after which a frenzied knife attack began. Mary Cox lived long enough to tell her tale to the surgeon and beadles. Found guilty of murder at the Old Bailey, Maria Theresa Phipoe was hanged outside Newgate on Monday 11 December 1797; and afterwards her body was publicly exhibited before she was anatomised.

George Foster, 1803

In 1802, George Foster lodged with Joseph Bradfield in North Row, Grosvenor Square. He worked for coachmaker James Bushwell and was described as being diligent and good natured. Foster was estranged from his wife but she called on him from time to time with their infant daughter. Foster's wife and daughter were last seen alive when they spent part of the afternoon of Sunday 5 December 1802 with him at the Mitre Tavern, situated near the canal at Paddington. Their bodies were found in the canal by boatman John Atkins about a mile from the Mitre, the baby's on Monday, the woman's on Thursday. There was sufficient circumstantial evidence against Foster for him to be charged with their murders.

Foster was tried at the Old Bailey on 14 January 1803. On being found guilty of the murders the recorder passed sentence on the prisoner: to be hanged by the neck until he be dead, and that his body be delivered to be anatomised, according to law in that case made and provided.

Before his execution, Foster admitted to the murders. He said he so hated his wife that he was determined to rid the world of a being he loathed. He said he had taken her twice before to the canal with the intention of killing her but his courage had failed him. He regretted the loss of the baby. Foster was executed outside Newgate on 18 January 1803. A contemporary account stated:

After hanging the usual time, his body was cut down and conveyed to a house not far distant, where it was subjected to the galvanic process by Professor Aldini ... On the first application of the process to his face, the jaws of the deceased criminal began to quiver, and the adjoining muscles were horribly contorted, and one eye was actually opened. In the subsequent part of the process the right hand was raised and clenched and the legs and thighs were set in motion.

John Bellingham, 1812

At about a quarter past five on the evening of 11 May 1812, Prime Minister and First Lord of the Treasury, the Right Honourable Spencer Perceval, was on his way to the House of Commons. As he and his associates passed through the Lobby (which in the old houses of parliament was opposite the south end of Westminster Hall), a thin-faced man, aged about forty, stepped forward, drew a pistol and shot the Prime Minister in the left breast. As he fell to the ground, he called out: 'Murder!' The assassin was quickly overcome and taken into custody by the Sergeant-at-Arms. His name was John Bellingham. Meanwhile, the Prime Minister was carried into the office of the Speaker's secretary, where he shortly died. Bellingham was recognised as a man who had in recent days made frequent visits to the Commons and had enquired about the identities of various members. When asked what his motive was for shooting the Prime Minister, Bellingham replied, 'It was want of redress and denial of justice on the part of the Government.' Bellingham had in recent weeks petitioned his MP, General Gascoyne, Member for Liverpool, concerning his grievances with the Government over injustices he said he had received in Russia, where his business dealings had landed him in trouble through no fault of his own.

Bellingham's trial took place at the Sessions House, Old Bailey, on 15 May 1812, just four days after Perceval's death, before Lord Chief Justice Mansfield. Bellingham made a speech to the jury and rambled on for two hours. Although it appears by his actions that Bellingham was insane and some witnesses said as much, he apparently showed no visible signs of insanity. Unless a person was obviously out of his mind, then a jury would have no alternative but to find a prisoner guilty, if they believed he had committed the crime for which he was being tried. The jury found him guilty after just fourteen minutes of deliberation. Sentence of death was passed on the prisoner. Bellingham was executed on Monday 18 May 1812 outside Newgate Gaol before an enormous crowd. The executioner was William Brunskill. Bellingham's body was afterwards conveyed on a cart to St Bartholomew's Hospital, where it was dissected in the anatomical theatre, before many spectators. Not everyone was content with Bellingham's fate, as this contemporary account shows:

> Bellingham has been convicted of murder and hanged, but some unease is now felt, since his wits had apparently been turned by the wrongs he suffered, and it is not the mark of a civilised society to execute lunatics.

The Cato Street Conspiracy, 1820

Travelling in a northerly direction from Marble Arch along Edgeware Road, on the right hand side, after about a quarter of a mile, is Harrowby Street. Second left, off Harrowby Street, is a narrow road known as Cato Street, famous for what is known to history as the 'Cato Street Conspiracy of 1820'. The plot was given that name because the conspirators met in a loft above the stable at No. 6. This ill-conceived plot seemed doomed to failure from the start and is probably more notable for the high profile execution of the perpetrators, than the actual purpose of the conspiracy itself. It nevertheless caused quite a stir at the time.

The plot involved a group of extreme radicals who were highly dissatisfied with government legislature, in the wake of the Napoleonic wars, a time when economic problems and high unemployment were rife.

The leader, Arthur Thistlewood, was a militia officer, who following visits to America and France, developed revolutionary sympathies and on 15 November 1816, had organized a demonstration at Spa Fields, intending to seize the Tower of London and the Bank of England. Thistlewood was arrested along with several others and tried before the King's Bench at Westminster, on 9 June. He was acquitted.

When Thistlewood began to recruit at Cato Street, he secured the support of about twenty-five men, including many hot-headed illiterates. One of the recruits was a government spy named George Edwards, so the authorities were aware of the plot from the beginning. Edwards probably joined the conspirators for personal gain and immediately after joining the group, went straight to Windsor to inform Sir Herbert Taylor. The conspirators planned to murder Lord Liverpool, the Prime Minister and his entire cabinet, while they dined at Lord Harrowby's (the President of the Council) house at 29 Grosvenor Square, on 23 February 1820.

Another conspirator, Thomas Hiden, also turned informer and gave the Government exact details of the plot. The plot involved one of the conspirators to knock at the door of Lord Harrowby's residence on the pretence of leaving a parcel. When the door was opened the whole band of men would rush into the house and, while a few took care of servants, the others would fall upon Lord Harrowby and his guests. Hand grenades were to be thrown into the dining room and during the noise and confusion the assassination of the entire cabinet would be accomplished.

Thistlewood and others were closely watched and once matters were sufficiently advanced so no doubt could remain as to their guilt, a detachment of soldiers, headed by Lord Frederick Fitzclarence, constables and Bow Street officials descended on Cato Street. During the ensuing fracas, Thistlewood killed one of the officers, Richard Smithers, with his sword, then promptly took to his heels and escaped.

Several other conspirators were captured and taken to Bow Street: Richard Bradburn, Charles Cooper, William Davidson, James Gilchrist, James Ings, John Monument, John Shaw-Strange and Richard Tidd. A large number of weapons was found in the loft and taken away. Thistlewood was caught the next day at 8 White Street, Little Moorfields, to the north of the present-day Moorgate station. He was in bed with his breeches on and in the pockets were found several cartridges. He was first taken to Bow Street, where he was examined and then appeared before the Privy Council. Other conspirators including John Thomas Brunt and John Harrison were arrested over the next few days. Thistlewood was taken to the Tower of London as state prisoners with his fellow ringleaders but most of the other conspirators were held in Coldbath Fields Prison.

Six weeks after the proposed assassination of the cabinet, the trial of the Cato Street Conspirators took place at the Old Bailey. Thistlewood made a long and rambling defence. He also described the 'informer' George Edwards as a 'contriver, instigator and entrapper'. It came as no surprise that the prisoners were all found guilty. Those conspirators who had pleaded guilty escaped execution but five were executed.

Thistlewood, Ings, Davidson, Brunt and Tidd were hanged outside Newgate Gaol on 1 May 1820. The five conspirators were spared being disembowelled and quartered but the law still required traitors to be decapitated. Arthur Griffiths's records in *The Chronicles of Newgate*:

A crowd as great as any known collected in the Old Bailey to see the ceremony, about which there were some peculiar features worth recording. The reckless demeanour of all the convicts except Davidson was most marked. Thistlewood and Ings sucked oranges on the scaffold; they with Brunt and Tidd scorned the ordinary's ministrations, but Ings said he hoped God would be more merciful to him than men had been. Ings was especially defiant. He sought to cheer Davidson, who seemed affected, crying out, 'Come, old cock-of-wax, it will soon be over.' As the executioner fastened the noose, he nodded to a friend he saw in the crowd; and catching sight of the coffins ranged around the gallows, he smiled at the show with contemptuous indifference. He roared out snatches of a song about Death or Liberty, and just before he was turned off, yelled out three cheers to the populace whom he faced. He told the executioner to 'do it tidy', to pull it tight, and was in a state of hysterical exaltation up to the very last. Davidson, who was the only one who seemed to realize his awful situation, listened patiently and with thankfulness to the chaplain, and died in a manner strongly contrasting with that of his fellows ...

After the men had been hanged, their bodies were taken down after half an hour and their heads removed by a masked man wielding a surgeon's knife. The severed trophies were each in turn displayed to the crowds of onlookers. Afterwards the bodies were placed in the coffins, with the heads in the correct position and taken inside Newgate Gaol, where they were buried in the narrow passage which linked the gaol with the adjoining Sessions House. There carved in the stones is a row of letters: T, B, I, D and T, for Thistlewood, Brunt, Ings, Davidson and Tidd, to mark the spot where they were buried.

George Edwards, it was said, after the conviction of the conspirators had been assured, went abroad, with an ample pension, provided on condition he did not return to England.

Dickens comments on Newgate's condemned cells in *Sketches By Boz*:

... The entrance is by a narrow and obscure staircase leading to a dark passage, in which a charcoal stove casts a lurid tint over the objects in its immediate vicinity, and diffuses something like warmth around. From the left-hand side of this passage, the massive door of every cell on the storey opens, and from it alone can they be approached. There are three of these passages, and three of these ranges of cells one above the other, but in size, furniture and appearance, they are all precisely alike ... We entered the first cell. It was a stone dungeon, eight feet long by six feet wide, with a bench at the further end, under which were a common horse-rug, a Bible, and prayer-book. An iron candlestick was fixed into the wall at the side; and a small high window in the back admitted as much air and light as could struggle in between a double row of heavy, crossed iron bars. It contained no other furniture of any description.

Patrick Carroll, 1835

This particular Newgate inmate has the distinction of being the first criminal to be tried at the court constituted as the Central Criminal Court. Patrick Carroll, from Ballihoy, Ireland, enlisted in the 7th Regiment of Fusiliers at the age of twenty-two. Seven years later, he switched regiments to the Marines and was stationed in Woolwich. There he frequented the Britannia, a public house kept by a widow, Mrs Browning. He repeatedly asked her to marry him and although she was not entirely averse to the idea, she refused to entertain his advances any further after he had abused her on more than one occasion while in a state of intoxication.

On Sunday 26 April 1835, Carroll, went to the Britannia and on finding she had invited some friends for tea, without having extended an invitation to himself, some angry words ensued and he was forcibly ejected from the house. He returned next morning and insisted on seeing Mrs Browning in private. Having been told she would not see him, he forced his way into the bar and repeatedly struck her with his hand before drawing his bayonet and stabbing her. She died. On Friday 15 May, Patrick Carroll was tried at the Central Criminal Court, Old Bailey, for murder. Found guilty, he was hanged outside Newgate on Monday 18 May 1835.

William John Marchant, 1839

Eighteen-year-old William Marchant worked as footman to magistrate Henry Edgell, at 21 Cadogan Place, Chelsea. On Friday 17 May 1839, under-housemaid Elizabeth Paynton was found with her throat cut in the drawing room, a razor laid by her side. When it was discovered Marchant had absconded suspicion immediately fell on him. On Sunday 19 May, Marchant gave himself up to a police officer in Hounslow. Although he appeared to be terrified at what he had done and on the journey back to London fancied he heard the murdered woman at his back, he never gave any explanation why he had killed Elizabeth Paynton. Marchant was tried at the Central Criminal Court, Old Bailey on Friday 21 June and pleaded guilty to the indictment of murder. He was hanged outside Newgate on 8 July 1839.

François Benjamin Courvoisier, 1840
François Benjamin Courvoisier, a valet who murdered his employer, Lord William Russell, was incarcerated at Newgate prior to his trial at the Old Bailey on 18 June 1840. Courvoisier was executed outside Newgate on 6 July the same year.

Thomas Cooper, 1842
In 1842, Hornsey Wood covered what is now the park itself in the part of the capital known as Finsbury Park. A hostelry known as the Hornsey Wood Tavern once stood close to the site of the present-day boating pond. Near this hostelry, on 5 May 1842, Thomas Cooper, a twenty-two-year-old bricklayer-turned-thief, was surprised by policeman Charles Moss while he was engaged in some felonious act. Without hesitation Cooper shot and wounded Moss. The sound of gunfire attracted the attention of another policeman called Mallet, and a baker called Mott, who was walking in the woods nearby.

Mallet and Mott gave chase as Cooper headed off in the direction of Highbury. Meanwhile, another baker, named Howard, was driving his post chaise down Hornsey Road. He saw Cooper being chased and raced after him, Cooper headed for Highbury Barn. As another policeman, Timothy Daly, closed in on Cooper near Highbury Cottage, Cooper jumped over a hedge into a short cul-de-sac called Black Ditch. This area was bounded by a paling fence which hemmed Cooper in long enough for Daly and Howard to catch up. Cooper, who was carrying two large horse pistols, fired both of them. One hit its target and Daly died instantly, but Hudson was unscathed and with the help of two gardeners was able to overcome Cooper and hold him. Cooper was tried at the Old Bailey, found guilty of murder and hanged outside Newgate on 4 July 1842.

Thomas Hocker, 1845
At around 7.00pm on 23 February 1845, Police Constable John Baldock on patrol near the bridle path that ran through the fields between Primrose Hill and Belsize Park, was alerted by a baker, Edward Hilton, to cries of 'Murder!' When he arrived at the scene (at today's junction of Belsize Park Gardens, England's Lane, Eton Avenue and Primrose Hill), accompanied by Sergeant Thomas Fletcher, in the dark they found the bloody and battered body of a well-dressed man. Whilst the sergeant went to get assistance, Constable Baldock stayed with the corpse.

A cloaked man, later identified as Thomas Hocker, approached the constable and uttered the words: 'Hilloa, policeman, what have you got there?' He offered the constable brandy, which he refused, but Hocker persuaded him to take a shilling to get a glass of brandy later. At no time did he indicate that he knew the victim, although it would become clear that in fact he knew him very well. Shortly after, William Satterthwaite, a Hampstead shoemaker appeared and Hocker left the scene. Dr Perry examined the body. His report stated:

> Death is attributed to concussion of the brain, the consequence of the external violence. I should imagine the wounds were inflicted by a heavy instrument, such as a stick ...

The man appeared to have been robbed, because the only item found on him was a letter written in blue ink addressed to J Cooper. The letter began 'Dear James' and in it the writer requested a meeting at their usual place; she also informed him that she was pregnant. It was signed Caroline. A coroner's inquest was held at the Yorkshire Grey in Hampstead, by which time the victim had been identified as James De La Rue. A verdict of wilful murder was recorded. Twenty-seven-year-old James De La Rue, a music teacher, lived in well appointed lodgings at 55 Whittlebury Street. The road no longer exists but in 1845 it led into Euston Square from Drummond Street, which straddles Hampstead Road. He earned his money principally giving piano lessons. James De La Rue was buried in St John's Churchyard, Hampstead, on 28 February. Thomas Hocker, aged twenty-two, was a close friend of De La Rues. He lived at 11 Victoria Place, situated near the western edge of Regent's Park, sharing a room with his brother, James. Although he considered his musical talents to be worthy of more, he scraped a living by giving the occasional violin lesson.

These friends were a pair of amorous aspiring gentlemen, dapper dressers, who had a penchant for collecting pornography in the form of prints. Using various aliases they had developed acquaintances with numerous women, mostly servant girls and those who, although not exactly prostitutes, had loose morals. They often indulged in orgies. Neither had any intention of cementing any of their relationships by marriage, hence the use of false names in their liaisons. During the police investigation that followed, De La Rue's friendship with Hocker emerged. Following the funeral, Hocker's apparent indifference to his best friend's death, threw suspicion his way. Both Thomas and James Hocker were questioned and as matters unfolded James Hocker was able to give information about the letter found in

De La Rue's greatcoat pocket. The letter, written in a supposedly girlish hand, had in fact been written by Thomas Hocker in one of his numerous false hands. The unusual blue ink was traced to his room, and this evidence, together with the discovery of De La Rue's watch and a pair of blood-soaked trousers, proved sufficient to convict him of his friend's murder.

Hocker was tried at the Old Bailey on 11 April, before Mr Justice Coleman, in a trial lasting less than ten hours. The jury found him guilty after just ten minutes deliberation. He protested his innocence to the end, blaming another he would not name. He was hanged at Newgate before a crowd of 10,000 on 28 April 1845 by William Calcraft.

The opening of Holloway Prison in 1852 resulted in Newgate's role being reduced to holding only prisoners awaiting trial at the Old Bailey, or awaiting execution. Further building work was undertaken there in 1857 and 1858 on the improvement of accommodation by replacing severely dilapidated and crowded wards with a block comprising five floors of cells built around galleries. A further block for women was built to a similar design in 1862. During the last years it housed some highly colourful, notwithstanding gruesome individuals, some of whom are described below.

Later inmates

Franz Müller, 1864

On Saturday 9 July 1864, seventy-year-old Thomas Briggs, chief clerk at the bankers Messrs Robarts & Co of Lombard Street, boarded a train on the North London Railway which left Fenchurch Street station for Chalk Farm at 9.50pm. He was on his way home to 5 Clapton Square, near to Hackney or Hackney Wick (Victoria Park) stations. He travelled in a first-class carriage, Carriage No. 69. The train arrived at Hackney at 10.11pm. Two bank clerks got into empty carriage No. 69 and found blood on the seats and on the window. The guard was summoned and he found a hat, a walking stick and a small black leather bag. He took these away and the carriage was locked. About the same time Mr Briggs was found barely alive lying in the 6ft way between the Up and Down lines near Victoria Park, by two railway workers. Help was summoned from the nearby Mitford Castle public house to where Mr Briggs was carried and received medical attention. He had several severe wounds to the head apparently inflicted by a blunt instrument to ferocious effect. He died of his injuries twenty-seven hours later.

It was established that Mr Briggs had been wearing gold-rimmed spectacles and a gold watch and chain. They were missing. The facts of the murder and the object, robbery, were thus conclusively proved. Of the items found in the railway carriage, the stick and bag were his but not the hat. It was established that the hat had been bought at Walker's, a hatters in Crawford Street, Marylebone, while within a few days Mr Briggs's gold chain was traced to a jeweller's at 55 Cheapside (Mr Death). In little more than a week after the murder, following newspaper reports, a cabman came forward and made a statement which drew suspicion to a German, Franz Müller, who had been the cabman's lodger. A photograph of Müller was shown to Mr Death. He identified Müller as the man who had exchanged Mr Briggs's chain. The cabman swore that he had bought the very hat found in the carriage for Müller. It was a distinctive hat of a new short design (a short top-hat instead of the usual stovepipe).

Franz Müller, aged twenty-five, was from Saxe-Weimar. In his native country he had been apprenticed as a gunsmith and had arrived in England in 1862 hoping to find work. Unable to get a job as a gunsmith, he found employment as a tailor in Threadneedle Street. At the time of the murder Müller was lodging at 16 Park Terrace, which was part of the Old Ford Road, Victoria Park. There was no mystery about his departure: he had gone to Canada by the *Victoria* sailing ship, starting from London docks and bound for New York. Two detectives accompanied by the jeweller and cabman, went to Liverpool and took the first steamer the *City of Manchester*, across the Atlantic. It arrived in New York before Müller's sailing ship. When the *Victoria* docked, Müller was identified and arrested. Mr Briggs's watch was found in his luggage and Müller was wearing Mr Briggs's hat, which he had cut down.

Müller was brought back to England and his trial followed at the next sessions at the Central Criminal Court, within the Old Bailey, beginning on 27 October 1864 and lasting for three days. He was found guilty of murder and hanged outside Newgate, by William Calcraft on 14 November 1864. This case is notable for being Britain's first railway murder.

John Wiggins, 1867
John Wiggins, a thirty-five-year-old lighterman, was found guilty at the Old Bailey of the murder of Agnes Oates of Temperance Cottage, Limehouse, in the early hours of Wednesday 31 August 1867, when her throat had been savagely slit open. Agnes, a young woman in her late teens, hailed from Liverpool. Wiggins met her when she was

working as a barmaid at the Crown Tavern, in Salmon Lane, Lime-house. She subsequently worked as a servant at the Cock, Wapping, leaving her position to live with Wiggins about six months before her death, after he seduced her and promised they would marry. Witnesses reported that the couple quarrelled over money. Wiggins, who had knife wounds to his neck and himself expected to die, later maintained that Agnes had attacked him with a knife and then cut her own throat. The evidence suggested otherwise. He was hanged outside the Debtors' Entrance at Newgate on Tuesday 15 October 1867, by William Calcraft. The execution was not without incident. The *Illustrated Police News* reported:

> ... the prison bell began to toll, and the convict was escorted to the scaffold, which he ascended with a light step, attended by the ordinary and the executioner. There a very unusual and very painful scene occurred. The crowd on seeing the convict, became very excited, and he began to resist the efforts of Calcraft to place him below the beam. First, one of the stalwart prison warders and then another were summoned to assist in restraining him, until four or five of them, with the executioner were upon the scaffold at any one time. After the cap had been drawn over his face, the convict shouted to the crowd 'I am innocent; on my dying oath. I am innocent. Cut my head off, but don't hang me. I am innocent.'

Wiggins continued to struggle and protest his innocence to the crowd, until at last he was overcome by sheer force. The rope was adjusted and the drop fell. The *Illustrated Police News* reported that the convict was soon dead.

Henry Wainwright, 1875
On the afternoon of Saturday 11 September 1875, a sensational chase began in the Whitechapel Road. A four-wheeled cab was followed on foot by a perspiring and breathless young brushmaker named Alfred Stokes. He called out from time to time for police assistance but none came. Stokes followed the cab to the Commercial Road, where it stopped briefly near the corner of Greenfield Street to pick up a female passenger. The chase continued through the city as the cab made its way to the river, then across London Bridge, before it ended its journey in High Street, Borough, coming to a halt at the junction with Southwark Street, at a group of buildings known as the Hen and Chickens.

A smartly dressed, bearded man got out of the cab and took from the front seat a parcel, which he carried into the Hen and Chickens. While this was happening, Alfred Stokes spotted a policeman and went to talk to him. A little later the man came back to the cab and took out another parcel. Stokes and the policeman approached him, joined by another policeman. They accompanied the man, still carrying the parcel, into the Hen and Chickens and emerged a few minutes later. The beaded man and the woman who remained inside the cab, were taken into custody and driven to Stone's End Police Station. The two parcels were taken to St Saviour's mortuary.

The bearded man was Henry Wainwright, a mat and brushmaker, who had until his recent bankruptcy operated from business premises at 84 and 215 Whitechapel Road. Back in 1871, thirty-three-year-old Henry Wainwright, a keen amateur actor and public speaker, was a successful businessman who was living with his wife and family in Chingford. By chance, he met twenty-two-year-old Harriet Louisa Lane, apprenticed to a milliner and dressmaker. She became his mistress. They conducted their affair using various aliases and he moved her into lodgings at 14 St Peter Street (now Cephas Street), Mile End. Well placed in business, Wainwright gave his mistress £5 a week. Harriet bore him a daughter on 22 August 1872. After Wainwright moved his family into 40 Tredegar Square, Bow, he moved Harriet to the West End. She later bore him another child, also a girl. Both children were looked after elsewhere, paid for by Wainwright.

As Wainwright's business dealings began to flounder Harriet became an increasingly irritating encumbrance. To economise he had moved her back to Whitechapel, to lodgings in Sidney Street. His business continued on the downturn and he had debts of over £3,000. Harriet's constant demands on his purse and her increasing bouts of drunkenness were beginning to cause him embarrassment, particularly as she had taken to calling in at his place of business. He decided to offload her and conceived a plan to procure a new lover for her. He persuaded his brother, Thomas, to pose as her admirer, and the name he chose for him was that of one of his acquaintances, Teddy Frieake. His plan was for Thomas, in the guise of Frieake, to endear himself to her and to take her to some far-flung place on the continent and leave her without means, so that her return to England would be impossible. This highly implausible plan was only partially put into operation with several liaisons between Teddy and Harriet. Meanwhile, Wainwright attempted to rescue his failing business, by mortgaging his warehouse at 215 Whitechapel Road, in September 1884.

Clearly by this time Wainwright had realised the continuance of his relationship with Harriet Lane posed too great a risk. On 10 September he ordered half a hundredweight of chloride of lime. At four o'clock the following afternoon, Harriet Lane left her lodgings. The living space above Wainwright's warehouse was vacant, she intended staying there. She was never seen alive again.

Three men working next door to Wainwright's warehouse swore that, on an evening about this time in September, between half-past five and six o'clock, they heard three pistol shots fired in rapid succession, which appeared to come from the direction of Wainwright's premises. The discoveries made almost exactly a year later would seem to bear that out. Certainly Harriet's body was buried in chloride of lime in an area towards the back of the warehouse, known as the 'paint shop'. Harriet Lane had been shot through the head and her throat had also been cut. Wainwright clearly believed that the chloride of lime would quickly dissolve the soft tissue and there would be no remains to link him to the murder. How wrong he was. Harriet's family made enquiries concerning her whereabouts and the real Teddy Frieake, appearing on the scene caused considerable consternation, which later was explained at the Wainwright brothers' trial.

On 27 November 1874, Wainwright's shop at 84 Whitechapel Road burnt down. He claimed £3,000 insurance money from the Sun Fire Office but they disputed the claim. He brought an action against them, which had not yet come to trial at the time of his arrest. On 30 June 1875, Henry Wainwright was declared bankrupt. A fellow Whitechapel businessman, Mr Martin, took over Wainwright's former business in an amicable way, and advanced him £300. He paid Wainwright a salary of £3 a week as manager, and intended to eventually restore his business to him. Wainwright had by this time moved from Tredegar Square to School Lane, Chingford. Mr Martin also took on Alfred Stokes, Wainwright's former long-term outworker.

The mortgagees having foreclosed on his warehouse, made Wainwright realise that Harriet's remains had to be removed. He still retained a key and gained unobtrusive access to the rear of the warehouse via Vine Court. Exactly when Thomas Wainwright became aware of what had happened to his brother's mistress is not known. But once Wainwright realised Harriet's remains were extremely well preserved, he enlisted his assistance. On 10 September 1875 the brothers purchased between then some American cloth, rope, a spade and a chopper, after which Harriet's body was crudely chopped up. About four o'clock that afternoon Henry Wainwright asked Stokes to help him remove some parcels from the warehouse. He did so and carried one heavy package into Whitechapel Road, Wainwright carried the other, all the time puffing on a cigar to disguise the offensive smell. While Wainwright went for a cab, Stokes untied the rope and peered into one of the parcels. He saw a human hand. When Wainwright put the parcels into the cab Stokes followed it and the chase began.

Henry Wainwright's shop was situated next to the Pavilion Theatre. He was very friendly with the artistes who appeared there, and often took them out. In the Commercial Road, when he saw Alice Day, who worked at the theatre as a seamstress, Wainwright stopped the cab and invited her to join him. He continued to puff on his cigar until the cab reached the Hen and Chickens in Borough High Street, where until recently his brother, Thomas, had run an ironmongery business. There were deep cellars there with plenty of places to secrete unwanted encumbrances. But as Wainwright attempted to dispose of Harriet once and for all, he was arrested, but not before attempting to bribe the two police officers who apprehended him in the act.

The remains were examined and three bullets were found in Harriet's skull. It was concluded that her throat had been cut either immediately before or immediately after death. Although her facial features were unrecognisable, she was positively identified by her father because of a scar on her right knee.

It soon became clear that Miss Alice Day knew nothing about the contents of the parcels and was released but Henry Wainwright's brother, Thomas, was also arrested. The Wainwright brothers' trial commenced at the Old Bailey on Monday 22 November 1875, before the Lord Chief Justice of England (Sir James Alexander Cockburn, Bart). The whole story of Wainwright's connection with Harriet Lane was revealed, as was his brother's involvement. Henry Wainwright was found guilty of murder and sentenced to death. Thomas Wainwright was found guilty of being an accessory and sentenced to seven years' penal servitude. After the prisoners had been removed from the bar, the Lord Chief Justice said:

I think it right to exercise a power which I have vested in me, sitting here upon the trial, by Act of Parliament, to order that a reward be given from the proper fund to the man Stokes. His conduct and his energy in the occasion of these remains being moved from Whitechapel to the Borough, and his perseverance in following up the cab in which those remains were being conveyed, have in reality led to the discovery of this crime and the conviction of the offenders concerned in it. I shall direct, therefore, that he shall receive from the proper fund the sum of £30.

Henry Wainwright, languishing out his final few days in Newgate, chose the hymns for the service in the prison chapel on his last Sunday. On the evening before his execution within Newgate's execution shed, he strolled up and down the yard in the company of the governor of the prison, Mr Sydney Smith, smoking a cigar, allowed as a special privilege, while he recounted his tales of his amorous adventures with numerous women. On the morning of his execution, Tuesday 21 December 1875, Wainwright stepped briskly from his cell, nodded cheerily to the governor and strode to the execution shed with a smile on his lips. His smile faded when he beheld the unexpected crowd of spectators, because the execution itself was only nominally private as some sixty-seven persons were present, admitted by special permission of the sheriff. There were unsubstantiated rumours that several women, disguised as men, were present. Wainwright's executioner was William Marwood who had only recently taken up his post in London. As Wainwright entered the execution shed, he said to the assembled company, 'Come to see a man die have you, you curs?'

Following his execution, towards the middle of the day, the body of Henry Wainwright was placed in a rough deal box, filled with wood shavings and quick lime. It was then carried by warders to a narrow, bleak gaol pathway, below massive cross-barred gratings, which almost shut out the light of day, connecting Newgate to the adjoining Sessions House. This grim corridor was known as Birdcage Walk but was more commonly referred to as Dead Man's Walk. Wainwright was buried there beneath the flagstones. The initial letters of the surnames of those buried there were carved into the wall, marking the spot beneath which they lay. This corridor was seldom visited, except by those who would walk down it on their way to their own execution.

Israel Lipski, 1882

Israel Lipski, a twenty-two-year-old Jewish immigrant, working as an umbrella manufacturer, lodged in the attic of a three-storey house at 16 Batty Street, Stepney. Among the fourteen other residents was eighteen-year-old Miriam Angel who occupied a second floor room. On 28 June 1887, Miriam was found on the bed by a relative with yellow foam coming from her mouth. A doctor suspected corrosive poisoning and a container of nitric acid was found, which confirmed this. Lipski was still alive and his claim that he and Miriam had been attacked by two labourers was not believed. Police suspected that Lipski had tried to rape Miriam, and having failed had forced her to drink the acid and then attempted to commit suicide. Considerable unrest among the immigrant community surrounded this case. After his trial and conviction at the Old Bailey the authorities were unsure whether Lipski should be reprieved. However, it became clear that justice had been served when Lipski admitted that robbery, not rape, had been his motive, shortly before he was being hanged at Newgate on 22 August 1887.

Dr Thomas Neill Cream, 1892

Known as the Lambeth Poisoner, profoundly cross-eyed Dr Cream was born at 61 Wellington Lane, Glasgow on 27 May 1850. Four years later the Cream family emigrated to Canada. Thomas Cream studied medicine graduating from McGill College, Montreal in 1876. Earlier, in 1874, he had insured his lodgings for $1,000, within a fortnight of graduation, as a result of a mysterious fire, Cream had put in a claim for almost the full amount. At first his insurers refused to pay but eventually forked out $350 for what they believed was a case of arson. Before long Cream met the daughter of a wealthy hotelier, Flora Elizabeth Brooks, who shortly became pregnant. The pregnancy was terminated by Cream and almost resulted in Miss Brook's death. Her father insisted they marry and Cream was virtually marched up the aisle on 11 September 1874. The day after the wedding Cream took to his heels and headed for England. He didn't get in touch again until he heard Flora had died of consumption just over a year later, and that was only to demand $1,000 from her father for the marriage settlement. He got £200 for his cheek.

On his arrival in England, Cream enrolled as a postgraduate student at St Thomas's Hospital. During this further period of study he also received honours from the Royal College of Physicians and Surgeons at Edinburgh and afterwards returned to Canada, where from premises in Dundas Street, London, Ontario, he began to earn a considerable income as an abortionist. However, after the deaths of two of his patients under very dubious circumstances his practice was ruined and he moved to the USA to set up practice in Chicago, where he was later arrested on a charge of murder but acquitted through lack of evidence. Then, also in Chicago, in 1881, he was charged with poisoning a patient, Daniel Stott, found guilty of murder in the second degree and imprisoned for life in the Illinois State Penitentiary at Joliet. Bizarrely, he incriminated himself by the self-advertising of his

crime through a series of anonymous letters. With the assistance of
his family his sentence was reduced on appeal to seventeen years;
and on 31 July 1891, taking into account his good behaviour, he
was released. His father had died in 1867 and, having collected his
$16,000 inheritance, Dr Cream boarded the *Teutonic* for Liverpool.

On Monday 5 October 1891, Dr Cream, now calling himself Dr
Neill, checked into the Anderton's Hotel in Fleet Street. On 6 October,
he went to Ludgate Circus where he met prostitute Elizabeth Masters
and spent the evening with her drinking before going back to her
rooms at 9 Orient Buildings, in Lambeth's Hercule Road. This sordid
district of London obviously took his eye because the following day he
moved into lodgings at 103 Lambeth Palace Road. From there this
suave, silk hat wearing, bespectacled, sexual deviant, known to his
victims as 'Fred', went on a rampage of killing south of the River
Thames that rivalled the Jack the Ripper murders in the East End.
He, like the Ripper, chose prostitutes as his prey, plying them with
poison, administered in pills containing strychnine. Ellen Donworth,
Matilda Clover, Emma Shrivell and Alice Marsh all fell victim to
Cream. Just as he had done in Chicago he began sending anonymous
letters, which put himself into the frame and with the help of prostitute
Louisa Harvey, who had managed to elude the doctor's attempts to
poison her, Cream was arrested on 3 June 1892 in Lambeth Palace
Road by Inspector Tunbridge. Seven bottles of strychnine were found
at his lodgings.

Dr Cream's trial began at the Old Bailey on 17 October 1892,
before Mr Justice Hawkins. He was charged with the murder of
Matilda Clover and, three days later, with overwhelming evidence
against him, the jury found Cream guilty.

On 24 October 1892, the *St James's Gazette* included a report of
Dr Neill (Cream) by 'one who knew him':

Women were his preoccupation, and his talk of them far from
agreeable. He carried pornographic photographs, which he was
too ready to display. He was in the habit of taking pills, which he
said, were compounded of strychnine, morphia and cocaine, and of
which the effect, he declared, was aphrodisiac. In short, he was a
degenerate of filthy desires and practices ...

Cream never confessed or gave any indication what had driven him
to murder. He was hanged at Newgate on 15 November 1892 and
buried in Dead Man's Walk.

Milson & Fowler, 1896

On the morning of 14 February 1896, seventy-nine-year-old retired engineer Henry Smith was found by his gardener, Charles Webber, gagged and brutally murdered, in the kitchen of his imposing house, Muswell Lodge, situated in Tetherdown, Muswell Hill. He had been tied up with strips of cloth, cut with two penknives left nearby, the safe had been rifled and there were signs of forced entry through the kitchen window. Significantly, as would later be shown, a broken toy lantern left in the kitchen sink, was to prove crucial in the detection of the culprits. The lantern had multi-coloured bull's eye glasses, and was similar to the type used by railway guards. There were several distinctive marks on the lantern indicating that it had been repaired. The murder victim, although attended by a servant during the day, chose to live alone. He had been a widower for twenty-four years and despite his advanced years, was a strong and remarkably fit man. Very security conscious he took various precautions regarding the protection of his home, which included a spring gun, activated by trip wires in the garden. Unfortunately, the criminals had not activated the gun and all signs pointed to a burglary that had gone disastrously wrong.

The police worked on the premise that they were looking for two men and the behaviour of two known felons immediately following the crime left the police with few doubts that they were the suspects they were looking for. Thirty-two-year-old Albert Milsom, although not by nature a violent man, had already been convicted of a long list of crimes, mostly burglary. He lived with his wife Emily and their two children at his mother-in-law's house, along with fifteen-year-old Henry Miller, Emily's brother, at 133 Southman Street, Kensal Town. Milsom had been for some time associated with another Kensal Town resident, Henry Fowler. Thirty-one-year-old Fowler had a long record and was known to be violent. Fowler had been released from prison on parole on 16 January. Fowler's renewed association with Milsom had been noticed by the local police and their disappearance drew further attention to themselves. Once Henry Miller had identified the lantern as his own, pointing out the repairs he had undertaken himself, the police knew they had their men. Milsom and Fowler managed to evade their pursuers until Saturday 10 April, having travelled to various parts of the country as part of a travelling show. They were captured in Bath, brought back to London and tried at the Old Bailey on 19 May before Mr Justice Hawkins. The evidence was heavily stacked against them. This case is notable for the violent outburst that came as the jury returned with their guilty verdict. Fowler flung himself across the dock at his accomplice very nearly succeeding in sparing the executioner the job of hanging him. Milsom and Fowler were hanged at Newgate on Wednesday 10 June with Whitechapel murderer William Seaman between them.

William Seaman, 1896

William Seaman was responsible for a double killing known as 'The Turner Street Murders'. The victims were Mr John Goodman Levy, aged seventy-seven and his housekeeper, Mrs Anna Sarah Gale, aged thirty-five. Mr Levy had retired just a few weeks previously, having been in business as an umbrella manufacturer, trading as M J Myers. It was generally believed that Mr Levy made a considerable fortune as a 'fence', which subsequent events seemed to confirm. This case was instrumental in bringing Detective Sergeant F P Wensley to the notice of his superiors. He later became the first Assistant Commissioner to be promoted from the ranks.

Early on the afternoon of Saturday 4 April 1896, the East End was plunged into a state of wild excitement by the harrowing details which came to hand of one of the most brutal double murders, accompanied by attempted burglary, that had been seen in Whitechapel since the Jack The Ripper murders of 1888. The scene of the outrage was 31 Turner Street, Commercial Road East. The first suspicion of foul play was aroused a little before one o'clock on Saturday when Mrs Martha Lawton, a cousin of Mr Levy, who lived in the same street at No. 35, went to the house to keep a luncheon appointment but there was no reply. The next-door neighbour, a tailor, named William Schafer, came out to see what was the matter. He went to his back-yard to see if he could ascertain anything and was astonished to see a strange man in a brown cloth cap inside the house. The constables on duty in the vicinity, having been summoned, gained entry to No. 31 and proceeded to search the premises. Half concealed behind the lavatory door at the back of the ground floor, they discovered the body of Mr Levy, lying in a pool of blood. His throat had been cut from ear to ear with some sharp instrument, while the back of his skull had been battered in with what appeared, from the terrible nature of the wounds, to be a hammer. In the second floor back bedroom the housekeeper Mrs Gale lay on the floor, also in a pool of blood. Her head had been almost completely severed from her body, and her skull unmercifully beaten with a blunt instrument.

In the front room of the second floor the police officers noticed that a hole had recently been made in the ceiling giving access to the roof. There was a loud cry from the street below that there was a man on the roof. Just as one constable had got his body half-way through the hole into the void to the roof, he caught sight of a man standing in the gutter which ran round the roof. Moments later, the man had mounted the coping, hauled himself over by his hands and dropped into the street below, a distance of between forty and fifty feet. As he fell, his body struck the back of a little girl, Leah Hyams, who was standing with her mother close under the wall at the Varden Street entrance to the house. Several gold watches, some rings, and other jewellery, as well as a quantity of money were found in two parcels he was carrying. He had sustained serious injuries. The injured man was taken to the London Hospital as was little Leah Hyams, where she received attention for injuries to her back and for fright. She was discharged from hospital later that day. The man was identified as William Seaman. On Saturday 2 May 1896 *The Times* reported:

Yesterday morning, William Seaman, 46, described as a lighterman of Claud-street, Millwall, was brought from the London Hospital and charged at the Thames Police-court with the wilful murders of Sarah Annie Gale and John Goodman Levy, of 31, Turner-street, Whitechapel on 4th ult. The prisoner was lifted into the Court seated on an armchair and was evidently suffering considerable pain. Seaman, who was undefended, was on Thursday night interviewed by Mr. Bedford, solicitor, but declined that gentleman's services.

Constable G Bryan, 176H, said in his evidence given at Thames Police Court that, on 11 April while he was in charge of the prisoner at the London Hospital, Seaman said to him: 'I suppose old Levy is dead by this time and buried?' Constable Bryan told Seaman that he didn't know. Seaman went on: 'I am glad I have done for him. I have been a good many times for the money, amounting to £70, and the old man always made some excuse. I made up my mind to do for him. I am not afraid of being hanged.' The next day, on waking up, Seaman said: 'I have been a frequent visitor to the house in Turner Street, where the job was done; and if the old Jew had only paid me the £70, the job would not have happened ...'

Dr Lewis Smith, house surgeon at the London Hospital, said that when Mrs Bowater, Seaman's landlady, was called to identify him he said to her: 'I am guilty. I did it for revenge. He swindled me years ago. I did it for revenge.'

The outcome of Seaman's trial at the Old Bailey was almost a foregone conclusion. Found guilty of wilful murder, he was sentenced to death. Seaman was hanged at Newgate on 10 June 1896, by James Billington, along with Albert Milsom and Henry Fowler, two petty thieves turned murderers, who had fallen out during their trial, Fowler having almost strangled Milsom in the block. At their execution, Seaman was placed between Milsom and Fowler. Seaman's last words are reputed to be: 'This is the first time I've ever been a bloody peacemaker.'

An unusual mishap occurred during the execution. Four warders were in close attendance on the scaffold. One of them obscured Billington's view of his assistant, Warbrick. Warbrick was still pinioning the feet of one of the prisoners when Billington operated the lever that opened the trap door. The three criminals plummeted to their deaths as Warbrick was catapulted into the pit. Fortunately, the latter heard the bolt beneath him being withdrawn and instinctively grabbed the legs of the man in front of him. He ended up swinging below the feet of the three dead men. The execution of Seaman, Milsom and Fowler was the last triple execution at Newgate.

Louise (or Louisa) Josephine Masset, 1900

In 1899, Louise Masset, the daughter of a Frenchman and an English woman, lodged with her sister at 29 Bethune Road, Stoke Newington. Aged thirty-six and unmarried, she was an attractive looking woman who earned her living either as a piano teacher or as a governess. She had a four-year-old son, Manfred Louis, the result of an affair she had in France, but the father's identity was never revealed, although according to the child's foster mother, Miss Gentle, he regularly sent money to support the boy. Manfred was lodged separately with Helen Gentle, in Clyde Road, Tottenham. Louise began an affair with a nineteen-year-old French student Eudore Lucas but after he found out about little Manfred his ardour waned and Louise decided to get rid of what she clearly regarded as an unwanted encumbrance, in order to retain Eudore's affections.

She informed Miss Gentle that his father was going to take over Manfred's upbringing in France and collected him on the morning of 27 October, along with a parcel containing his clothes. Louise Masset was last seen with her son at London Bridge station. Later that same day his battered and naked body was found wrapped in a black shawl in the ladies' lavatory on Platform No. 3 at Dalston Junction station. Nearby was a bloodstained stone that had been used to kill him. After reading a report about the dead child in a newspaper, Miss Gentle came forward and identified him.

When questioned by police Louise Masset told them that she had handed her son over to two ladies at London Bridge, a Mrs Browning and her associate who were opening a new orphanage in Chelsea. She said she had handed over the boy and £12 to the two women, but could not produce a receipt, nor could the women be traced. She had then caught a train to Brighton, where she spent the weekend in the company of her lover. The weight of evidence was stacked against her. A paper parcel containing Manfred's clothes was found in the waiting room at Brighton station and the black shawl in which the boy's body had been found was identified as having been bought by Louise Masset in a shop in Stoke Newington. Ever more damming was the stone used to kill little Manfred. It fitted a hole in the rockery at 29 Bethune Road.

The public were outraged by this uncaring mother's cruel act, compounded by the fact that having killed her son she had gone immediately to the arms of her lover. They could not find a grain of sympathy for her and there was no outcry when she was hanged at Newgate on 9 January 1900. Louise Masset was the first person to be hanged in Britain in the twentieth century. Her executioner was James Billington.

The last few Newgate hangings

Ada Chard Williams was hanged on 6 March for the murder of Selina Ellen Jones. Henry Grove was hanged on 22 May for the murder of Henry Smith. Alfred Highfield hanged for the murder of his girlfriend Edith Margaret Poole, on 17 July. Wife-murderer William Irwin was hanged on 14 August for killing Catherine Amelia Irwin; and John Charles Parr was hanged on 2 October for the murder of his girlfriend Sarah Willett.

The year 1901 saw two hangings at Newgate. Samson Salmon was hanged on 19 February for murdering his cousin Lucy Smith; and on 19 November, Marcel Fougeron became Newgate's penultimate criminal to be executed, when he was hanged for the murder of Hermann Francis Jung.

George Woolf has the dubious distinction of being the last person to be hanged at Newgate. He became friendly with Charlotte Cheeseman while her own sweetheart was fighting in the Boer War. When the soldier returned from active service an unpleasant confrontation took place after he discovered her connection with Woolf and he and Charlotte broke off their relationship. Twenty-four-year-old Woolf callously ditched Charlotte having promised to marry her, after she became pregnant. He sent her a letter in which he informed her he had met someone else he liked better and not to try and put the blame on him if she found herself in a 'certain condition'. The letter went on:

> I hope I shall never hear of you or see you again, as I am indeed thankful I have got rid of you so easily.

Charlotte sent a reply:

> Dear George,
>
> Don't be offended because I am writing this letter to you. Will you go out with me again as you know what you have done to me. I think it is a shame how you have treated me, but I will forget that and think of you all the more. You don't know how much I love you ...

Woolf had also written to Charlotte's employer at the cigar factory in Hoxton, where she worked, implying she was not of good character and should not be trusted. Her employer thought otherwise and showed the letter to the police.

Woolf met Charlotte on the evening of 25 January 1902. They were seen drinking together in the Rosemary Branch, in Southgate Road, Hoxton. The following morning some children discovered Charlotte's blood-soaked, battered body in a ditch on Tottenham Marshes. She had been brutally killed with a chisel. Woolf attempted to escape by enlisting in the Army but justice caught up with him and he was tried at the Old Bailey and hanged 6 May 1902.

Shortly afterwards, work began on Newgate's demolition.

When Newgate was demolished the remains of the ninety-seven executed prisoners recorded to have been buried in Dead Man's Walk, were lifted and reburied in the City of London Cemetery.

CHAPTER 3

The Marshalsea

ituated on the south bank of the River Thames, the Marshalsea was a prison from *c.*1329. Its name is derived from the court once held by the Steward and Marshall of the Royal Household, which held special jurisdiction from *c.*1290. The court effectively went with the king wherever he travelled and had jurisdiction over a 12-mile radius from the king's person, wherever the king happened to be lodging. Members of the king's household were subject to his court rather than the local court. The Marshalsea prison was specifically built to house prisoners of this court. It acquired an unsavoury reputation for the harshness of the regime there and the original buildings were destroyed by Wat Tyler's rebels in 1381. The buildings of the Marshalsea were either repaired or completely rebuilt and in addition to its original function, began to take in debtors. Its site was at the present day 161 Borough High Street, between King Street and Mermaid Court. Its buildings, some acquired later as the prison grew in size, were set back from the street, and covered an area no more than 150ft by 50ft.

In external appearance the Marshalsea looked more like an Oxbridge College than a prison, with a turreted building known as the Lodge at the entrance, containing a side room known as The Pound, in which new prisoners were kept until they were allocated a room. Behind the Lodge was a courtyard known as the Park. This was divided in two by a high wall, built there so that the two classes of prisoner kept at the Marshalsea in the more commodious Master's Side, occupied by well-to-do debtors and the somewhat gruesome Common Side, occupied by poor prisoners, could not see each other. However, it was not uncommon for prisoners in the Master's Side to hire prisoners from the Common Side to act as their servants.

Although the Marshalsea technically fell under control of the Knight Marshall, in keeping with the practice at London's other prisons, it was rented out to private individuals who ran it for profit. There was some comfort available for those prisoners who could afford to pay but poor prisoners lived in squalor. In 1639, a revolt occurred in the Common Side following complaints by prisoners that twenty-three women were being held in one small room with insufficient space for them to lie down.

Punishments could be harsh. Prisoners were regularly whipped with a 'bull's pizzle', a whip made from a bull's penis. Thumbscrews were sometimes used, as was a device known as the skullcap, a vice placed on the head weighing 12lb. Possibly the most unpleasant punishment of all was being forced to lay in the Strong Room. This windowless shed was situated near the main sewer and contained cadavers awaiting burial. Of this most fearful place Dickens wrote that it was '. . . dreaded by even the most dauntless highwaymen and bearable only to toads and rats . . .'.

During the Reformation both Catholics and Protestants were imprisoned there, some of them being treated with extreme brutality. Despite most of the prisoners at the Marshalsea being debtors the Marshalsea became regarded as second in importance only to the Tower of London. During the reign of Elizabeth I, Bishop Bonner was brought to the Marshalsea as a prisoner in 1559 and died still a prisoner there in 1569. As the last Catholic Bishop of London he had been responsible for the imprisonment of many in the Marshalsea, as well as several other of London's prisons. In the Marshalsea the most unfortunate of Bonner's prisoners were placed in the lowest dank, dark dungeon, for sometime fearsomely known as 'The Hole' but from Bonner's time more commonly referred to as 'Bonner's Coal Hole'. Ben Jonson, the playwright, was imprisoned in the Marshalsea in 1597 for writing and having performed a play, *The Isle of Dogs*, which was regarded by the authorities as being seditious. In 1601, the poet Christopher Brooke was jailed for helping the seventeen-year-old Ann More marry the poet John Donne, without her father's consent. In 1541, Nicholas Udall, vicar of Braintree and headmaster of Eton College, was sent to the Marshalsea for buggery and suspected theft. His stint in the Marshalsea didn't seem to do him any lasting harm, as he was appointed headmaster of Westminster School in 1555. In 1557, a Protestant martyr named Gratwick was imprisoned in the Marshalsea before being burned in St George's Fields. The Vice Admiral of Devon, Sir John Eliot, the leading figure in the Commons opposition to royal policies in the first three Parliaments of Charles I, was firstly imprisoned in the Tower of London in 1632 before being tried at the King's Bench and brought to the Marshalsea after being sentenced to be detained during His Majesty's pleasure, for questioning the right of the king to tax imports and exports. Sir

John famously commented, 'I am leaving my palace in London for my country house in Southwark'. Sir John was soon returned to the Tower, where he died of consumption later that year.

The Marshalsea's separate areas for its two classes of prisoners, the Master's Side, which contained about fifty rooms for rent, was for some prisoners almost like a home from home. In 1728, rent for the rooms was ten shillings a week. These rooms were often shared, the rent being split between the prisoners occupying the respective room. Whereas, the Common Side was hugely different to the Master's Side. It contained nine rooms, which were not very large, into which were crammed as many as 300 prisoners, who were locked up from dusk until dawn. The Marshalsea was referred to by the inmates as The Castle, on account of the appearance of its buildings.

On 25 March 1729, the recently formed Gaols Committee visited the Marshalsea. The committee were shocked by the conditions the prisoners were living in and reported back to parliament that they had found:

> ... the sale of offices, breaches of trust, enormous extortions, oppression, intimidation, gross brutalities, and the highest crimes and misdemeanours ...

In the Common Side the committee were horrified at the conditions and quickly formed the opinion the prisoners were being routinely starved to death:

> ... All the Support such poor Wretches have to subsist on, is an Accidental Allowance of Pease, given once a week by a Gentleman, who conceals his Name, and about Thirty Pounds of Beef, provided by the voluntary Contribution of the Judge and Officers of the Marshalsea, on Monday, Wednesday, and Friday; which is divided into very small Portions, of about an Ounce and a half, distributed with One-Fourth-Part of an Half-penny Loaf: Each of the Sick is first served with One of those Portions, and those that remain are divided amongst the wards; but the numbers of the People in them are so great, that it comes to the Turn of each Man but about once in fourteen Days, and of each Woman (they being fewer) once in a Week. When the miserable Wretch hath worn out the Charity of his Friends, and consumed the Money, which he hath raised upon his Cloaths, and Bedding. And hath eat his last Allowance of Provisions, he usually in a few Days grows weak, foe want of Food, with the symptoms of a hectic Feve; and when he is

no longer able to stand, if he can raise 3d to pay the Fee of the common Nurse of the Prison, he obtains the Liberty of being carried into the Sick Ward and lingers on for about a Month or two by the assistance of the above mentioned Prison Portion of Provision, and then dies.

The extensive report made by the Gaols Committee and the enquiries that resulted, led to several key figures at various gaols being tried for murder. These included Thomas Bainbridge of the Fleet and William Acton, the Keeper of the Marshalsea. Four cases of death caused as a result of Acton's ill treatment of those placed in his charge were featured in his trial, involving the deaths of Thomas Bliss, a debtor unable to pay the prison fees, who was left in the Strong Room for three weeks wearing a skullcap, thumb screws, iron collar, leg irons and irons around his ankles. Captain John Bromfield, Robert Newton and James Thompson, also received similar treatment at the hands of Acton. Despite overwhelming witness evidence against Acton, the government favoured an acquittal to protect the good name of the Knight Marshall, Sir Philip Meadows, who had hired John Darby as prison governor, who had in turn leased the Marshalsea to William Acton, a butcher, for an annual rental of £400. A large number of witnesses came forward to speak in Acton's defence, including his butcher, brewer and confectioner. His coal merchant described Acton as being 'improper for the post he was in from his too great compassion'. Perhaps overwhelmed by the sheer volume of good character references, the jury saw fit to find Acton not guilty on all charges. Although the Gaol's Committee had highlighted the many shortcomings at the Marshalsea, they failed to have any significant impact on the improvement in conditions there.

In 1799 the government acknowledged that the Marshalsea was in a state of decay. When the Marshalsea was visited by prison reformer James Neild, in December 1802, the prison population had dwindled to just thirty-four debtors, along with eight wives and seven children. In his observations Neild commented that the Marshalsea was in:

... a most ruinous and insecure state, and the habitations of the debtors wretched in the extreme ...

A decision was made to rebuild the Marshalsea, on a new site 130 yards south of the old prison, to the north of St George's church, on the site of the White Lion Prison. It was built at a cost of £8,000 and opened in 1811. It contained two sections, one for Admiralty

Prisoners, the other, for debtors. Some features in the Admiralty section contained surviving parts of the White Lion Prison, which were in essence no longer fit for the purpose they were put to. The chapel, shared by both sections, was also a remnant of the old prison. As well as housing prisoners under court martial, the Admiralty section also held a few prisoners for mutiny, desertion, piracy and what was termed 'unnatural crimes', which presumably meant buggery.

The Debtors' section provided accommodation that was cramped as that in the original Marshalsea, consisting of a brick barracks, measuring about 99ft by 30ft, divided into eight houses, each with three floors, containing fifty-six rooms in all; a yard measuring 177ft by 56ft, a kitchen, a public room, and a tap room or snuggery, where debtors could drink as much beer as they could afford to pay for. Women debtors were housed in rooms over the tap room. Most of the rooms for men measured either 10ft 6in square or 8ft 6in square. Each had a window and fireplace. Most of these room housed two or three prisoners, usually in shared beds. The wealthier prisoners were allocated the better accommodation.

The presence of women, wives, daughters and even prostitutes in the Marshalsea was the accepted form. Visitors, including women, were free to come and go as they pleased and to live with the prisoners if they wished. Female prisoners living on the women's side of the barracks were free to mix with the male prisoners. The prison gates were closed at ten o'clock at night until eight o'clock the following morning. Half an hour before closing time an officer walked round the prison calling out, 'Strangers, women and children all out!'

On 20 February 1824, John Dickens, the father of novelist Charles Dickens (1812–70), became a prisoner at the Marshalsea, having been sent there under the Insolvency Debtor's Act of 1813, for a debt owed to a baker, James Kerr, of £40 10s. While Dickens' mother, Elizabeth, went to live at the Marshalsea, along with their three youngest children, in April, twelve-year-old Charles was sent to live in lodgings in Camden Town. From there he walked five miles every day to Warren's blacking factory, at 30 Hungerford Stairs, owned by a relation of his mother. He worked for ten hours each day, wrapping bottles of shoe polish, for which he was paid six shillings a week. Each Sunday he would visit his family in the Marshalsea. He found lodgings closer to the prison in Lant Street, in the attic of a house belonging to the vestry clerk of St George' church. From there he was able to break-fast with his family in the Marshalsea before going to work and to dine with them each evening. Although John Dickens' stay in the

Marshalsea was relatively short, he was released on 28 May 1824, the experience having a lasting effect on his son, Charles.

It is thanks to Charles Dickens that the Marshalsea is very well known, even though the prison that was familiar to him had a relatively short life and only existed as a prison from 1811 until 1842. In 1827, of the 630 debtors imprisoned there, 414 were there for debts of less than £20. The authorities were beginning to take a different view towards an individual's indebtedness. Dickens highlighted the sorry plight of debtors in several of his books, the Marshalsea featuring in three of them, *The Pickwick Papers* (1836/37), *David Copperfield* (1849/1850) and *Little Dorrit* (1855/57), in which the main character, Amy, is imprisoned in the Marshalsea. One small passage from *Little Dorrit* which is particularly moving, is where Dr Haggage tells another prisoner:

> We are quiet here; we don't get badgered here; there's no knocker, sir, to be hammered at by creditors and bring a man's heart into his mouth. Nobody comes here to ask if a man's at home, and to say he'll stand on the door mat till he is. Nobody writes threatening letters about money to this place. It's freedom, sir, it's freedom!

The Marshalsea Prison was closed by an Act of Parliament in 1842, its inmates being transferred on 19 November to either the Hospital of Bethlem (for those who were mentally ill) or the Queen's Prison (which the King's Bench Prison had become known). A little over seven years later, on 31 December 1849, the Court of the Marshalsea of the King's of England was abolished, and its powers transferred to Her Majesty's Court of Common Pleas at Westminster.

In July 1843, the Marshalsea's buildings and land were sold by auction, realising £5,100. Although most of the prison buildings were demolished in the 1870s, parts of it survived until as recently as 1955. All that remains today is a brick wall that once marked the southern boundary of the prison, which can be viewed in a small public garden that was once St George's churchyard. There is a plaque recording that the Marshalsea Prison once stood there.

CHAPTER 4

The Gatehouse

The Gatehouse was built in 1370 by Walter Warfield, cellarer to Westminster Abbey. Situated in Broad Sanctuary, very close to Westminster Abbey itself, it had two wings built at right angles to each other. Both had gates and gaols. The north wing was the Bishop of London's prison, meant to house 'clerk convicts', the other wing to the south was for lay offenders. The duty of running the Gatehouse fell upon the shoulders of the abbey janitor, who undertook the task for an official salary of a daily ration of bread and ale, and a new robe annually.

Although only a relatively small prison, being close to Westminster Hall it was convenient for holding state prisoners. The Irish Jesuit of the Counter Reformation, Christopher Holywood (1559–1626), was imprisoned in the Gatehouse in 1598 before being moved to the Tower of London and later to Wisbech Castle, before being shipped to the continent following the death of Elizabeth I in 1603. Sir Walter Raleigh (1552–1618) spent the last night of his life in the Gatehouse before his execution on 29 October 1618. When neither legal precedents nor logic could be opined as to why Raleigh must die, rhetoric was resorted to give a reason for his death: 'You have lived like a star, at which the world hath gazed. And like a star you must fall, when the firmament is shaked.'

The Cavalier metaphysical poet Richard Lovelace (1618–57) was imprisoned in the Gatehouse from 30 April to 21 June 1642, following his presentation of a Royalist petition to Parliament favouring the restoration of the Anglican bishops, who had been excluded from the Long Parliament. During his incarceration he wrote one of his finest works, *To Althea from Prison*:

> *When love with unconfined wings*
> *Hovers within my gates,*
> *And my divine Althea brings*
> *To whisper at the grates;*

When I lie tangled in her hair
And fetter'd to her eye.
The birds that wanton in the air
Know no such liberty.

When flowing cups run swiftly round
With no allaying Thames,
Our careless heads with roses bound,
Our hearts with loyal flames;
When thirsty grief in wine we steep,
When healths and draughts go free
Fishes that tipple in the deep
Know no such liberty.

When, like committed linnets, I
With shriller throat shall sing
The sweetness, mercy, majesty,
And glories of my King;
When I shall voice aloud how good
He is, how great should be.
Enlarged winds, that curl the floods,
Know no such liberty.

Stone walls do not a prison make,
Nor iron bars a cage;
Minds innocent and quiet take
Than for an hermitage:
If I have freedom in my love
And in my soul am free,
Angels alone, that soar above,
Enjoy such liberty.

Lovelace was released on bail on condition that he avoid communication with the House of Commons without permission.

In 1690, Samuel Pepys (1633–1703) spent three weeks in the Gatehouse 'on suspicion of being affected to King James' (being suspected of Jacobitism). No charges being successfully proved against him, Pepys was released after he became ill. In November 1727, Richard Savage, William Merchant and James Gregory were imprisoned there following the murder of James Sinclair, before being transferred to Newgate.

One peculiarity of the Gatehouse was an occasional income the prisoners received, the benefit by means of an alms box placed by the door of the gaol. In addition to the usual alms deposited in the box, by tradition the scholars of nearby Westminster School were obliged to place any coins they were seen to be playing with during school hours in the alms box at the Gatehouse as a punishment for this misdemeanour.

In 1761, Dr Samuel Johnson (1709–84) wrote the Gatehouse was 'so offensive that, without any particular reason, it ought to be pulled down, for it disgraces the present magnificence of the capital, and is a continual nuisance to neighbours and passengers'.

In 1768, notorious mother and daughter Sarah and Sarah Morgan Metyard were imprisoned at the Gatehouse following their arrest for the murder of the Naylor sisters, before they were transferred to Newgate.

Having been a feature of Westminster for some 406 years, the Gatehouse was demolished on the orders of the Dean and Chapter of Westminster in 1776. During the demolition process, when it was realised a sufficiently wide passage had been cleared for pedestrians, one of the Gatehouse's walls was allowed to remain in situ for another seventy years. Today the site of the Gatehouse is partly occupied by the Westminster scholar's Crimean War memorial.

CHAPTER 5

The Prisons at Clerkenwell

lerkenwell was once a hamlet situated to the north of the walls of the City of London, being sandwiched between Holborn and Isleden, the village from which the present-day Islington, as well as the London Borough bearing the same name, is derived. By 1500 Clerkenwell had grown into a much larger settlement and in 1612, sessions of the Justices of the Peace were being held there, in Hick's Hall on John Street. They were later held at the Sessions House on Clerkenwell Green.

Middlesex Bridewell
The Middlesex Bridewell was built at Clerkenwell following the 1609 Act of Parliament, requiring all counties to build a house of correction on the model of Bridewell to set 'rogues and idle persons' to work. It opened its gates to take its first prisoners in 1615, originally to incarcerate, put to work and punish the rogues and vagabonds of the County of Middlesex. By the beginning of the following century the function of Bridewells had been extended to include the holding of those suspected of crimes and offenders awaiting trial. At Clerkenwell two such prisoners were Lowther and Keele.

Twenty-three-year-old Will Lowther, born in Whitehaven, Cumbria, had spent ten years at sea, latterly as master on a collier given to him by his father, which traded between Newcastle and London. He was seduced by the seedier elements of London's docks and took to robbing ships as they lay at anchor. He also indulged in petty thieving elsewhere in the capital, whenever the opportunity arose, and struck up a friendship with another thief, Dick Keele, with whom he was apprehended in the act of stealing; and incarcerated in Clerkenwell Bridewell, where they caused a riot, during which Edward Perry, a servant to Mr Boreman, the keeper, was killed. Moved to Newgate, Lowther and Keele were found guilty of murder at the Old Bailey and hanged on Clerkenwell Green on 23 December 1713. Middlesex Bridewell was demolished in 1804.

The New Prison (Clerkenwell House of Correction and Detention)

The New Prison was built in *c.*1617 on an adjacent site to the south of the Middlesex Bridewell. In 1679 the prison was burned down by the inmates and rebuilt. In May 1724, Jack Sheppard (he of the genre of criminal folk heroes) and his accomplice Elizabeth Lyon (known as Edgworth Bess, because of where she originated from, Edgworth once being the name for Edgeware), having being brought from St Ann's Round House, Soho, posing as man and wife, were held together in a room in part of the prison known as Newgate Ward. There they were visited by friends, who were able to pass some tools to Sheppard to help him escape. On 25 May, Sheppard filed through his fetters and made a hole through the cell wall large enough for himself and Bess to squeeze through. Then, having fashioned a rope from the bed sheets, he and Bess climbed down 25ft into the yard of the adjacent Middlesex Bridewell and somehow managed to scale the 22ft-high wall and escaped.

One of the New Prison's most notable inmates was Theodore Gardelle (also see page 45), a Swiss painter who specialised in miniatures. He lodged on the western side of Leicester Fields, today's Leicester Square, with his landlady, Mrs King, close to the home of Sir Joshua Reynolds. From available accounts he appears to have been an otherwise inoffensive man. Some say he killed Mrs King in order to rob her, others because she spurned his attempts to seduce her; and, by his own admission, he killed her following a quarrel after she repeatedly poured scorn on a miniature portrait of her which he had executed. He was goaded into this fit of frenzy early in February 1761. Gardelle maintained that Mrs King came into the parlour and began to verbally abuse him about the miniature. The quarrel continued to the adjacent bedroom. When Gardelle told Mrs King that she was a very impertinent woman, she struck him a very violent blow on the chest. He pushed her away and Mrs King's foot caught in the floor-cloth and as she fell backwards her head hit a sharp corner of the bedstead with great force. As blood streamed from her mouth, Gardelle went to assist her. Mrs King threatened him with charges of assault and continued to rant and rage, at which point Gardelle panicked, picked up a sharp-pointed ivory comb and drove it into her throat. Her cries faded away and she died.

Horrified at what he'd done, Gardelle said he covered Mrs King's body with the bedclothes, before swooning away and hitting his head on the wainscot, which raised a bump over his right eye. A maid-servant who lived in the house was out on an errand. The only other residents another lodger and his servant, were out of town. When the maid returned Gardelle paid her wages on behalf of Mrs King and discharged her, telling her that her mistress had gone away to the country and would be bringing back another servant with her. When he eventually summoned up the courage several days later, Gardelle stripped the body and laid it out on the bed. He disposed of the bloodstained bedclothes by putting them in soak in a tub in the back washhouse. He then carved up Mrs King's body, disposing of blood and some pieces of flesh in various sinks. He burned several body parts and laid other pieces out in the cock loft. Callers to the house were informed that he expected Mrs King to return any day. He hired a woman to help him clean up but on finding a quantity of 'meat' in blocked up sinks and the blood-soaked bed linen, she reported her suspicions that foul play was afoot to the Bow Street Runners.

When the house was properly searched conclusive evidence was found, both in the cock loft and elsewhere in the house. Gardelle was committed to the New Prison at Clerkenwell, where he attempted to commit suicide twice, firstly by taking forty drops of opium, then by swallowing twelve halfpennies, hoping the verdigris would kill him. It only resulted in severe stomach pains. For greater security, he was removed to Newgate and closely watched, until his trial could take place at nearby Old Bailey. Subsequently found guilty of murder, he was hanged on a specially erected scaffold in the Haymarket, near its junction with Panton Street, close to the scene of his crime. After-wards his body was gibbeted on Hounslow Heath.

The New Prison was rebuilt in 1846 and renamed the Clerkenwell House of Correction and Detention. Richard Burke and Joseph Casey, two leading Fenians (the secret Irish society founded in 1858, bent on the overthrow of the British Government in Ireland, and the establishment of an independent republic) were incarcerated here following their arrest in London in 1867. A plot was hatched to free them while they were exercising in the prison yard. On 13 December 1867 a wagon filled with explosives was drawn up outside Clerkenwell House of Correction and Detention. The ensuing explosion blew a 60ft-wide hole in the prison wall and demolished or damaged several houses in the vicinity. There were twelve fatalities and 120 people were injured. However, the prison governor having received advance information that an escape attempt was likely, had unbeknown to the Fenians, suspended prisoners' exercise. Three suspects were arrested as they fled the scene and another three were arrested during the ensuing police investigation. The suspects charged with the bombing were held at Millbank Prison. One, Michael Barrett was convicted of actually lighting the fuse, and went down in history as the last person to be hanged in public in England. He was hanged outside Newgate on 26 May 1868. The other five suspects were acquitted.

In 1877, when local prisons were placed under the control of the Prison Commissioners, Clerkenwell House of Detention was closed. Its site is presently occupied by Hugh Myddleton School, in Woodbridge Street.

Coldbath Fields Prison
Designed by John Howard, Coldbath Fields Prison, a house of correction, was built in 1794 in Coldbath Fields, Clerkenwell, situated north of the Middlesex Bridewell and the New Prison, to house convicted criminals, in the Mount Pleasant area of London. Built to contain 232 cells, at a cost of £65,656, its name was derived from a medicinal spring discovered in 1697, known as Cold Bath Spring. Although Coldbath Fields Prison was built for the County of Middlesex, the City of London authorities made a contribution towards costs so that they might also have use of it. For a period the prison was used to gaol petty offenders of both sexes, but after 1850 only men were imprisoned there. This prison soon developed a reputation for the severity of its regime and the brutality of punishments meted out to the inmates. This prompted one visitor to Coldbath Fields to nickname it 'The Bastille'. The adherence to 'silence' was vehemently encouraged and the use of the treadwheel (called by the prisoners 'grinding the wheel') and later the treadmill, was worked by the unfortunate inmates for six hours each day, three hours at a time. The original treadwheel was the invention of a gentleman of science known as Cubitt of Lowestoft. At first, each male prisoner was apportioned 12,000 feet of ascent per day. However, it was eventually realised that such was the debilitating capacity of the treadwheel, that the required 'labour' was reduced by 90 per cent to 1,200 feet per day. There were six treadwheel yards with a total of twenty treadwheels, which could accommodate 350 men. Labour at Coldbath Fields, unlike at some other prisons in London, was intended only as a punishment. Very little of the valuable energy expended by the inmates was ever put to good use.

The treadwheel comprised a large hollow cylinder of wood on an iron frame, around the circumference of which were steps placed 7½ inches apart. Isolation of criminals was maintained by screens of wood placed on each side of the mill, converting each working area into a separate compartment. The criminal steadied himself by handrails, placed on either side, then trod on the steps, his weight causing the wheel to revolve. At first the necessary resistance was obtained using weights. All this meant was that the criminal was compelled to hour after hour of useless toil. Later on, when the treadwheel became the treadmill, it was utilised for grinding corn and pumping water. The speed was regulated by a brake, its usual speed being set so that the treadmill revolved at thirty-two feet per minute. Each criminal was on the wheel for fifteen minutes and then rested for five; and in the course of his day's labour climbed 8,640 feet.

The crank, an alternative to the treadwheel and treadmill, consisted of a small wheel, rather like the paddle wheel of a steamer. A handle, turned by the prisoner, made the wheel revolve in a box partly filled with gravel. The resistance was provided either by the amount of gravel in the box or by a brake, which usually exerted a pressure of 12lb. During his six hours, the prisoner was required to make between 8,000 and 10,000 revolutions, depending on his strength, the number of revolutions being registered on a dial. Later on, the crank was made to serve more useful purposes.

Oakum-picking was also carried out at Coldbath Fields, in a room accommodating 500 men, in complete silence. There was also a water pump, which involved the turning of a large wheel, operated by two prisoners at a time.

Coldbath Fields Prison is associated with the Ratcliffe Highway Murders, which rank amongst the most brutal of all London murders. They occurred on 7 and 19 December 1811 in what is today simply known as The Highway, described by Thomas De Quincey (1785–1859) as:

A public thoroughfare in the most chaotic quarter of eastern, or nautical London; and at this time, when no adequate police service existed except the detective police of Bow Street, admirable for its own peculiar purposes, but utterly commensurate to the general service of the capital, it was a most dangerous quarter.

The first victims were the Marrs and an apprentice boy. Mr Marr, a young man who kept a lace and hosiery shop at No. 29, sent his servant girl out to buy some oysters. When she returned she found Mr Marr's body and those of his wife, baby and thirteen-year-old apprentice boy, all violently slaughtered, their heads smashed in and their throats cut. On 19 December, a man named Williamson, landlord of the King's Arms, 81 New Gravel Lane (now Garnet Street), his wife and an elderly maidservant were similarly murdered. A sailor's maul, or hammer, and a ripping chisel were discovered at the murder scene. Identified as belonging to a labourer named John Williams, he was apprehended at the Pear Tree Tavern in Cinnamon Street and remanded in Coldbath Fields Prison, pending further investigation. On 28 December, Williams was found hanging from a beam in his cell. Some said he had cheated justice, others took a different view and it was suggested that John Williams was not guilty of the killings and that he did not commit suicide but was himself murdered, to prevent him telling the truth. On 31 December, Williams' remains were taken to St George's watch-house, in preparation for his internment. The body was placed on a cart on an inclined platform, so as to afford the public a better view and the maul and ripping chisel placed on either side of his head. Escorted by the High Constable of Middlesex, hundreds of constables, officials and parish officers, the procession, watched by thousands of onlookers, many of whom carried torches, took a circuitous route passing the scene of the crimes until the cart stopped at St George's Turnpike, which is now the crossroads of Cable Street with Cannon Street Road, which was where Williams was buried in a grave over which the main water pipe ran. During the hours of darkness between twelve and one o'clock the body was taken from the platform and lowered into the grave and then a stake was driven through it, piercing the heart before the grave was filled in, a common practice at that time for suicide.

Under the authority of Coldbath Fields' second governor, George Chesterton, the prison was gradually expanded to become the largest in England and could accommodate 1,150 prisoners. In 1834, Chesterton introduced a regime of total silence. Punishments for breaking this strict code included being loaded with leg-irons, solitary confinement and a diet of bread and water.

By the 1850s Coldbath Fields had sufficient accommodation for 1,450 prisoners and was run by 122 officers. However, the regime of the silent-associated system, where prisoners worked together but were not allowed to communicate, could not be fully implemented because of the lack of single cell accommodation. In an attempt to prevent prisoners talking to each other, the governor posted officers in each dormitory.

On arrival at Coldbath Fields a prisoner's clothes were fumigated. The firing of guns signalled the start of each day's work. Many prisoners spent hours doing 'shot drill', which involved the carrying of cannon balls up and down and round a yard, serving no useful purpose whatsoever. A prisoner was allowed to receive only one letter and one visit every three months. In 1854, it was recorded that the prison contained 1,495, persons, 919 in separate cells. So strict was the regime there that in that same year, when the prison population for the entire year totalled 9,180, no fewer than 9,023 were punished, 5,421 for noise making, insolence and bad language.

Coldbath Fields Prison held very few prisoners of any importance, one exception being in February 1820 when some of the Cato Street Conspirators were brought there for a few days before they were removed to the Tower of London. Of the many thousands of others, virtually all were petty offenders, a third of which were serving at least their second sentence there. On average, 9,000 prisoners were kept at Coldbath Fields each year.

During the 1870s as many as 1,700 men were being imprisoned at Coldbath Fields. The petty offences for which some were imprisoned were so minor they hardly warranted a prison sentence and as many as half of the inmates were imprisoned because they couldn't pay or had failed to pay small fines.

Coldbath Fields Prison came under the control of the Prison Commissioners in 1877. It was closed in 1885 and demolished in 1889. Today, Mount Pleasant Post Office and Sorting Office covers its site. There are some surviving subterranean chambers that once formed part of Coldbath Fields Prison within the Post Office complex.

CHAPTER 6

Holloway Prison

olloway Prison originally opened as the City of London House of Correction. Built at a cost of £91,547 10*s*, 8*d.*, to the designs of James Bunstone Bunning, construction began in 1849 and the prison was completed in 1852, opening in October that same year. The original prison contained 436 cells for the reception of men, women and juveniles, built with three wings for males and one for females and juveniles. Of these cells 283 were allocated for male occupation, sixty for females and sixty-two for juveniles. In addition there were eighteen refractory cells, fourteen reception cells and the same number of workrooms. Between 1881–82, two wings, B Wing and C Wing, were extended to provide 340 additional cells and in 1883–84 a new Hospital Wing was built. Oscar Wilde was held on remand at Holloway in 1895 awaiting his trial. One of Holloway's most notorious inmates, a criminal lunatic known as Richard Archer Prince, brought about the death of one of the most gifted and popular actors to grace the stage in late Victorian London. It involved the tragic consequences of a practical joke that went seriously wrong, of baseless jealousy arising from another actor's cruel hoax. The principal players in this tragedy are fifty-year-old William Terris (William Charles James Lewin), actor and murder victim; Richard Archer Prince, a supernumerary, stagehand and murderer; and William L Abingdon, actor and perpetrator of the joke that turned sour.

William Terris was affectionately known by the British public as 'Breezy Bill' and also as 'No. 1 Adelphi Terris' (Adelphi Terrace being one of London's most fashionable streets and, after the Adelphi Theatre, where Terris mainly worked). He was a good-natured, handsome, athletic and an accomplished swimmer and rescued several people from drowning resulting in him being presented with the medal of the Royal Humane Society.

Richard Archer Prince was born in Dundee. At his trial, his age was given as thirty-two, but his mother maintained that he was her eldest son, born in 1858. This would have made him thirty-nine. In any event, he looked considerably older than his years. Richard Archer (he adopted the name of Prince later, because he thought the name was more becoming of a future great actor), was short of stature, with a slight cast in his right eye and a heavy, dark, droopy moustache, which he waxed at both ends. He dressed eccentrically and often wore the attire associated with a stage villain. Many of his acquaintances simply regarded him as a harmless eccentric. Others, who perhaps saw deeper into his psyche, nicknamed him 'Mad Archer'. He had a wretched, poverty-stricken childhood and nurtured a burning ambition to become a great actor. Apprenticed to a Dundee shipbuilder, sometime later he secured a walk-on part, swelling the ranks of a visiting company to the Theatre Royal. This was the beginning of his undistinguished theatrical career. Prince's sister, Maggie, moved south to London, where she became a lady of easy virtue. One of her regular gentleman friends was the actor William L Abingdon.

Billy Abingdon as he was known by his intimates, had joined the Adelphi Company in 1887 and had been largely in the employment of that company ever since. Prince found his way to London in 1881. He sought out his sister, who it is believed sweet-talked Abingdon, to secure her brother some employment. It seems Abingdon did indeed manage to secure work for Prince from time to time. One such job was in the company of *The Silver Falls*, which opened at the Adelphi Theatre in December 1888, with Terriss as leading man. Prince was in the cast as a supernumerary. After the run ended Terriss left the Adelph for five years. He went on a tour of America and Prince found himself out of work. However, it was as 'R. A. Prince, late Adelphi Theatre' that he presented himself to potential employers. He established a connection with the provincial manager J F Elliston, a reputable manager who was based in Bolton, Lancashire and remained with Elliston's company for several seasons until the end of the 1894–95 tour. After this, unable to find work, he returned to Dundee where he obtained a job at an ironworks. He began writing abusive and threatening letters to numerous theatrical figures accusing them of 'blackmailing' him. He uses this expression many times and presumably meant 'blackballing'. Towards the end of 1895, Prince returned to London, where he secured an engagement as a supernumerary in Seymour Hicks' *One of the Best*, opening on 21 December. Terriss was leading man. During this engagement a cruel practical joke was formulated. Abingdon was appearing in a principal role in the play. He and a couple of his cronies found Prince's inflated opinion of himself quite hilarious. They encouraged his caprices, adding fuel to spark the fire of hatred, already smouldering and soon to burn ferociously in Prince's twisted brain. They convinced Prince that in their opinion he had true greatness and he only needed the right opportunity to stake his claim. *One of the Best* closed and Prince's services were not required in the following play. He sent several begging letters to various actors, including Terriss, who sent him money. By the summer of 1896 Prince's situation was becoming desperate. Unable to find work, he ventured north to his own town, Dundee, where he obtained work at the Wallace Foundry, which he left after he managed to secure a theatrical engagement. Prince's general behaviour and his inability to remember lines resulted in his dismissal when the company reached South Shields. Prince's last engagement followed. He was engaged for 25 shillings a week by Ralph Croydon. Before the end of the first day of rehearsals he had been dismissed.

Prince made his way back to London by sea. It was reported that of the many and various jobs which Prince took between theatrical engagements, that he had served as a ship's steward and also as a valet. Short of money, he may have used his contacts to secure his passage. He found lodgings in Eaton Court, Buckingham Palace Road – a room at 3 shillings a week, knocked down by his sympathetic land-lady, Mrs Charlotte Darby, from 4 shillings. Shortly afterwards, Prince went to the business premises of Mr George Lauberg, a cutler in Brompton Road, where he purchased a knife for 9d. Prince also paid a visit to the stage door of the Adelphi Theatre on 9 November and asked the stage doorkeeper, Henry Spratt, if a note could be sent to Mr Terriss. The note was taken to Terriss's dressing room and a reply returned to Prince. This took the form of a reference to the Actor's Benevolent Fund. It was later given in evidence. It read:

I have known the bearer, R. A. Prince, as a hard-working actor.

Prince made frequent requests to the Actor's Benevolent Fund. His begging letters were produced at his trial. On the morning of 16 December, Prince left his lodgings, after being refused hot water by Mrs Darby. He was behind with his rent and she had had enough. He paid a final visit to the Actor's Benevolent Fund, but was told that his application for assistance had been rejected. Prince went to see the agent C St John Denton, in Maiden Lane, seeking work. His visit proved fruitless. He walked into the Strand and by an unlucky chance, came face to face with his sister, Maggie. He asked her for money. She replied, 'I would rather see you dead in the gutter than give you a farthing.' This final rejection was too much for him. He walked back to Maiden Lane and positioned himself opposite the private entrance.

During this period Terriss had every reason to be pleased with himself. His company was to appear in a Command performance on Christmas Eve, before the Queen, at Windsor Castle. The word was out, he was to be knighted. On 16 December, Terriss was discussing moving from his West London home in Bedford Park, in Turnham Green to a larger house in Maida Vale, with John Graves. They played poker with Fred Terry at the Green Room Club and afterwards went to Jessie Millward's (Terriss's leading lady and mistress) flat in Prince's Street, Hanover Square. She provided them with a light meal and left them playing chess. Terriss and his companion were dropped off at the end of Maiden Lane and walked the short distance to the private entrance, which allowed quick access to the four principal dressing rooms. It was a little after seven o'clock that, as Terriss was bending to put his key in the lock, a figure emerged from across the narrow lane and hurriedly stabbed him twice in the upper back. Terriss turned to confront his assailant and in doing so, received a third blow to the chest, which pierced his heart. Then, when Terriss cried out, 'My God! I am stabbed,' Graves took hold of Prince and held him until Police Constable Bragg arrived and took Prince into custody at Bow Street.

Medical help was quick to arrive from nearby Charing Cross Hospital. Terriss died a few moments before eight o'clock. The funeral took place five days later at Bromptom Cemetery, being preceded by a service at the Chapel Royal of the Savoy. Terriss was laid to rest on the East Terrace, sharing a vault with his mother and his baby grandson who had been buried there two weeks previously. *The Times* reported that some 50,000 people lined the streets to watch the funeral procession and pay their respects to their lost favourite of the London stage. Nothing was mentioned to the police about the practical joke that was at the root of the tragedy and Abingdon was not called to give evidence at the trial. However, Prince's Sister Maggie conveniently disappeared, sometime between the murder and the trial.

The trial took place on 13 January 1898, less than a month after the murder, and lasted one day. It was an extremely disturbing affair. Prince was tried at the Old Bailey before Mr Justice Channell. The jury retired at 6.35pm, and having considered the evidence, returned after just half an hour. They found Prince guilty of wilful murder, but taking the medical evidence into account, not responsible for his actions. He was ordered to be retained as a criminal lunatic at

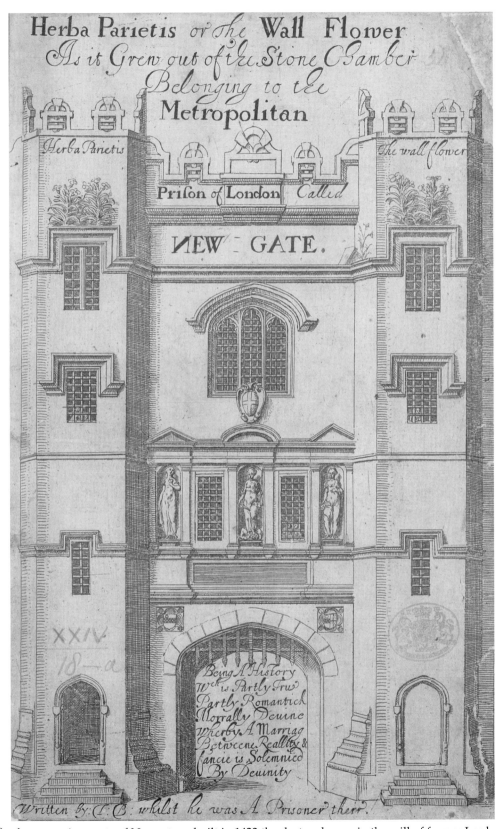

The famous prison gate of Newgate, rebuilt in 1423 thanks to a legacy in the will of former Lord Mayor, Sir Richard Whittington.

A defendant being branded on the hand in the Sessions House, Old Bailey, following his trial. Branding on the hand in lieu of a far more severe penalty was common practice, especially for those pleading Benefit of Clergy (see Ben Jonson, p. 29). (*Author's collection*)

An eighteenth-century engraving of the Sessions House, Old Bailey, where John Price was found guilty of murder during the Old Bailey Sessions of 23–26 April 1718 (see p. 32). Trials were held in the open air to prevent disease spreading from the pestilence-ridden criminals to the judge, lawyers and court officials. (*Author's collection*)

The burning of Newgate during the Gordon Riots of 1880. This replacement for Whittington's Newgate had only recently been completed to the designs of architect George Dance on the same site as its predecessors in Old Bailey. The new prison sustained considerable damage but was quickly repaired. (*John D Murray collection*)

This early nineteenth-century engraving shows Newgate and Old Bailey.

Public executions had taken place outside Newgate since 1783, after the centuries old tradition of executing criminals at Tyburn ended. John Wiggins is seen here struggling on the scaffold on Tuesday 15 October 1867. Executioner William Calcraft places the noose around his neck. (*Illustrated Police News*)

The execution of Henry Wainwright in the Execution Shed at Newgate on 21 December 1875.
(*Illustrated Police News*)

An eighteenth-century view of the first Marshalsea which served as a prison from c.1329 until 1811. (*Author's collection*)

NORTH VIEW OF THE
MARSHALSEA, SOUTHWARK

A present-day view of the remains of the second Marshalsea, from St George's Churchyard (now a public park). Only a brick wall, this was once the southern boundary of the prison that replaced that replaced the original bearing the same name, on a site across the present day Borough High Street, just a short distance away. This second Marshalsea, made famous worldwide due to the works of novelist Charles Dickens, served as a prison from 1811, until its closure by Act of Parliament in 1842. (*The Author*)

In May 1724 Jack Sheppard and his accomplice Elizabeth Lyon (known as Edgworth Bess), having being brought from St Ann's Round House, Soho, posing as man and wife, were held together in a room in part of the prison known as Newgate Ward. There they were visited by friends, who were able to pass some tools to Sheppard to help him to escape. On 25 May, Sheppard filed through his fetters and made a hole through the cell wall large enough for himself and Bess to squeeze through. Then, having fashioned a rope from the bed sheets, he and Bess climbed down 25 feet into the yard of the adjacent Middlesex Bridewell and somehow managed to scale the 22 feet-high wall and escaped. (*John D Murray collection*)

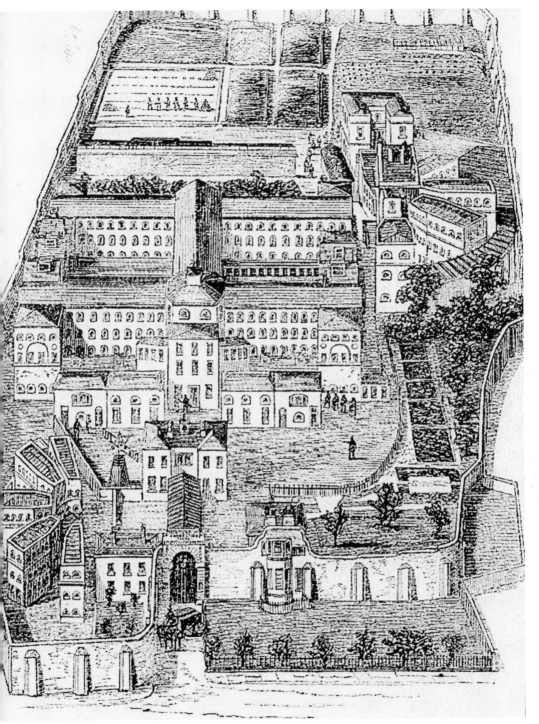

Coldbath Fields Prison, 1860. (*John D Murray collection*)

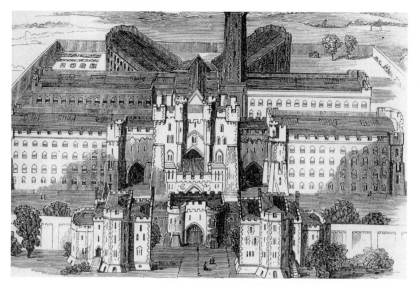

A nineteenth-century bird's eye view engraving of Holloway Prison. (*Author's collection*)

A modern view of HMP Holloway. (*The Author*)

Pentonville Prison, seen here not long after its opening in 1842. (*Author's collection*)

Inside one of Pentonville Prison's cell blocks during the mid-Victorian period. (*John D Murray collection*)

Margaret Seddon visiting her husband in the condemned cell at Pentonville in April 1912.
(*Illustrated Police News*)

A nineteenth-century engraved view of the Fleet Prison. The Fleet was the first prison built in London to be specifically designed as a gaol. Built in 1197, it remained in operation until 1842.
(*John D Murray collection*)

An early nineteenth-century engraving showing a debtor begging at the grate at the Fleet Prison. (*John D Murray collection*)

An eighteenth-century view of the gatehouse known as Ludgate. Built as a replacement for the original in 1215, Ludgate was rebuilt in 1586 and again after it was destroyed in the Great Fire of London in 1666. Ludgate was demolished in 1760.

(*Author's collection*)

Poultry Street Compter. Built in the fourteenth century, it closed in 1812. (*John D Murray collection*)

Wood Street Compter, built in 1555 as a replacement for Bread Street Compter. It burnt down in the Great Fire of London in 1666, but survived until 1897, when its prisoners were transferred to Giltspur Street Compter. (*Author's collection*)

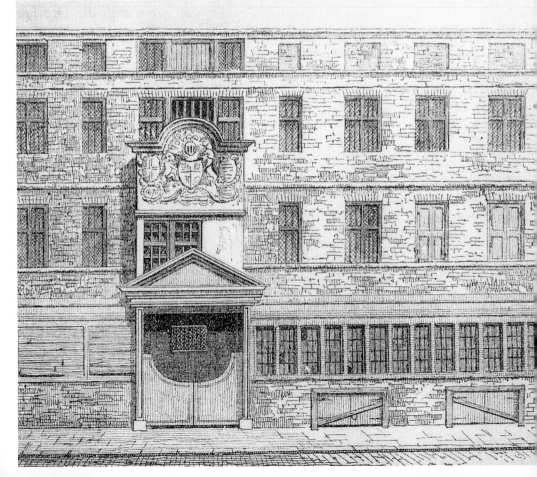

The women's pass room at Bridewell. This sad dormitory was where paupers and vagrants from outside London were incarcerated for seven days before being carted off to their own parishes.
(*John D Murray collection*)

A cell at Millbank Prison. This beautifully conceived building, opened with the best intentioned and most grandiose ideas concerning the incarceration of criminals, soon proved to be an abysmal failure as a prison.
(*John D Murray collection*)

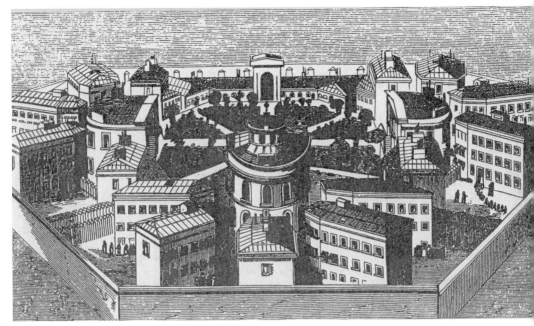

A mid nineteenth century engraved bird's eye view of Tothill Fileds Prison. (*Author's collection*)

Wormwood Scrubs, seen here shortly after it was completed in 1890. (*John D Murray collection*)

The Surrey House of Correction in Horsemonger Lane, also known as Horsemonger Lane Gaol. Built between 1791–98, as the county gaol for Surrey, it remained operational until 1878 and was demolished in 1880. (*Author's collection*)

Female convicts exercising at Brixton Prison. (*John D Murray collection*)

London Bridge Cage. Queen Mary I ordered cages and stocks to be erected in every parish in London. These were used to hold drunks or those breaching the peace, especially at night, before they could be taken before magistrates the following morning. (*Author's collection*)

The Parish Lock-Up, set in the perimeter wall of Cannon Hall, Hampstead, viewed from Cannon Lane, in 2011. Constructed in 1730, this lock-up was in operation for about a century. (*The Author*)

Holloway until Her Majesty's pleasure be known. Richard Archer Prince was not kept at Holloway for very long before he was transferred to Broadmoor, where he remained until his death in 1937. Billy Abingdon, having moved to America died by his own hand. He was found at his apartment at 235 West 76th Street, New York, having slit his throat, on 19 May 1918.

When Holloway became a women only prison in 1902 it had a capacity for 949 prisoners. In 1905, a new extension, known as DX Wing, was built, providing accommodation for an additional 101 prisoners. Many suffragettes were imprisoned at Holloway, including Christabel Pankhurst, Anne Miller Fraser, Mary Richardson and Hanna Sheehy-Skeffington. Holloway Prison was widely referred to as Holloway Castle because of its appearance. Its famous gatehouse was said to have been modelled on Warwick Castle; others referred to it as Camden Castle.

With the closure of Newgate Prison in 1902 and the subsequent alterations to Holloway for female use, it became necessary to provide an execution facility. An execution shed was erected at the end of B Wing and contained a gallows which could accommodate two prisoners side by side. In all, there were three executions in this facility. In 1903, Amelia Sach and Annie Walters, known as the Islington baby-farmers, were hanged together. This was the last double female hanging in Britain; and in 1922 Edith Thompson was also hanged there. Following this third execution a spacious condemned suite and execution shed was fashioned out of five first-floor cells and two ground-floor cells. On the first floor there was a Visitor Cell, with a glass partition to separate the condemned prisoner from their visitor. Next door was a bathroom, beyond which was the Condemned Cell itself, twice the size of the other two cells. A strategically placed wardrobe hid a door which led to an empty cell, through which the execution chamber was reached, the condemned being required to walk fifteen paces from the Condemned Cell to the drop. On the ground floor immediately below the Execution Chamber was the Gallows Pit, and, adjacent to it, beneath the empty first-floor cell, the Autopsy Room. The lights were kept on 24 hours a day and the condemned prisoner was guarded around the clock by at least two wardresses at any one time. Executions customarily took place at 9.00am after which the body of the executed prisoner was left hanging for an hour. Following this it was cut down by the executioner and his assistant, stripped of its clothing and wheeled on a gurney to the adjacent autopsy room. Following the autopsy an inquest was held and around lunchtime of the day of execution the women's bodies were buried in unmarked graves within the precincts of the prison.

Holloway Prison's first clients of the hangman were possibly its most hated, they were Sach and Walters, the notorious Islington baby-farmers. Baby-farming was a peculiarity of late Victorian England: unwanted babies and children, whether illegitimate or simply a burden to their parents, were farmed out to women who acted as foster mothers. These women were paid to 'adopt' the children or to look after them for a specific period, before they were moved to permanent homes. Large financial rewards could be obtained by taking these unwanted children and the result was that some women obtained money to place a child in a good home and, having found none, 'took care' of their charges simply by killing them. Rivers, canals, reservoirs and even rubbish tips were common dumping grounds for these unfortunate innocents. Two such baby-farmers were Amelia Sach and Annie Walters.

Mrs Amelia Sach, aged twenty-six, lived at Claymore House, Hertford Road, East Finchley, which she had converted to serve as a private lying-in hospital. There she operated a successful business as an *accoucheuse*. She claimed to be a certified midwife and nurse and attended to her female patients herself. In difficult cases she arranged for a doctor to be present. She had a ready supply of unwanted babies to baby-farm. Her accomplice in crime was fifty-one-year-old Annie Walters, who described herself as a 'short stay foster parent'. Exactly how many babies were killed by these evil women will never be known. Some have speculated it could amount to hundreds of such unfortunate infants. Annie Walters often changed address, probably so her activities were not subjected to too close a scrutiny. While lodging at 11 Danbury Street, Islington with a police constable named Sale and his wife, her many accounts of how babies were given new homes made them suspicious. Her fanciful stories did not ring true with PC Sale. He and a colleague Detective Constable Wright decided to watch her. On 18 November 1902 she had in her possession a baby boy, believed to be the child of Ada Galley, a single young woman and a patient at Claymore House. Walters was followed to South Kensington railway station by DC Wright, who arrested her after the child was found to be dead. It had been dead for between 8 and 12 hours. Chllorodyne, a painkiller containing morphia, chloroform and prussic acid, mixed with a baby's milk in sufficient quantity would soon cause death. Walters said to police: 'I never murdered the dear. I only gave it two drops in its bottle, the same as I take myself.' A whole catalogue of grim events unfolded and Amelia Sach was also arrested. Both were charged with murder. Their trial commenced before Mr Justice Darling at the Old Bailey on 15 January 1903. Found guilty of murder, they were sentenced to death. Mrs Sach's plea for clemency on the grounds that it was most unusual to be hanged as an accessory was turned down and the two women were executed together at Holloway, by the Billington brothers, on 3 February 1903; and afterwards their bodies were buried within the precincts of the prison.

On the evening of 3 October 1922, thirty-two-year-old shipping clerk, Percy Thompson, had taken his twenty-eight-year-old wife Edith, who worked in Aldersgate Street in the City of London as the manageress-bookkeeper for Carlton & White, a firm of wholesale milliners, to the Criterion Theatre in London's Piccadilly Circus and returned with her afterwards by train to Ilford. They reached the local station about midnight and from there set off to their home in Kensington Gardens. As they were walking down the long and dark Belgrave Road between Endsleigh Road and Kensington Gardens, a man came out of the darkness and stabbed Percy Thompson in the head and neck before vanishing into the darkness. Immediately afterwards, Edith Thompson, in a state of hysteria, appealed to some passers-by for help, saying she had no idea who the assailant could be. Although medical aid was sent for, when Mrs Thompson and others, including Miss Dora Finch Pittard and Dr Maudsley, returned to Percy Thompson's side, he was already dead. During the subsequent enquiry when Chief Inspector Frederick Wensley learned that neighbours were scandalized by Mrs Thompson's liason with P & O laundry steward, twenty-year-old, Frederick Bywaters, he arranged to have Bywaters arrested and Mrs Thompson brought to Ilford Police Station where she could glimpse her lover in another room. Immediately, Mrs Thompson betrayed her complicity when she blurted out, 'Oh, why did he do it? I did not want him to do it!' Stupidly Bywaters had kept a large quantity of Edith's letters (some sixty-two formed exhibits at the trial) the contents of many of which had been foolish for Edith to write and even more foolish for her lover to have kept. Some letters mentioned poisoning Percy and others even claimed Edith had put ground up light bulbs in his food. At 9.00am on the morning of 9 January 1923 Edith Thompson was hanged by John Ellis. Half a mile away at Pentonville Prison, at exactly the same hour, her lover Freddy Bywaters (also see page 119) was being hanged by Thomas Pierrepoint.

In the Notable British Trial Series the *Trial of Bywaters And Thompson*, Filson Young commented:

He went to his death with firmness and assurance. She was taken to hers in a state of collapse and, I hope, of merciful oblivion. For, on the most sober consideration of the case, her execution seems to have been without other than merely legal justification, and to have been the result of a kind of frozen moral inertia which seized those whose business and responsibility it should have been to avoid an act that, though technically justifiable on legal grounds, was, in the considered judgement of public opinion, as essentially unjust as it was inexpedient.

Notwithstanding Edith Thompson's physical state at her execution (she had to be carried from the Condemned Cell to the drop by four male warders), the execution itself was not without incident and in its aftermath the remaining women to hang in British prisons were required to wear a special garment, in order to prevent a reoccurrence of the unpleasantness that occurred as Thompson breathed her last breath. When the bolts had been drawn by John Ellis and Thompson plummeted to a swift death, a copious amount of blood haemorrhaged from her vagina. Many of those present in the Execution Chamber who witnessed it were severely distressed, the hangman John Ellis included. Afterwards, because Edith Thompson had gained weight during her incarceration in Holloway's Condemned Cell, despite a considerable loss of appetite, this caused some to speculate that she was pregnant. The fact that she was pregnant at the time of her execution was not mentioned in the autopsy report. Others have suggested that a previous self-induced abortion had damaged the lining of her uterus and the force of the drop had caused massive internal damage. Some have been quick to point out it was merely a particularly heavy menstrual flow. These assertions were being based on research conducted in Germany both before and during World War Two, where it was showed that menstruation was often interrupted by the stress of being tried and sentenced to death, but could resume on being informed of the actual date of the execution. After Edith Thompson's execution all women executed in Britain were obliged to wear special canvas knickers, to prevent any such bleeding being visible.

Sir Henry Curtis-Bennett, Thompson's leading counsel, commented after the trial and execution:

She spoiled her chances by her evidence and demeanour ... I had a perfect answer to everything, which I am sure would have won an acquittal if she had not been a witness. She was a vain woman and an obstinate one. Also her imagination was highly developed, but it failed to show her the mistake she was making ... In short, Mrs Thompson was hanged for immorality.

There would be a lapse of over thirty-one years before the next execution took place at Holloway, although no fewer than twenty-five women had occupied the Condemned Cell in the intervening years. There would then be two executions, in fact those of the last two women to be executed in Britain, their executions taking place within eight months of each other.

In 1939, shortly after the outbreak of World War Two, Holloway's inmates were transferred to Aylesbury Prison and Holloway was then used to hold people who for some reason or other, through either their actions or professed views, were likely to be unbeneficial or prejudicial to the war effort. Prisoners included Sir Oswald Mosley (leader of the British Union of Fascists), who was arrested on 23 May 1940 and interned under Defence Regulation 18B as a threat to the security of Britain, firstly at Brixton Prison and then with his wife, Lady Mosley (the former Diana Mitford), who lived in a house within the precincts of the prison until they were released for health reasons in November 1943.

In 1941 Dorothy Pamela O'Grady was caught in a 'sensitive area' of the Isle of Wight from which the public had been banned. She was also accused of cutting an Army telephone line and of being in possession of a document concerning defence measures. She was found guilty of treason at the Old Bailey and the mandatory death sentence was duly passed on her. The death sentence was commuted at her appeal, and she served fourteen years in Holloway.

Another prisoner detained in Holloway, who had her death sentence commuted to life imprisonment, was involved in the sensational wartime murder which became known as the 'Cleft Chin Murder' (see pages 124–5). Eighteen-year-old exotic dancer Elizabeth Jones, known by her stage name Georgina Grayson, had her death sentence commuted two days before her scheduled execution. She served her sentence in Holloway, being released in January 1954.

Of the two final women to be executed at Holloway, the first was a Greek Cypriot woman, Mrs Christofi. In 1954, the ground floor and first floor of 11 South Hill Park, Hampstead was occupied by the family of a Greek Cypriot named Stavros Christofi, who worked as a wine waiter in the West End at London's famous Café de Paris. Stavros lived with his German wife Hella and their three children.

After about fifteen years of marriage, the family were joined in 1953 by Stavros's mother, Mrs Styllou Christofi. Styllou Pantopiou Christofi was illiterate even in her own native language. Unable or unwilling to learn either English or German, she had great difficulty communicating with her daughter-in-law, who became the object of her hatred and obsessive jealousy.

On the evening of 29 July 1954, while Stavros was at work and the children in bed, Mrs Christofi murdered Hella by hitting her on the head with a cast-iron ash plate from the kitchen stove, then strangling her. She then set about burning the body in the garden. John Young, a neighbour, witnessed Mrs Christofi poking what appeared to be a tailor's dummy. Some time later, Mrs Christofi stopped a passing motorist, restaurateur, Mr Burstoff, and his wife and in broken English she told a pathetic tale. She said, 'Please come, fire burning, children sleeping.' When the Burstoffs arrived at the house and were taken through to a yard outside the kitchen, they saw the naked body of a woman, covered in ash and blood and burning on the ground. When the police came, the blood and other evidence in the kitchen told an entirely different story to the pathetic tale Mrs Christofi attempted to relate to them in broken English. There is no doubt that Mrs Christofi was a horrible woman to have as a mother-in-law. In 1925, while two fellow villagers had held open the mouth of her own mother-in-law, Mrs Christofi had rammed a blazing torch down her throat, killing her. On that occasion she was acquitted. However, this time she was not so lucky. She was tried at the Central Criminal Court before Mr Justice Devlin. Christofi refused to plead insanity and was found to be sane by three doctors. Indeed, she had, vociferously proclaimed this fact during an angry rant to her counsel, when she told him, 'I am a poor woman, of no education, but I am not a mad woman. Never, never, never!' On 28 October, she was found guilty of murder. Having considered the evidence it took the jury just two hours to bring in a guilty verdict. Mrs Christofi was hanged on 13 December 1954. Her executioner was Albert Pierrepoint.

The next occupant of Holloway's Condemned Cell was to be its last inmate to be hanged there. If she cannot claim to have been Holloway Prison's most famous ever inmate, Ruth Ellis might easily be regarded as one of its most glamorous, at least in the eyes of the general public. In itself the case of Ruth Ellis is not all that remarkable. Indeed, other than the subject is noted for being the last woman to be judicially hanged in Great Britain, the murder she committed is regarded by many as nothing more than a crime of passion. Ruth Ellis was a 5ft 2in tall, twenty-eight year old, bleached platinum blonde, nightclub manageress and mother of two, who shot her twenty-four-year-old racing car driver lover, David Blakely, outside the Magdala Tavern, Hampstead on Easter Sunday 10 April 1955. Ruth was born in the North Wales seaside resort of Rhyl. The name on her birth certificate was Ruth Neilson, her father being Arthur Hornby, a musician who worked professionally as Arthur Neilson. Ruth had a peripatetic childhood and the remainder of her relatively short life was crammed full of incident. She became pregnant aged seventeen, giving birth to an illegitimate daughter, Clare Andrea Neilson, in September 1945, who in early life was mostly looked after by her sister, Muriel, while Ruth moved to London's West End, where she worked as a model and later as a nightclub hostess, experiencing both the high life and the seedier aspects that such occupations can bring.

She married an alcoholic dentist, George Ellis, in November 1950, producing a daughter, Georgina, in October 1951, who was later adopted. Her marriage ended in divorce. Ruth embarked on a social life full of drink, high living and sex. The abuse and deceit she endured from her younger lover David Blakely, who promised her marriage and stability in her troubled life, only brought sadness, disappointment and jealousy, which resulted in Ruth's last desperate act. She neither denied or tried to justify her actions; and during her trial which began at the No. 1 Court at the Old Bailey on Monday 20 June 1955, before Mr Justice Havers, when asked by the leading prosecuting counsel, Mr Christmas Humphreys, 'Mrs Ellis, when you fired that revolver at close range into the body of David Blakely, what did you intend to do?' her fate was sealed when she replied: 'It is obvious that when I shot him I intended to kill him.' Some less generous-spirited commentators have said that had this 'ice-cool' murderess not been a young woman with undoubted physical attractions, then the case would not have warranted so much media attention, nor indeed prompted the degree of public indignation following her conviction for murder and subsequent execution.

For much of her time at Holloway, Ruth Ellis abandoned the customary paperback novels she avidly consumed and instead read the Bible, studying some passages in great detail, believing she would be at peace with God if she were executed. Following her conviction for murder and sentencing on Tuesday 21 June, Ruth saw her father and solicitor at the Old Bailey before she left for Holloway for the final time, to occupy the Condemned Cell, situated immediately next to the adjoining execution shed. There she would spend the last three weeks of her life, constantly watched and observed by day and by night. During her stay in this death cell Ruth remained outwardly composed. To occupy her time she also made dolls out of materials brought to Holloway by her mother, did jig-saw puzzles and wrote letters. She was allowed an hour's exercise each day, given the customary ration of cigarettes but declined to drink the beer made available to the condemned. Ruth Ellis was executed on Wednesday 13 July 1955. When the time came, Ruth met her end with that same stoical courage she had displayed during the previous weeks of her incarceration in Holloway.

The story of Ruth Ellis and David Blakely has continued to arouse considerable curiosity. Albert Pierrepoint in his autobiography *Executioner Pierrepoint* commented:

> When I left Holloway after the execution of Ruth Ellis, the prison was almost besieged by a storming mob. I needed protection to get me through. I knew I would have walked out of Strangeways [where a forty-year-old woman, described by some as a harridan, had just been reprieved] a week earlier into an empty street. At Euston Station a crowd of newspapermen were awaiting me. I shielded my face from the cameras as I ran for my train. One young reporter jogged alongside me asking, 'How did it feel to hang a woman, Mr Pierrepoint?' I did not answer. But I could have asked: 'Why weren't you waiting to ask me that question last year. Sonny? Wasn't Mrs Christofi a woman too.

Although Ruth Ellis is widely known for being the last woman to be executed in Britain, she was not the last occupant of Holloway's Condemned Cell. Freda Rumbold was convicted of the murder of her husband in November 1956 and sentenced to death. Because of legislation going through Parliament at that time all death sentences were being commuted. This legislation resulted in the Homicide Act of 1957. Freda Rumbold was reprieved and given a life sentence.

Another glamorous inmate at Holloway was seventeen-year-old Mandy Rice-Davies, who had become involved through association with the political scandal known as the 'Profumo Affair', in 1963. Ongoing police investigations and supposed security implications caused the authorities to believe it would be expedient to detain her and she was arrested at Heathrow Airport, en route for Palma, Mallorca, on 23 April and detained on the dubious charge of 'possessing a document so closely resembling a driving license as to be calculated to deceive', for which 'offence' she subsequently received a fine of £42 with £16.12s costs.

In her autobiography *Mandy* she writes:

I was remanded in custody, which as the court was going into recess, meant nine days in Holloway Jail before my case could be heard.

First there was the depersonalising process of being removed from freedom and locked away. Then came the indignity of the search, the body search (what was I supposed to be smuggling in?) and to submitting to the strange ritual of the shaving of pubic hairs. This was the ultimate violation. 'Touch me and I'll scream bloody murder.' I said I would do my own shaving, thank you very much. They did not insist, and later I discovered that they had not even the right to inflict this on remand prisoners.

In *Mandy* Miss Rice-Davies goes on to say:

I was locked in my cell for twenty out of every twenty-four hours, allowed out to change my library books and once to go to the Warden's office. Earl Felton had sent me a gift. Chocolates, oranges and a pack of 200 Peter Stuyvesant. He'd forgotten I didn't smoke. The rule was ten cigarettes a day. I took them back to my cell and within a few minutes there was a strange face at the door.

'You've cigarettes, then?'

'Yes, but no matches'

Give me a cigarette, I'll give you a match,' she said. The deal was done. I had never smoked before. I disliked being in the company of people who smoke, and Christine's [Keeler] smoking when we shared drove me wild with exasperation. By the time I left Holloway I was addicted to cigarettes and I have never been able to give them up.

Mandy Rice-Davies gives an account of the state of Holloway during the old prison's latter years, taken from the notes she made following her incarceration there in 1963 and included in her autobiography *Mandy*, published in 1980, a decade after the Holloway Prison she knew had been completely demolished:

As if the fact of imprisonment wasn't bad enough, Holloway is a disgustingly depressing building. Dirty, falling to pieces, the immediate impression is that it really is like the inside of a prison as seen in films: floors stacked one above the other with safety nets to catch the people who are hurled or hurl themselves over the railings . . . Lesbianism was the prevailing force. Mannish women in trousers with butch haircuts were in charge: in the kitchen, in the garden, eyeing me in a way that made me nervous.

Holloway's by then notorious but no longer required Condemned Suite and Execution Chamber was dismantled in 1967.

During the rebuilding work that went on at Holloway it was decided that the removal of the remains of the five women who had been executed and buried within the prison's precincts between 1903 and 1955 was essential. Ruth Ellis's remains were exhumed by the London Necropolis Company at 5.00am on 1 April 1971 and subsequently reburied in the churchyard extension of St Mary's, Amersham, Buckinghamshire. The remains of the four other executed women, Amelia Sach, Annie Walters, Edith Thompson and Styllou Pantopiou Christofi were also exhumed by the London Necropolis Company that same morning and transported to Brookwood Cemetery, Surrey, where they were interred in a single grave in Plot 117 later in the day. Amid much controversy a memorial stone was placed over the gravesite and dedicated on 13 November 1993. The grey granite memorial was placed there in a defiant attempt to commemorate the life of Edith Thompson by those wishing to exonerate her from complicity in her husband's death. The names of the three other executed women are also included in the memorial.

Holloway Prison was completely rebuilt between 1971–75, to the designs of architect Gavin Stamp, on the same site as the original. The new prison opened in 1977 with a capacity for 532 convicted and remanded female adults and young offenders. It was equipped with a mother and baby unit. The majority of accommodation is for prisoners in single cells with some dormitory accommodation being provided. Full and part-time education courses are offered at the prison and skills training workshops are also available to inmates. There is also a family-friendly Visitor Centre.

CHAPTER 7

Pentonville Prison

Two Acts of Parliament made provision for the building of Pentonville Prison and construction began on 10 April 1840. When it opened in 1842, in Caledonian Road, Barnsbury, about a mile to the north of King's Cross Station, in what is today within the London Borough of Islington, Pentonville was known as a model prison. Built to an American pattern, with a central hall and five radiating wings, it was completed at a cost of £84,186.12s 2d., and originally held prisoners in readiness for transportation to Australia. Pentonville was designed to hold 540 prisoners in isolation. Known as the 'separate system' and based on that first used at Eastern State Penitentiary in Philadelphia, each prisoner had a cell measuring 13ft long by 9ft wide, with a ceiling height of 9ft, and a small window placed on the outside wall.

Conditions at Pentonville were considerably better and generally healthier for prisoners than those at Newgate and several of London's other prisons. Originally operated using the separate and silent system, prisoners were required to wear masks to prevent them either communicating or recognising each other. Each prisoner was put to work from 6.00am to 7.00pm, being given tasks such as picking coir or weaving. Food rations comprised three meals: breakfast, consisting of 10 ounces of bread and three-quarters of a pint of cocoa; dinner – half a pint of soup or four ounces of meat, five ounces of bread and one pound of potatoes; and supper – a pint of gruel and five ounces of bread.

Prisoners served the first part of their sentence in solitary confinement, working, eating and sleeping alone in their cells. Exercise was also conducted alone in the prison yard. Prisoners were later allowed to walk around a yard with other prisoners but any form of communication between prisoners was expressly forbidden. Prolonged solitary confinement and deprivation from communicating did not have any beneficial effect regarding the reform of Pentonville's prisoners. Indeed, some were driven mad, others committed suicide. Nevertheless, despite its shortcomings, such was the success of Pentonville that it became the model for British prisons and for those throughout the British Empire.

In 1902, shortly after the entire site was cleared to build the present Central Criminal Court in the Old Bailey, the gallows were moved from the demolished Newgate Prison to Pentonville and located in a newly constructed execution room and condemned cells were created. Thereafter, men were hanged at Pentonville for crimes committed north of the River Thames.

The first execution to take place at Pentonville was that of John MacDonald, who was hanged on 30 September 1902, for the murder of Henry Groves. The second execution took place some six weeks later, on 11 November, when Henry Williams was hanged for the murder of his daughter, Margaret Anne Andrew; and the third followed on 9 December, when Thomas Barrow was hanged for the murder of his step-daughter cum girlfriend, Emily Coates.

Other executions at Pentonville included:

Charles Jeremiah Slowe, 1903

At ten o'clock on the night of Wednesday 23 September 1903, Mary Jane Hardwick, who was assisting her sister Mrs Jane Starkey, landlady of the Lord Nelson public house in Whitechapel Road, was violently attacked in the public bar by a customer who then stabbed her with a knife, before fleeing the scene. Miss Hardwick died almost immediately. The man was identified as Charles Slowe of Rowton House, Whitechapel, referred to by many locally simply as Jerry. Slowe, a man without a trade or regular employment, had taken a shine to Miss Hardwick but she would have nothing to do with him and did not like having to serve him. Slowe was quickly apprehended nearby and taken into custody. Robert Musgrave, a potman at the Lord Nelson said he had heard Slowe say in the bar one night, some seven or eight months before the murder: 'I'll put her light out one of these days.'

Slowe's trial began at the Central Criminal Court, Old Bailey on Wednesday 21 October 1903. The defence attempted to have the charge reduced to manslaughter by claiming a lack of premeditation, but Mr Justice Bingham said: 'In the eye of the law, if a person used a knife with the intent to do an injury, and death ensued, he was guilty of murder.' After fifteen minutes deliberation the jury found Slowe guilty of murder. Before passing sentence the judge said the prisoner had been guilty of a cruel and barbarous murder, and he must suffer for the consequences of his act. As he was leaving the dock, Slowe said: 'I shall meet it without fear.' He became the fourth prisoner to be executed at Pentonville, when on Tuesday 10 November 1903, he was taken from the condemned cell and hanged by James Billington.

Conrad Donovan and Charles Wade, 1904

On 12 October 1904, half-brothers Conrad Donovan and Charles Wade decided to rob a newsagent and tobacconist's shop at 478 Commercial Road, Stepney run by Miss Matilda Emily Farmer. Unknown to them, the two men had been seen acting suspiciously outside the premises two days previously by a Sunday school teacher, who was later able to identify them. Miss Farmer was well known in the area for owning and wearing jewellery. During the course of the robbery she was bound and gagged. When she was discovered the following day she had choked on the gag and her jewellery was missing. The two culprits were quickly apprehended and brought to trial. As the judge pointed out, accidental homicide consequent on robbery is murder. Donovan and Wade were hanged on 13 December 1904.

Dr Hawley Harvey Crippen, 1910

This case is notable for the murderer being the first to be caught by wireless telegraph. Hawley Harvey Crippen was born in Coldwater, Michigan. When he met his future wife he was a thirty-one-year-old widower. Doctor Crippen was 5ft 4in tall, with piercing blue-grey eyes, which due to an affliction bulged slightly. Compelled to wear thick-lensed glasses, he constantly blinked. He married his colleague's secretary, Brooklyn-born Cora Turner (of Polish descent who had changed her name from Kunigunde Mackamotzki and was fourteen years his younger), on 1 September 1892. Cora had aspirations to become an opera singer but the American stage did not welcome her.

In 1900, Crippen was given the opportunity to go to London for Munyon's Remedies, a patent medicine business on a salary of £3 a week. The Crippens took rooms at 37 Store Street, off Tottenham Court Road, Bloomsbury. While the doctor was dispensing quack medicines, the wife was visiting theatrical agents. Doctor in name only, his professional qualifications did not allow him to practice in England, so he knuckled down to work as a glorified salesman. If Cora was not quite Covent Garden material, London and the provinces had the Music Halls. She managed to get some periods of regular employment under her new stage name, Belle Elmore, which meant on occasions she was away from home, sometimes for several weeks, which enabled her to indulge her nymphomaniac inclinations. Not a great success on stage, in off-stage theatrical activities, she became something of a personality, rising to become Honorary Treasurer of the Music Hall Ladies' Guild, enabling her to befriend such stars as Marie Lloyd and Vesta Tilley. Her constant entertaining and her expensive tastes in stage attire and gowns were a drain on the Crippens' finances. In September 1905, they moved to a large semi-detached house in Holloway. Number 39 Hilldrop Crescent was rented for £52 10s a year. To supplement their income the Crippens took in paying guests. A delivery of clothing to the Crippens' household in January 1909 was carefully documented by Jones Brothers, of Holloway, who delivered three suits of pyjamas.

In September 1908, Miss Ethel Le Neve became Crippen's secretary at Albion House, 61 New Oxford Street. She was tiny, dark, attractive, demure and genteel – almost the exact opposite of what Cora had become. Ethel and Doctor Crippen found that they were soul mates and fell deeply in love.

On 17 January 1910, Crippen went to the chemist's Lewis and Burrows in New Oxford Street, asked for five grains of hyoscine hydrobromide for Munyon's Remedies and put down the use he wished the drug in the Poison Register, 'homeopathic preparation'.

The last people to see Cora Crippen alive were retired mime artistes Paul and Clara Martinetti. They were invited to Hilldrop Crescent on the evening of 31 January 1910. The little dinner party broke up at about 1.30am. On the afternoon of 2 February, Belle Elmore failed to appear at a meeting of the Music Hall Ladies' Guild, held in a room at Albion House, loaned by her husband. Two letters were delivered by the hand of Ethel Le Neve, both were signed 'Belle Elmore' but neither was in her handwriting. The letters informed the Guild that she was resigning her membership, owing to an urgent visit to America due to a family illness.

It was on 20 February when Crippen took Ethel to the Music Hall Ladies' Guild annual ball, at the Criterion, that Belle's friends began to take a little more interest in the doctor. Ethel was wearing one of Belle's brooches. Crippen told Belle's friends that his wife had developed pneumonia in California and was dangerously ill. On 24 March, Doctor Crippen and Ethel Le Neve went on a five-day Easter holiday to Dieppe as Mr and Mrs Crippen. Before they left, Crippen sent a telegram to the Martinettis saying 'Belle died yesterday at six o'clock ...'

On their return from France, Belle Elmore's friends bombarded him with questions. 'She passed on of pneumonia, up in the high mountains of California,' he told them. A friend of Lil Hawthorne (member of the Music Hall Ladies' Guild and something of a busybody) happened to be Detective Superintendent Froest, of Scotland Yard. He was in charge of the recently formed Serious Crimes Squad and since Hawthorne was suspicious that something was amiss, he promised to look into the matter. Chief Inspector Walter Dew was assigned to make general enquiries. Inspector Dew explained the reason for the visit and Crippen told him: 'I suppose I'd better tell the truth.' A lengthy statement was taken over five hours. Crippen stated that by the time he came home from work on 1 February his wife had gone. She had run off with another man. To add insult to injury she had left most of her clothes and the jewels he had given her. Crippen and Ethel accompanied Inspector Dew and Sergeant Mitchell to Hilldrop Crescent, where they looked around. They were satisfied nothing was amiss. However, Crippen must have felt uneasy about this police attention. He panicked and fled with Ethel to Rotterdam.

On Monday 11 July, Chief Inspector Dew returned to Albion House to clear up some final points. Crippen's associate, Doctor Rylance, informed Dew that on Saturday 9 July, he had received a letter from Crippen instructing him to wind up his affairs. Included in the letter was the ominous sentence: 'In order to escape trouble I shall be obliged to absent myself for a time.' A dental mechanic employed at Albion House told Dew, that Doctor Crippen had sent him out to purchase clothing for a boy of sixteen.

When the inspector visited Hilldrop Crescent, the house was searched from top to bottom and again, during the 12 and 13 July. On a third inspection of the coal cellar after Dew had been prodding the floor with a fire-poker, he discovered that there were some loose bricks. The presence of quicklime urged him to dig deeper. It was not long before the gruesome discovery of what little remained of Cora Crippen was made. Just a stinking heap of human flesh, viscera and hair, wrapped in a pyjama jacket.

The remains were examined by Doctor Pepper and Doctor Bernard Spilsbury. Tests were carried out on the tissue samples by a toxicologist Dr William Willcox. The discovery of hyoscine hydrobromide led them to conclude that poisoning by the same was the cause of death and that the remains were those of a stout female, who bleached her hair. Part of the flesh from the abdomen showed a scar consistent with the ovariectomy undergone by Cora Crippen. A warrant was issued on 16 July for the arrest of Doctor Hawley Harvey Crippen and Ethel Le Neve for murder and mutilation.

Meanwhile, Crippen and Le Neve were in Belgium and were staying at the Hotel des Ardennes in Brussels. On Wednesday 20 July, having boarded the SS *Montrose* at Antwerp, as Mr John Philo Robinson and Master John Robinson, they set sail for Quebec. Crippen had shaved off his moustache and removed his spectacles. His failure to refrain from being over affectionate towards his 'sixteen-year-old son', with whom he shared a double cabin, aroused the suspicion of Captain Kendall, who quickly came to the conclusion that Master Robinson was a woman. Kendall, who had seen a police notice about the fugitives, communicated the news to Scotland Yard, via the new Marconi Electric Telegraph.

Chief Inspector Dew and his sergeant, made arrangements to travel to Quebec by a faster ship. They set sail from Liverpool on 23 July aboard the SS *Laurentic*, and arrived in Quebec ahead of the SS *Montrose*. Dr Crippen and Ethel Le Neve were arrested on Sunday 31 July and brought back to London after three weeks' detention in Canada, aboard the SS *Megantic*.

Cora Crippen's remains were interred at Finchley Cemetery on 10 October 1910. A few bits of flesh were retained for the trial, where they were passed round in a soup plate. Crippen's trial began on Tuesday 18 October 1910, at the Old Bailey, before the Lord Chief Justice, Lord Alverstone. Ethel Le Neve was to be tried separately with being an accessory after the fact. Mr Richard, for the defence suggested that the remains had been buried in the cellar at 39, Hilldrop Crescent, sometime before September 1905, when the Crippens had moved into the house. However, the tell-tale label on the pyjama jacket, bearing the words 'Jones Brothers Ltd' in which the remains had been wrapped, proved they could only have been buried there after the Crippens' occupancy, as Jones Brothers did not become a Limited Company until 1908. On the fifth day of the trial, having heard all the evidence, the jury retired and returned after only twenty-seven minutes, with a guilty verdict. Sentence of death was pronounced.

The trial of Ethel Le Neve began on 25 October and lasted one day. She appeared before the same judge and had the same prosecutor as her lover. She was defended by F E Smith KC, afterwards, 1st Earl of Birkenhead. She gave no evidence but was acquitted and set free. Doctor Crippen's appeal was heard on 5 November. It failed. He was hanged on the morning of 23 November 1910 by John Ellis.

Frederick Seddon, 1912

Lancashire-born Frederick Henry Seddon was employed as District Superintendent of Canvassers for North London with the London and Manchester Industrial Assurance Company, a position he had occupied since 1901. A freemason, one time chapel-goer and preacher, this hard-working, thrifty man had a shrewd eye for business and took pride in meticulously attending to even the simplest of transactions. He was not particularly likeable as his general manner and air of superiority tended to alienate him. By 1909, in addition to his insurance work, Seddon owned a second-hand clothes business, which he ran in his wife's name at 276 Seven Sisters Road, Finsbury Park and he and his family lived above the shop. Seddon invested his additional income in mortgaged property and regularly sold it on at a profit. After one successful business deal he bought a fourteen-roomed house at 63 Tollington Park, situated north of his shop between Stroud Green Road and Hornsey Road. He and his family moved in, along with Seddon's elderly father in November 1909. Seddon decided to rent out the top floor, the basement office he rented to his employers, who finding him scrupulously honest, allowed him to bank their money in his own account and paid him 5*s* a week rent.

On 12 August 1910, Miss Eliza Barrow became Seddon's tenant. She was a forty-nine-year-old spinster of independent means with private property amounting to about £4,000, which included the Buck's Head, Camden Town. Miss Barrow had taken on the responsibility of looking after two orphaned children, an adolescent girl named Hilda Grant, who was away at boarding school and her little brother Ernie, aged eight. They had lived with Miss Barrow in a succession of lodgings, ending up with her cousins, the Vonderahes, at 31 Evershot Street but they did not get on, so Miss Barrow moved around the corner to Tollington Park. Seddon said that Miss Barrow had become increasingly worried about her investments since 1909 when she believed Lloyd George's budget and 'soak the rich' policies might reduce her to penury. Miss Barrow eventually signed over all her property to Seddon in exchange for an annuity and subsequently increased this by signing over her India Stock, which she was apparently highly delighted with. London sweltered in a heatwave in late August and early September 1911.

On 1 September, Miss Barrow was taken ill with what Dr Sworn diagnosed as epidemic diarrhoea and added that her mental state appeared to be as bad as her physical health. Her condition gradually deteriorated. She refused hospitalisation insisting that Mrs Seddon could nurse her just as well. On 4 September, Mrs Margaret Seddon said Miss Barrow instructed her to go and get some flypapers. The smell of her offensive motions was attracting swarms of flies. The stench became so bad that it was necessary to hang sheets soaked in carbolic in all the rooms in an attempt to fumigate the air. Miss Barrow began to worry about what would happen to little Ernie and Hilda if she were to die. She asked Seddon to draw up a will for her. He did so and the will was witnessed by his married sister, Emily Longley and Mrs Seddon. The will made Frederick H Seddon sole executor, 'to hold all my personal belongings, furniture, clothing and jewellery in trust' until Ernest and Hilda Grant came of age. Miss Barrow died at about 6.15am on Thursday 14 September. Dr Sworn made out the death certificate giving the cause of death as 'epidemic diarrhoea'. Seddon arranged the funeral. William Nodes, undertaker, commented as follows at Seddon's trial:

> ... having regard to the state that the body was in and the diarrhoea that had taken place, the warmth of the weather, and the fact that there was no lead lining to the coffin, it seemed quite reasonable that the body should be buried on Saturday ... I explained to him what kind of funeral it would be for the price; it was a £4 funeral really ... it would mean internment in a public grave ... it is used for more than one person.

Seddon pointed out to Mr Nodes that Miss Barrow was not a relation and in consideration for the business he had brought him, accepted 12s 6d commission. The funeral took place on the afternoon of Saturday 16 September. Miss Barrow was buried in East Finchley in a public grave. When the Vonderahes learned of their cousin's death they wanted to know why they had not been informed and expressed astonishment that she had not been buried in the family vault in Highgate Cemetery. Seddon produced a copy of a letter he had sent them to Evershot Street but the Vonderahes had changed address. They also wanted to know what had happened to her money and were not satisfied with Seddon's answers. They caused such a fuss that the police, unbeknown to the Seddons, arranged to have Miss Barrow's remains exhumed on 15 November. Examined by Dr Bernard Spilsbury and Dr William Willcox, arsenic was found in the hair and various organs. Further detailed tests took place, resulting in forty-year-old Frederick Seddon's arrest for murder on 4 December.

Various financial attractions involving £5 notes endorsed by Margaret Seddon using false names, were investigated. Thirty-three fivers, through their serial numbers, were traced to Miss Barrow. Thirty-eight-year-old Mrs Margaret Seddon was arrested on 15 January 1912. The trial of the Seddons opened at the Old Bailey on 4 March 1912 before Mr Justice Bucknill. Arsenic found in flypapers used in the Seddon household and in Miss Barrow's room formed the basis of the prosecution's case. Although the formidable Edward Marshall Hall put up a convincing defence, the trial resulted in Mrs Seddon's acquittal and her husband's conviction for wilful murder. Fred Seddon's lack of affability went strongly against him. The jury simply did not like him. His flippant response to cross-examination did not endear him. Before sentence of death was pronounced, Seddon gave a long and powerful speech, quoting facts and figures and a full protestation of his innocence. He concluded by raising his hands as if he was taking a freemason's oath. The judge, too, was a freemason. He was moved to tears.

An appeal was heard on 1 April and dismissed the following day. Despite a petition containing over 250,000 signatures protesting his innocence, Seddon was hanged on 18 April 1912, by John Ellis. Considerable doubt has been expressed about Seddon's guilt by some criminologists and true crime authors, many suggesting in all probability that if it was indeed murder, Mrs Seddon was the guilty party.

Edward Hopwood, 1913

Edward Hopwood was a married man who took as his mistress Florence Silles, better known as the actress Florence Dudley. Hopwood had passed himself off as a wealthy bachelor. In reality he was nothing of the kind and was wanted by police for passing bad cheques. Miss Dudley was appearing at the Tivoli Theatre. On the morning of 28 September 1912, when she learned the truth about her lover, horrified at the thought of bad publicity, she broke off the affair. That afternoon, pleading forgiveness, Hopwood took a cab with Miss Dudley to Fenchurch Street station. When she would not submit to his wishes he pulled a gun out and shot her dead. He then turned the gun on himself. He did not die and was nursed back to health. Hopwood was tried at the Old Bailey, found guilty of murder and hanged on 29 January 1913.

In 1915, George Joseph Smith, the notorious 'Brides in the Bath Murderer' was held at Pentonville during trial then removed to Maidstone to hang.

Roger Casement, 1916

During the First World War, Roger Casement having been found guilty of treason, for seeking German support for Irish nationalists, was stripped of his knighthood and incarcerated in Pentonville prior to him being hanged there on 3 August 1916.

Louis Voisin, 1918

On 2 November 1917, a road-sweeper was at work in Regent Square, Bloomsbury. He noticed a large parcel covered in sackcloth, behind the iron railings in the shrubbery of the central gardens. He opened the parcel and discovered, wrapped in a bloodstained sheet and dressed in delicate lace underwear, the headless torso of a woman. On a paper wrapper was scribbled the miss-spelled message 'Blodie Belgiam'. Nearby, wrapped in brown paper, was a second parcel and this contained the woman's legs. There was one clue that was to prove crucial in the identification of the remains. On the bloodstained sheet in which the torso had been wrapped, was an embroidered laundry mark: 'II H'. It was established that the remains had been dismembered by someone who had knowledge of anatomy, and the time of death was established as being within the previous two days.

Chief Inspector Frederick Wensley was placed in charge of the case. The usual rounds of launderers were instigated and eventually the laundry mark was traced down to a house in Munster Square, situated off Albany Street, Regents Park. At number 50 a young Frenchwoman lodged. Thirty-two-year-old Emilienne Gerard, estranged from her husband, Paul, had been missing from her rooms since 31 October. A search revealed an IOU for the sum of £50, signed by Louis Voisin, who was discovered to be her lover.

Voisin was traced to the basement flat at 101 Charlotte Street, Fitzroy Square. When the police called there, he was in the company of Berthe Roche, who apparently lived with him. They also discovered that his trade was a butcher. As Voisin spoke hardly any English, it was decided to conduct the interview through an interpreter and Chief Inspector Wensley had them brought to Bow Street for questioning. There it was established that Voisin had known Emilienne Gerard for about eighteen months and an intimate relationship had developed between them. On 31 October they had met to say their goodbyes, on the eve of Madame Gerard's departure for France. She was going to see her husband who was a cook in the French army. For the moment all that had been established was the fact that Voisin and Madame Gerard were lovers. It had not at that point been established that the dismembered remains were actually those of Madame Gerard. Nevertheless, Voisin was detained at Bow Street overnight.

The following morning, through an interpreter, Chief Inspector Wensley asked Voisin if he would mind writing out the words 'Bloody Belgium'. Louis Voisin was a hulking brute of a man, who had great strength but little intelligence. He laboriously wrote down the words five times. The last effort was strikingly similar to that written on the parcel. On seeing this, Chief Inspector Wensley was confident he was on the right track.

After a further visit to Charlotte Street there was no doubt at all as to whose remains had been discovered in the parcels found in Regent Square. The kitchen contained the tools of Voisin's trade. As well as saws and knives hanging on the walls, there was also a big knife-sharpening wheel. The walls of the kitchen were spattered with blood. This proved to be human. An earring was found caught in a towel. It was later established this belonged to Madame Gerard. Further searching revealed even more damning evidence. In a little arched recess in the coal cellar the police found a cask of alum which also contained Madame Gerard's head and hands. Voisin owned a pony and trap. The trap was covered with blood. When questioned about the discoveries, Voisin said he had found Madame Gerard's body in its dismembered state on the previous Thursday at her flat, adding, 'I did not know what to do. I thought someone had laid a trap for me.'

However, his story did not tally with the evidence and what Voisin had intended to be a false clue, to suggest a xenophobic anti-war motive, served only to trap him. Semi-literate, and not at all bright, he was clearly unaware of the mis-spelling of what he had intended to read 'Bloody Belgium'. His inability to spell, in part, proved to be his downfall. The theory put forward by Home Office pathologist Bernard Spilsbury, based on the evidence provided by the wounds to the body, was that a large number of wounds had been inflicted by a far weaker hand than the powerful brute of a man, Voisin. However, what the police believed may have happened was never admitted by Voisin or Roche. This theory, or at least something very like it, seems the most likely explanation, based on the known facts. On the night of the 31 October 1917, London suffered one of the worst Zeppelin raids of the war. It is believed that Emilienne Gerard was in the vicinity of Charlotte Street that night, and in fear of her life; she called at her lover's home seeking shelter and comfort from the raids but an argument resulted in her being murdered.

Voisin's trial before Mr Justice Darling, at the Old Bailey, was only remarkable for the fact that after being found guilty of murder, the judge pronounced sentence of death in French. Louis Voisin was hanged on 2 March 1918. Berthe Roche was tried separately before Mr Justice Avory on 1 March 1918. She was acquitted of murder but charged as an accessory. The jury found her guilty and she was given a seven-year prison sentence. However, she didn't serve it, as within a very short time she was certified insane. Berthe Roche died on 22 May 1919.

Henry Julius Jacoby, 1922

In the Spring of 1922, eighteen-year-old Henry Jacoby took the position of pantry boy at the Spencer Hotel, in the heart of the West End. Before he had been there a month, young Henry decided to avail himself of some of the wealthy residents' property. With robbery in mind, on the night of Monday 13 March 1922, he put his plans into action. The Spencer Hotel, a private hotel (now the Mostyn Hotel), was situated in Portman Street. It was a comfortable place, dignified and quiet, the kind of hotel where retired people of good standing could spend the remaining years of their lives, being well taken care of, in pleasant surroundings. One of the residents was sixty-year-old Lady White, the well-off widow of Sir Edward White, a former Chairman of London County Council. That evening, Lady White had been playing bridge in the drawing room. She had been at the hotel since the previous November. The forty or so other guests liked her and as Lady White received the domestic attention she required, the Spencer Hotel evidently suited her. She retired to her room at about eleven o'clock.

At five past eight on the morning of the 14 March, chambermaid Sarah Ann Pocock went into Lady White's room, number 14, as part of her usual routine. The room was in semi-darkness, as the curtains were drawn; when she opened them she saw that Lady White was covered in blood and had serious head injuries. Police Divisional Surgeon, Dr Percy Bertram Spurgeon, was called to the hotel and found Lady White still breathing. She had an extensive fracture of the skull. The bone had been splintered and brain matter and blood clots were protruding. There was a laceration about 8-inches long across the scalp and the edges were gaping. He concluded that the injuries were caused by more than one blow with a blunt instrument and that Lady White must have been rendered unconscious by the first blow. There was also an injury to Lady White's left hand. There were no signs of a struggle and no traces of forced entry. Lady White died during the early hours of the following morning. She never regained consciousness.

On the night of the murder, eighteen-year-old pantry boy, Henry Jacoby, told the porter he had heard some men whispering outside his basement room. However, nothing untoward was found and the porter returned to his duties, and young Henry to his bed.

The inquest was opened at Marylebone Coroner's Court, by Mr H R Oswald, on 16 March. Meanwhile, police enquiries were continuing. Young Henry's all too eager enthusiasm to help and, his theories as to how the murder might have been committed, along with his tale of hearing men whispering outside his room, threw suspicion his way. When his room was searched, two bloodstained handkerchiefs were found. Henry caved in and told the police what had happened. Robbery was the motive. He entered the room and before he had the chance to steal anything, Lady White woke up. He saw her in the beam of his torch, panicked and hit her with the hammer he had taken from a toolbox, which he had later returned after cleaning it.

The trial opened on 28 April at the Old Bailey. The jury consulted for some time in private, then the foreman said they were all agreed that Jacoby went into the room without intending to murder, but for the purpose of robbery. They wanted to know whether, bearing this in mind, they could bring a manslaughter verdict. Mr Justice McCardie said, that if Jacoby went into the room for the purpose of stealing, then the next question was, did he strike Lady White intending either to kill or inflict grievous bodily harm? Yet inasmuch as the victim had died from the injuries inflicted by Jacoby, he would be guilty in law of murder. They brought in a guilty verdict. There was to be no reprieve and Henry Jacoby was hanged on 7 June 1922.

In the Condemned Cell, Jacoby wrote several letters, one of which concluded:

> H. J. 382 – please excuse this curious signature, as this is what I shall be buried under.

Frederick Bywaters, 1923

On the evening of 3 October 1922, thirty-two-year-old shipping clerk Percy Thompson, had taken his twenty-eight-year-old wife Edith, who worked in Aldersgate Street in the City of London as the manageress-bookkeeper for Carlton & White a firm of wholesale milliners, to the Criterion Theatre in London's Piccadilly Circus and returned with her afterwards by train to Ilford. They reached the local station about midnight and from there set off to their home in Kensington Gardens. As they were walking down the long and dark Belgrave Road between Endsleigh Road and Kensington Gardens, a man came out of the darkness and stabbed Percy Thompson in the head and neck before vanishing into the darkness. The assailant was Frederick Bywaters (for the events surrounding this place please see pages 99 to 101). At 9.00am on the morning of 9 January 1923 Freddy Bywater's accomplice in crime, Edith Thompson, was hanged by John Ellis at Holloway prison. Half a mile away at Pentonville Prison at exactly the same hour, her lover Freddy Bywaters was being hanged by Thomas Pierrepoint.

Ewen Stitchell, 1926

On New Year's Day 1926, in a house in Arlington Road, Camden Town, seventeen-year-old Polly Edith Walker was discovered lying beneath her bed in her nightdress, by her widowed mother. She had been strangled with one of her own silk stockings by her twenty-five-year-old, French Canadian, one-legged street musician lover Ewen Stitchell, also known as Eugene de Vere. In addition to being strangled, Polly had also sustained several head injuries. A copper-handled poker was found lying on the blood soaked eiderdown, as were some broken fire tongs. Stitchell had a charismatic personality but lived life almost like a vagrant. Polly was attracted to him and felt sorry for him and had taken him under her wing. Following his arrest at Hitchin in Hertfordshire, on Sunday 3 January, Stitchell admitted killing Polly. He said he had done so out of jealousy having discovered that she had taken another lover. *The Times* reported that, despite his artificial leg, Stitchell is believed to have walked the thirty-two miles to Hitchin, following the murder. Ewen Stitchell was hanged on 24 March 1926.

John Robinson, 1927

At a little after 1.50pm on Friday 6 May 1927, a man described by luggage attendant Mr Glass as being of military bearing, arrived by taxi-cab and deposited a large black trunk in the left luggage office at Charing Cross Railway Station. The letters F and A were painted on either end of the trunk and a label read 'F AUSTIN to ST LENARDS', actually St Leonards-on-Sea and, as later discovered, pertaining to the quite innocent previous owner.

On Monday 9 May, attention was drawn to the trunk when an unpleasant smell was noticed. The next morning the police were summoned. When opened and emptied at Bow Street Police Station it was discovered that the trunk contained five brown paper parcels tied up with string, a pair of woman's shoes and a black handbag. The parcels contained five portions of a woman. Her limbs had been severed at each shoulder and hip joint and wrapped in items of female clothing and a towel, before being wrapped and tied up with string. A duster had been wound around the victim's head, which was still attached to the torso. The remains were moved to Horseferry Road Mortuary and on Wednesday 11 May a post-mortem examination was carried out by Dr Rose and Dr Henry Bright Weir. Home Office Pathologist Sir Bernard Spilsbury also examined the remains. There were several bruises on the woman's forehead, stomach, back and limbs. These, Spilsbury concluded, had been inflicted before she died and he suggested that she had been beaten unconscious and that the cause of death was asphyxia. He further concluded that the woman had been dead for perhaps a week, that she had been short and stout and was aged about thirty-five.

Two of the items of clothing bore a laundry mark and a name-tag on a pair of slate coloured knickers bore the name 'P Holt'. Investigations led to a former cook once employed by a Mrs Holt of Chelsea. Her name was Mrs Minnie Alice Bonati, the estranged wife of an Italian waiter. Bianco Bonati told the police that Minnie had left him to go with a roadworker, Frederick Rolls, on 21 September 1923 and they had lived at various addresses until the relationship came to an end in July 1926. The police were able to satisfy themselves that neither Mr Rolls nor Mr Bonati were in any way connected with the murder and mutilation of Mrs Bonati.

Enquiries about the trunk and the taxi in which its depositor had left, led police to 86 Rochester Row, Westminster. One of the occupants of a two-roomed, second floor office that overlooked the street, was one John Robinson, who traded as an estate agent under the business name 'Edwards and Co., Business Transfer Agents'. Mr Robinson had not been seen for several days. Apart from a cracked window pane and a broken fender in the fireplace, nothing seemed amiss and, the police could find no traces of blood.

When police visited Robinson's lodgings in Camberwell Gate, they discovered he'd left without leaving a forwarding address and discovered a telegram addressed to 'Robinson, Greyhound Hotel, Hammersmith', had been returned marked addressee unknown. As was later discovered, the telegram had been returned to sender by a new maid at the Greyhound Hotel, unaware that the Robinson mentioned in the telegram actually worked there. However, this was not John Robinson himself, but *Mrs* Robinson.

Thirty-six-year-old John Robinson was born in Leigh, Lancashire. He left school at the age of twelve and began his working life as an errand-boy for the Co-op. He also worked as a clerk, a tram conductor, bartender and butcher's assistant. He had four children by his first wife, whom he married in 1911. He later bigamously married a Tasmanian girl from whom he was estranged. She worked at the Greyhound Hotel, Hammersmith. She cooperated with the police and when Robinson contacted her, at his request, she agreed to meet him. On Thursday 19 May, they met at a public house the Elephant and Castle, Walworth. She was escorted by Chief Inspector George Cornish of Scotland Yard. Robinson denied any knowledge of either buying the trunk or of Mrs Bonati. At the identity parade, of the three witnesses who attended, the station porter, the taxi-driver and Mr Ward, the dealer who had sold the trunk, not one of them recognised him. The police had no alternative but to release him.

The bloodstained, dirty duster, in which the murder victim's head had been wound was washed to see if it revealed any further clues. A small tab on the hem of the duster revealed the name 'GREY-HOUND'. A further painstaking search of Robinson's office suite revealed a bloodstained match, which had been caught in the wicker-work of a waste-paper basket. A small clue, yes, but the bloodstained match, combined with the duster proved sufficient to break Robinson's confidence and, having been brought back to Scotland Yard from his lodgings in De Laune Street, Kennington, on Monday 23 May, he decided to make a statement. He said that Minnie Bonati had propositioned him at Victoria railway station at about 4.15pm on the afternoon of Wednesday 4 May. At his office suite, she asked him for money and when he told her he hadn't any, she was abusive and threatened violence. There was a struggle in which he broke a window pane as he stumbled backwards and his head hit it. She fell, knocking herself insensible as she struck her head on a chair. Fearful of the racket they had made and well aware of the close proximity of the police station, in a panic, Robinson said he decided to leave the office building. On his return to the office the following morning he found Mrs Bonati was lying face-down on the carpet dead. At no time did Robinson ever admit to killing her but he did not deny that he had cut up her body and placed the remains in the trunk.

Robinson's trial was held at the Old Bailey and began on Monday 11 July 1927, before Mr Justice Rigby Swift. The defence was unable to convince the jury that Minnie Bonati was the victim of an unfortunate accident. In his own evidence Robinson admitted everything that was put to him, excepting an intention to kill. Sir Bernard Spilsbury's contention that the bruises on Mrs Bonati had been caused by direct blows and pressure and that she had been asphyxiated after a violent assault, seemed to hold more water with both the judge and the jury. On Wednesday 13 July the jury returned a verdict of 'guilty'. John Robinson was hanged on 12 August 1927 and buried within Pentonville's precincts.

Maurice Freedman, 1932
Ex-policeman Maurice Freedman had hopes of marrying young typist Annette Friedson. However, Freedman was already married and Miss Friedson's family were not impressed by the unemployed Freedman's hand-to-mouth existence. He pawned his clothes to raise money for gambling and even Annette wondered when he would divorce his wife as promised. Realising that he was a hopeless case she told Freedman that she wished to end the relationship. His reaction to this severing of ties frightened Annette and each day her brother took her to the office where she worked in the City of London. On the morning of 26 January 1932, Freedman waited inside the building and cut her throat with a razor. When he was arrested Freedman claimed he had intended to kill himself and that Annette had died accidentally. He also claimed he had thrown the razor in the canal. However, the razor was found on a bus. As well as her blood group it had traces of fibres from Annette's coat. The bus conductor was able to identify Freedman. He was found guilty of murder at the Old Bailey and hanged on 4 May 1932.

John Stockwell, 1934
In 1934, the Eastern Palace Cinema stood in Bow Road, Mile End. On 7 August an employee, nineteen-year-old John Stockwell, attacked the cinema's owner Dudley Horde and his wife, Maisie, with an axe and stole a little under £100. Mr Horde was found lying in a pool of blood unconscious, in the circle of the cinema. He died without regaining consciousness. Mrs Horde had only been knocked out and recovered. Stockwell had formulated an elaborate fake-suicide by drowning plan, which might have worked if only he had got the chronology right. After stealing the money from the safe he fled the scene and went to Aldgate East station, where he deposited a suitcase in a left luggage locker. Establishing that he was still alive and on the run, was made easy for the police, partly through a slip he made in signing a hotel register and, through the discovery of his clothes on the seashore, before the time the postcard sent by himself to police was postmarked, on which he announced his attention to commit suicide. Discovered under an alias, Stockwell was arrested at the Metropole Hotel, Great Yarmouth. He was tried at the Old Bailey, convicted of murder and hanged on 14 November 1934.

Udham Singh, 1940

Indian independence activist Udham Singh, who shot Sir Michael O'Dwyer (Governor of the Punjab) during the Amritsar Massacre, was detained at Pentonville and hanged on 31 July 1940.

Karl Gustav Hulten – The Cleft Chin Murder, 1954

At 2.30am on Saturday 7 October 1944, nightwatchman Bill Hollis was at work at a Chiswick car depot. He heard the distinct sound of a single gunshot. At about 8am, apprentice electrician John Jones found several items scattered along the grass verge of the Great Southwest Road. They included an identity card, cheque book and driving licence, all belonging to George Heath. Jones handed them in to the police. Not long afterwards, a man's body was found in a ditch at Knowle Green near Staines. He had been shot in the back at close range. The body was quickly linked to the items found by the road-side at Chiswick and the dead man identified as thirty-four-year-old freelance cab-driver, cleft-chinned George Heath. His missing Ford V8 saloon was found in Lurgan Avenue, Fulham on 9 October. The car was placed under observation and within a short time of its discovery, a dark haired young man came out of a house and got into it. Three policemen quickly moved in and the man was discovered to have a Remington automatic pistol in his possession and several rounds of ammunition. He was arrested and taken to Hammersmith police station.

The man, an American, gave a false name, claiming to be Second Lieutenant Richard Allen. Under the Visiting Forces Act a potential serious diplomatic problem emerged. An officer from the American Army Criminal Investigation Department interviewed Allen and after several hours of questioning he broke down and confessed to being Private Karl Gustav Hulten, aged twenty-two, who was absent with-out leave. He alleged to have found the car near the army barracks where he was stationed in Newbury and said at the time of the murder he was with a girl, Georgina Grayson. She was tracked down to a bedsit at 311 King Street, Hammersmith and brought in for question-ing. Eighteen years old, her real name was Elizabeth Jones. She hailed from Neath in South Wales and worked as an exotic dancer at the Blue Lagoon Club in Carnaby Street, using the stage name Georgina Grayson. She said she did not know a man named Hulten, but after being shown a photograph she confirmed that she knew Hulten as 'Ricky' and they had met the previous week in a café, since when they had been out on several dates. She also said he had spent the entire night of 7 October with her, in her flat. Satisfied with her answers, the police allowed her to leave. On her way home she bumped into an old acquaintance, Henry Kimberley, who happened to be a Reserved Constable. He said she looked tired. She told him about being questioned by police and he told her not to worry if she had nothing to do with the murder. However, his suspicions were aroused when she remarked:

It's no wonder I look tired. If you'd seen someone do what I've seen done, you wouldn't be able to sleep at night either.

Kimberley went with police officers to bring Jones in for questioning once again, this time she told in detail how Hulten had shot George Heath and how from 3 October she had accompanied him on a campaign of crime and violence in the army vehicle he had commandeered. She said he had told her he was connected with Chicago gangsters and she, according to Hulten had incited him to commit robbery and murder as she wanted to 'do something exciting'. They had hailed Heath's taxi near Olympia and Hulten had shot him in Chiswick – to impress her. The US government waived its right and allowed Hulten to be tried in a British court. Hulten and Jones' trial commenced at the Old Bailey on Tuesday 16 January before Mr Justice Charles. It lasted six days, both were found guilty of murder and sentenced to death. Jones was reprieved two days before her scheduled execution and her sentence commuted to life imprisonment. She was released in January 1954. Hulten was hanged on 8 March 1945.

Neville George Clevely Heath, 1946
Twenty-nine-year-old, 5ft 11in tall, handsome, charming, Neville Heath, on the surface the perfect escort for ladies, was in reality a confidence trickster with a long record of petty criminality, which included housebreaking, passing bad cheques, using a string of false identities and jewellery theft. During World War Two Heath served as an officer in the RAF and later the South African Air Force but was cashiered from both services for fraud and other offences. He had a fondness for passing himself off as high-ranking officers and laying claim to honours and medals he had not earned. More disturbingly, he also had perverted sexual tastes extracting gratification from cruel and sadistic acts, which came to a climax when he murdered two women in horrific circumstances.

After the war, Heath led a raffish life. He met a would-be actress and film extra, known as 'Ocelot Margie', at the Panama Club, Knightsbridge. Thirty-two-year-old Margery Gardiner had left her husband and child in Sheffield and come to London to pursue an acting career. Her nickname resulted from the fake ocelot coat she often wore. Known to the police, Mrs Gardiner mixed with pimps, thieves and black-marketeers and was known to be a masochist with sadistic inclinations. Heath and Mrs Gardiner enjoyed at least one date at which the binding and beating being satisfactory to both parties resulted in this last fatal encounter on Thursday 20 June 1946. The following afternoon Margery Gardiner's body was found in room No. 4 at the Pembridge Court Hotel, Notting Hill Gate, which Heath had booked the previous week under the names of Lieutenant Colonel and Mrs Heath. Mrs Gardiner's naked body was lying on its back, her feet were tied together with a handkerchief and marks on her wrists suggested her hands had also been tied. Her face was extensively bruised and there were seventeen lash marks on various parts of her body, which had left distinctive diamond patterns on the flesh. Her nipples had almost been bitten off and a rough object had been savagely forced into her vagina causing severe bleeding. Home Office Pathologist, Dr Keith Simpson, confirmed that the mutilation was inflicted while Mrs Gardiner was alive. The actual cause of death was suffocation, which may have been the result of a gag or from the victim's face being forced into a pillow.

Meanwhile, Heath went to Worthing where he met with his fiancé, Yvonne Symonds, who had stayed overnight with him at the Pembridge Court Hotel the previous week, when he had proposed to her. In Worthing he again used his own name at the Ocean Hotel. He told Yvonne that a terrible murder had occurred in London, in the hotel room he had booked and that he had lent the room to a woman to entertain a friend named Jack. He also claimed that he had been invited by police to view the body the following morning.

When newspaper reports contradicted this and mentioned wanting to interview Heath, he took to his heels. The police later discovered an RAF uniform and some medals in his room. Heath arrived in Bournmouth on Sunday 23 June, where he booked into room No. 81 at the Tollard Royal Hotel, booking himself in as Group Captain Rupert Brooke. He sent a postcard to Inspector Barrett at Scotland Yard in which he claimed to have lent his hotel room to Margery Gardiner, having later '. . . found her in the condition of which you are aware . . . I have the instrument with which Mrs Gardiner was beaten and am forwarding this to you today'. The 'instrument' never arrived.

On the afternoon of Wednesday 3 July, 'Brooke' met Doreen Marshall on the promenade. She was a pretty, twenty-year-old former Wren, who was staying at Bournemouth's Norfolk Hotel recuperating from a bad bout of influenza. He entertained her to afternoon tea and invited her to dinner at his hotel. After dinner witnesses stated at about 12.15am she asked him for a taxi to be called for her but Heath insisted on walking her back to her hotel. She was not seen alive again. Heath's attempt to establish an alibi by climbing into his room via scaffolding and a ladder, failed.

On 5 July, the manager of the Norfolk Hotel reported Miss Marshall missing. Heath, still claiming to be Group Captain Rupert Brooke, called into Bournemouth Police Station and confirmed when shown a photograph, that it was indeed the missing girl he had dined with. However, he was quickly identified as Heath and arrested. A metal-tipped riding crop found among Heath's possessions matched the marks on Margery Gardiner's body and there was also some blood-stained clothing. Doreen Marshall's body was found by a walker among rhododendron bushes at Branksome Dene Chine on 8 July. She had been attacked with even more bestial savagery than Heath's previous victim.

An imitation pearl found in Heath's pocket was identical to a broken string of imitation pearls found with Miss Marshall's body. Heath's trial began in the No. 1 Court at the Old Bailey on 24 September 1946 before Mr Justice Morris. Heath was charged only with the murder of Mrs Margery Gardiner, he pleaded not guilty. In an attempt to save him from the gallows, his defence claimed that a man would simply have to be mad to commit such crimes. However, medical experts disagreed and put him outside the scope of the McNaghten Rules (widely used in British courts since 1843 as the accepted definition of insanity in law), declaring him definitely not insane. In his summing up the judge said:

A strong sexual instinct is not of itself insanity. Mere love of lust, mere recklessness, are not in themselves insanity. Inability to resist temptation is not in itself insanity. A perverted impulse could not be excused on the ground of insanity. Legal insanity could not be permitted to become an easy or vague explanation of some conduct which was shocking because it was also startling.

At the end of a three-day trial the jury's verdict was unanimous. They found Heath guilty after one hour's deliberation. Heath wrote to his parents:

My only regret at leaving the world is that I have been damned unworthy of you both.

He did not appeal and was hanged on 16 October by Albert Pierrepoint.

The Antiquis Murder 1947

A little after 2pm on 29 April 1947, father of six Alec de Antiquis, a thirty-four-year-old mechanic who ran a motor repair shop in Colliers Wood, South London, was in the West End on business, when he saw a robbery in progress at Jay's Jewellers, situated at 73–75 Charlotte Street. The robbery had been a violent one, in which shots were fired. As he tried to foil the robbers' escape at the junction of Tottenham Street, by driving his motorcycle in front of the fleeing three masked raiders, one of the gang shot him through the head. The robbers made their escape through the crowds and traffic. The police were quickly on the scene, led by Superintendent Robert Fabian ('Fabian of the Yard'). Mr Antiquis died in the ambulance before he reached hospital. The murder weapon was found by a schoolboy on the Thames foreshore at Wapping at low tide. Another gun found nearby was also identified as being used in the robbery. A taxi driver reported seeing two masked men entering a building in Tottenham Court Road. A search produced a raincoat and a scarf, folded to create a mask. The raincoat was traced to twenty-three-year-old Charles Henry Jenkins, who had a criminal record (younger brother of Thomas Jenkins, involved in the killing of Commander Ralph Binney), two of his associates were also picked up. Christopher James Geraghty, aged twenty (who had been in borstal with Jenkins) and Terence Peter Rolt, aged seventeen, and both incriminated themselves. All three were members of a gang of young thugs who called themselves the 'Elephant Boys'. They were charged with the murder of Alec de Antiquis.

The trial of Geraghty, Jenkins and Rolt began at the Central Criminal Court, Old Bailey, on Monday 21 July 1947, before Mr Justice Hallet. It lasted a week. The jury took fifteen minutes to reach a verdict in all three cases. Sentence of death was pronounced on Geraghty and Jenkins. Although it was Geraghty who fired the gun that killed Mr Antiquis, Jenkins was an accessory engaged in a joint enterprise of armed robbery, Rolt, who was too young to be hanged, was sentenced to be detained during His Majesty's Pleasure. Geraghty and Jenkins were hanged on Friday 19 September 1947 by Albert Pierrepoint. After serving less than nine years, Rolt was released from prison on licence in June 1956.

Timothy John Evans, 1950

Throughout the long history of London's prisons there has undoubtedly been many unknown and unrecorded miscarriages of justice, some unfortunate victims paying the supreme penalty for a crime they neither committed nor had anything to do with. One such victim was Timothy John Evans. This case involved a double murder at what was soon to become one of London's most notorious addresses. 10 Rillington Place, Notting Hill. On 2 December 1949 the bodies of nineteen-year-old Beryl Evans and her fourteen-month-old baby daughter, Geraldine, were found by police, dumped in the outside washhouse. At this same address the notorious serial killer John Reginald Halliday Christie lived on the ground floor. The Evans family lived in the top floor flat. On 30 November Timothy Evans, a twenty-four-year-old illiterate van driver, had visited Merthyr Tydfil police station and made a voluntary statement, in which he said he had returned home from work on 8 November and found his wife, Beryl, dead. He also said he had disposed of the body down a drain.

After the discovery of the bodies in the washhouse, Evans made a new statement, in which he accused John Christie of killing his wife while carrying out an illegal abortion. Then, after the pathologist, Dr Teare, found no evidence of an abortion, Evans changed his statement again and confessed to both murders. Evans was known to quarrel with Beryl and to beat her up. The violent arguments were often about money

At the Old Bailey on 11 November 1950, Evans retracted his confession and blamed Christie for both murders. However, the prosecution's chief witness was John Christie and at the conclusion of Evans's trial, it took the jury just forty minutes to find him guilty of murder. Evans was hanged on 9 March 1950. After the dreadful events of 1953 when Christie himself was charged with murder, some doubt was cast on Evans' guilt, but Dr Francis Camps, pathologist in the Christie case, entertained no doubt about Evans' guilt. Christie admitted to killing Beryl but not to the baby and various scenarios have been suggested for both killings. Timothy Evans was posthumously pardoned on 8 October 1966.

John Reginald Halliday Christie, 1953

By 1953, the one-time neat, three-storey houses of well-to-do Victorian families in Rillington Place, Notting Hill, had become run down and most were divided into flats, many of them being occupied by members of London's growing immigrant community. On 24 March 1953, new tenant Beresford Brown, recently arrived from Jamaica, was examining the kitchen on the ground floor of No. 10. The previous tenants, an Irish couple, the Reillys, had been evicted by the landlord after just one day's occupancy as they had taken over the tenancy from John Christie who had lived there with his wife since 1938; but Christie, who took £7 deposit from the Reillys had no right to sub-let and had disappeared owing several months' rent. Beresford Brown noticed there was a strange mixture of unpleasant smells, which were being partially disguised by disinfectant. These smells were most potent in the kitchen and seemed to originate from a section of wall, which he tapped. It had a hollow sound and further investigation revealed a papered over door. He peeled back the wallpaper and shone his torch into a cut out section. In the torchlight Brown could see what appeared to be the body of a woman.

The local police being summoned were quick to call in Scotland Yard and Detective Chief Inspector Griffin and pathologist Dr Francis Camps were soon on the scene. When the door had been fully opened a largish alcove was revealed. The dead woman was in a sitting position with her back towards the room. When the body was removed two more dead women were found wrapped in blankets. A fourth body was discovered beneath the floorboards in the front room. The first body was identified as twenty-six-year-old Hectorine MacLennan, the others in the alcove were Kathleen Maloney, also twenty-six and Rita Nelson, aged twenty-five. All three women were prostitutes. The body beneath the floorboards was Christie's wife, Ethel, who had not been seen for over three months. While these bodies were being examined, the police concentrated on the small garden at the rear of the house. There they unearthed a large quantity of bones, which turned out to be those of Ruth Fuerst, aged twenty-one, who had disappeared in July 1943 and Muriel Eady, a woman in her early thirties, who was reported missing in October 1943.

During their search the police discovered a tobacco tin which contained four locks of pubic hair. One lock matched that of Ethel Christie. The former occupant of the flat, fifty-five-year-old office worker John Reginald Halliday Christie had already been at the centre of a murder enquiry, being principal witness for the prosecution at the trial of fellow resident Timothy John Evans, who was hanged for murder. Christie was born in Halifax, Yorkshire, in 1898 and was known in his teens, due to his sexual inadequacy, as 'Reggie-no-dick'. He served in the First World War, where he was gassed in

France in 1918, which affected his voice and left him softly spoken thereafter. He married Ethel Waddington in 1920 but, according to several accounts his sexual inadequacies continued and he often visited prostitutes. He had a criminal record for various petty offences including in 1929, assaulting a woman with a cricket bat. His wife left him, but by the late 1930s he had settled down to work as a stock clerk and the Christies were reunited. Christie also professed some medical knowledge and was eager to advise anyone willing to listen to him. During World War Two he concealed his criminal record and joined the police force as a special constable.

Following the gruesome discoveries in Rillington Place a nation-wide hunt for Christie was instigated. On the morning of Tuesday 31 March Christie, who had been staying at a nearby doss house made his way to Putney Bridge, where he was spotted staring into the River Thames by police constable Thomas Leger, who arrested him. Once in custody Christie did not deny his guilt and at his four day trial at the Old Bailey before Mr Justice Finnemore, despite having confessed to the murders of seven women, including Evans's wife, Geraldine, was charged only with the killing of his wife, Ethel. Christie spoke quite candidly about how he had enticed the women home and, having plied them with alcohol, rendered them unconscious with coal gas before strangling them. Evidence suggested he had sexual intercourse with them, indulging a taste for necrophilia. His occasional lapses into vagueness were seen as an attempt to bolster up his plea of 'not guilty by reason of insanity'. However, the jury were not convinced and found Christie guilty of murder after less than an hour and a half's deliberation. An inquiry into Christie's mental state upheld the jury's views. He was hanged on 15 July 1953.

Ronald Henry Marwood, 1959

On 14 December 1958, in the early days of the 'Teddy Boy' era, Ronald Marwood, a twenty-five-year-old scaffolder, was celebrating his first wedding anniversary. He lived with his twenty-year-old wife Rosalie, in Huntingdon Street, Islington. Trouble flared up between two rival gangs, the Angel Mob and the Finsbury Park Lot, outside Eugene Gray's Dancing Academy at 133 Seven Sister's Road near that part of Holloway known as Nag's Head. Amongst other weapons, knives, bottles and knuckledusters were used. When matters got out of hand, the police intervened. While 6ft 5in, twenty-three-year-old Police Constable Raymond Henry Summers was arresting his best friend, Marwood was said to have pulled a 10-inch knife out and stabbed him in the back. The policeman died of his injuries.

Eleven youths were charged with brawling but Marwood, who denied any involvement was released. However, he attracted attention to himself when he disappeared. The killing of a policeman was a very serious matter indeed and Marwood's unexplained absence from home threw suspicion his way. He hid out with some friends in Chalk Farm. The police issued a picture on 3 January 1959 and he gave himself up on 27 January, when he walked into a police station and allegedly admitted: 'I did stab the copper that night.' This claim was later denied by Marwood who insisted the police 'put down things' he did not say. At his trial, which took place at the Old Bailey in March 1959, Marwood said he heard Police Constable Summers telling the brawlers to break it up and he struck out at the constable intending to push him away. He also said he did not know he had a knife in his hand. It transpired that on the night of the murder during his anniversary celebrations Marwood visited various pubs where he consumed ten pints of brown ale. The defence claimed there was no evidence connecting the accused man with the fatal blow, but if in the excitement of the fight he did stab the constable, whilst his brain was clouded with drink, then the verdict should be one of manslaughter. On 19 March, Ronald Marwood was convicted of the capital murder of a policeman and became the first person to be sentenced to death under the section of the Homicide Act of 1957 that protected police officers and warders. He was hanged on Friday 8 May 1959. There is a widely held belief in pockets of North London communities that Marwood was in fact innocent of the killing of PC Summers – the alleged killer being one of Marwood's close associates, who later achieved national fame and indeed celebrity status more than two decades after Marwood was hanged.

Edwin Albert Bush, 1961

On 3 March 1961, fifty-year-old Mrs Elsie May Batten, wife of renowned sculptor Mark Batten, was found stabbed to death in a shop situated at No. 23 Cecil Court, the narrow walkway which straddles Charing Cross Road and St Martin's Lane, occupied then, as it is today, by mostly second-hand book, antique print and curio shops. For the past two years Mrs Batten, who lived in Castletown Road, Fulham had been helping out as a part-time shop assistant, mostly to fill her days while her husband, who usually spent four days a week out of London, worked at his studio in Dallington, Sussex. No. 23, an antique and curio shop was owned by Louis Meier and run by his manageress Mrs Marie Gray; both were often away attending auctions.

On the morning of the murder, Mrs Batten unlocked the iron gates outside the shop and began arranging the display. When Mr Meier arrived after midday to pay Mrs Batten's wages, he found that the usual outside display was incomplete and when he entered the shop the light was on but Mrs Batten was nowhere to be seen. He discovered her body in a curtained-off area towards the rear of the shop, when he noticed Mrs Batten's legs sticking out from beneath the thick brocade drapes. An 18-inch antique dagger was protruding from her chest and another from her neck. There was a wound to her shoulder and another to her back. She had also been hit over the head with a heavy stone vase, which was found nearby. A piece of board under Mrs Batten's body had the imprint from the heel of a man's shoe. Neighbouring shopkeepers remember having seen a young coloured man who had been making enquiries about dress swords. Mr Meier remembered that the previous day a young Indian-looking man had expressed interest in a dress sword costing £15 and also several daggers. The same man had also tried to sell a sword to an adjacent shop, which was subsequently proven to have been stolen from Meier's shop that morning and had been used to inflict some of the injuries on the murder victim.

With so many witnesses, the police used a technique for the first time in England, the Identikit picture. Although the concept had been introduced to Scotland Yard in 1959, this was the first time it had been put to practical use. This first Identikit picture was widely circulated. On 8 March, PC Cole was on duty in Old Compton Street, when he saw a young man who looked very similar to the Identikit picture. He was taken into custody and picked out in an identity parade. His name was Edwin Albert Bush, a twenty-one-year-old Eurasian. The heel of one of his shoes was an exact match for the heel mark found at the murder scene. He was charged with murder. He admitted killing Mrs Batten in order to steal the sword. At his trial, which began at the Central Criminal Court, Old Bailey, on 12 May, Bush tried to play the race card, saying he had killed Mrs Batten after she had made an offensive remark about his colour, but this contradicted his earlier statement when he admitted he had killed her in order to obtain the sword. He was found guilty of murder on 13 May. An appeal failed and he was hanged on 6 July 1961. This was to be Pentonville's final execution.

Today, Her Majesty's Prison Pentonville is a local prison designated to hold adult male Category B & C, accommodating up to 1,250 prisoners remanded by local magistrates' courts and crown courts, as well as those serving short sentences or beginning long sentences. The prison is divided into four main wings:

A wing, used for Induction and a First Night Centre, for newly arrived prisoners.

B wing, used as a resettlement wing.

C wing, used for prisoners on remand and for convicted prisoners.

D wing, designated for enhanced prisoners.

In addition there is:

E wing, used as a detoxification unit overflow.

F wing, used as a detoxification unit.

G wing, used for education, workshops and offending behaviour courses.

As well as the usual habitual offenders, for some of whom 'the ville' as Pentonville is commonly known, has become almost like a second home, in recent years the prison has held some high profile inmates, including Boy George, in 2009, sentenced for false imprisonment of a male escort; and George Michael, in 2010, sentenced for driving while under the influence of drugs.

CHAPTER 8

Wandsworth Prison

andsworth was built in 1851, as a House of Correction for the county of Surrey, to hold 1,000 prisoners, on the separate and silent system and was originally known as the Surrey House of Correction. The male section had five wings radiating from a central building. The female section was similarly designed but had only three wings. The cells were well appointed, each prisoner having his or her own toilet facilities. However, in order to increase inmate capacity these facilities were subsequently removed, requiring Wandsworth's prisoners to indulge in what was a perfectly normal practice for the majority of prisoners held at other London's prisons, the deliberately humiliating process of 'slopping-out', which remained part of the daily routine at Wandsworth until as recently as 1996.

Wandsworth contained 100 cranks to be worked by male prisoners sentenced to hard labour, they remained in use until they were abolished in 1898. Female prisoners were usually put to work in the laundry. In keeping with the separate and silent system, male prisoners were required to wear masks and females to wear veils. Even more curious, each prisoner's number was painted on their uniforms and the number of their cell was displayed on a brass disc on a man's arm or a woman's belt, each individual prisoner being addressed by the warders using their cell numbers rather than their name. From 1877 Wandsworth was used to hold short-term prisoners. After Horsemonger Lane Gaol closed in 1878, executions for South London crimes were carried out at Wandsworth. In 1895, Oscar Wilde was held there for the first six months of his sentence before his removal to Reading Gaol. Wandsworth gradually expanded to become the largest prison in Britain.

Wandsworth's profile was considerably raised when it became a place of execution. Some of the high profile cases involving Wandsworth are:

Thomas Smithers, 1878
Smithers was the first prisoner to be hanged at Wandsworth, for the murder of Amy Judge. His execution took place on 8 October 1878.

Dr George Henry Lamson, 1882

Twenty-nine-year-old Dr George Lamson was not content with the share of his late parents-in-law's fortune that his wife had brought. He coveted his eighteen-year-old brother-in-law's share also. Percy Malcolm John, a cripple, was a boarding pupil at Blenheim House School, at 1 and 2 St George's Road, Wimbledon. On 31 December 1881 Lansom visited Percy and in company with the headmaster, Mr Bedbrook, and some fellow pupils, partook of some ready cut slices of Dundee cake, supplied by Dr Lamson. The doctor also gave Percy a capsule, which he had ostentatiously filled with sugar, evidently a ruse to draw attention away from Percy's slice of cake, laced with aconite. The doctor then left for Paris. Within hours Percy was taken ill and died later that night. The police suspected foul play. Percy had certainly been poisoned. When it was discovered that Lamson had bought a quantity of the little-known vegetable poison aconite from a manufacturing chemist on 24 November, on his return from Paris on 8 December he was brought in for questioning and subsequently charged with Percy's murder. Tried at the Old Bailey and found guilty, Dr Lamson was hanged on 28 April 1882. He confessed to the prison chaplain that he had injected Percy's slice of cake with the poison.

Robert Ward, 1899

On Thursday 20 June 1899, twenty-seven-year-old out of work bricklayer Robert Ward, returned to his home in Boundary Road, Camberwell Gate after indulging himself in a heavy drinking session, which had been his wont for the last six months or so since he had been out of work. He was very depressed, having been unable to find any permanent employment. This last drinking session had lasted for a full week. On 20 July, having left the house at about 6am to seek work in Peckham, he returned home about noon and asked for some food. His wife, Florence, a somewhat delicate, though hard-working woman, maintained the household by charring and other labour; and always managed to keep her children, two little girls, clean and tidy. She went out immediately to make some purchases. Meanwhile, Ward called his daughters, Mary and Violet, who were playing in the street, into the house and took them to an upstairs bedroom, where he hacked at their throats with an ordinary clasp knife. Great force must have been used, as the knife was not sharp. He then tried to commit suicide by slitting his own throat. Mrs Mills, the landlady heard the commotion and cries of 'Don't Daddy' and went to investigate.

As her horrified gaze fell on three bodies surrounded by blood, she fled the scene and fetched a policeman, who returned with her and sent for the divisional surgeon. Both little girls were dead but their murderer was still alive. Ward said to policeman PC 165L:

I have done it and I want to die as well. I did it with that penknife that lies at my feet.

His throat was bandaged up and he was able to walk to the ambulance, which took him to Guy's Hospital. Robert Ward was charged with the murder of his daughters, Margaret Florence (Mary), aged five and Ada Louisa (Violet), aged two; and with attempting to commit suicide (still a criminal offence, remaining so until 1961). Ward was tried at the Central Criminal Court, before Mr Justice Phillimore. The only reason he could give for his appalling act of cruelty was that his wife was too friendly with a soldier. After he discovered she had once been the sweetheart he became very jealous. Evidence of insanity in his family did not sway the jury. He was found guilty of murder and sentenced to death, the judge adding, he could hold out no hope that the law would not take its course. Ward was hanged at 9am on Wednesday 9 October 1899, by James Billington, assisted by his son Thomas.

Edgar Edwards, 1903

On 23 December 1902, Edgar Edwards was apprehended after assaulting John Garland, a grocer, from Godrell Road, Victoria Park, with a lead window weight, at 89 Church Road, Leyton. Mr Garland had gone to meet Edwards to discuss the purchase of a grocery business. Later, police discovered a business card in the name of John W Darby, a Camberwell grocer, in the bedroom. When police went to Camberwell to talk to Mr Darby they discovered that Darby, his wife Beatrice and their ten-month-old baby, Ethel, were nowhere to be found and most of the contents of their living quarters had disappeared. A bloodstained window weight was also found. The shop was being managed on behalf of Mr Edwards by a dwarf and his wife.

When attention was turned to the garden of Edward's recently acquired house in Leyton, a grim discovery was made. The remains of the Darby family had been buried in six sacks, having been brought there in wooden crates from Camberwell by a hired horse-drawn van along with some furniture. Evidence suggested that Edwards was intent on building up a chain of grocery shops without having to pay for the business he had planned to take over. He had lined up several potential prospects. Edwards' trial began at the Central Criminal Court, within the Old Bailey before Mr Justice Wright on Thursday 12 February 1903. The jury retired just before twelve o'clock on Friday 20 February 1903 and returned after half an hour with a guilty verdict. Edward was hanged by Billington on Tuesday 3 March 1903. His last words were 'I've been looking forward to this lot.'

George Chapman, 1903

George Chapman was the name adopted in 1892 by Severin Klosowski, the son of a Polish carpenter. He came to London aged twenty-three, in 1888, and found work as a barber's assistant in Whitechapel High Street. He married Lucy Baderski in 1889 but, shortly afterwards, a woman arrived from Poland and claimed to be his wife. A lawsuit was settled in Lucy's favour and in 1891 she and her husband emigrated to America. He returned alone the following year and took up with a woman named Annie Chapman, with whom he lived for about a year. He adopted her name and claimed to be an American. He later lived with a married woman, Elizabeth Spink, who had parted from her railwayman husband, Shadrach, and using her money firstly set up in business in Hastings as a barber, before returning to London, where as Mr and Mrs Chapman, they ran the Prince of Wales in Bartholomew Square, near Old Street. Mrs Chapman became ill with vomiting and abdominal pains. In December 1897, she died.

In 1898, Chapman, having become acquainted with Bessie Taylor, moved to run The Grapes of Wrath in Bishop's Stortford before returning once again to London in 1900 to The Monument Tavern, in Union Street, Lambeth, where Bessie became ill and died in February 1901. Chapman next moved to The Crown in Borough High Street, where Maud Marsh came into his life. She became ill. Her mother suspected poisoning. When Maud died on 22 October 1902, the doctor refused to grant a death certificate. When a post-mortem revealed that she had died of antimony poisoning, the bodies of Elizabeth Spink and Bessie Taylor were exhumed. Their bodies were remarkably well preserved, characteristics of antimony poisoning, which was confirmed as the cause of death. When it was discovered that Chapman had purchased tartar emetic from a local chemist, he was charged with the murder of Maud Marsh. Tried at the Old Bailey, he was hanged on 7 April 1903. Chapman was one of the many possible candidates suggested as being the unidentified Jack The

Ripper, the theory being he had changed his *modus operandi* for fear of detection.

Stratton Brothers, 1905

In the early hours of Monday 27 March 1905, a pair of petty criminals, the Stratton brothers, Alfred, aged twenty-two and Albert, aged twenty, broke into the business premises of Mr Thomas Farrow, at 34 Deptford High Street. Next morning, when his assistant arrived at the paint shop, he found Mr Farrow dead in the parlour, with his head battered in. Mrs Ann Farrow lay unconscious in one of the bedrooms. She died four days later. A cash box had been forced open. On its metal tray was a thumbprint. A milkman had seen two men hurrying from the shop early that morning. The brothers were arrested and their fingerprints taken. This case is a landmark case in British legal history, as Alfred and Albert Stratton were the first criminals to be convicted of murder by fingerprint evidence. The brothers were hanged together on 23 May 1905. Each blamed the other.

Reginald Dunn and Joseph O'Sullivan, 1922

On 22 June 1922, Field Marshall Sir Henry Wilson was gunned down on the doorstep of his Belgravia home by two English-born members of the IRA. Sir Henry Hughes Wilson (1864–1922) was born in Edgeworthtown, County Longford. After serving in Burma and the Boer War, he was commander of the Staff College (1910–14), rising to chief of the Imperial General Staff (1918–22). He was made a baronet in 1919. When he left the Army in early 1922 he entered politics, as MP for North Down, Ulster. He had recently returned from Belfast, where he had been advising the Northern Irish authorities on how to deal with bomb outrages perpetrated by Southern Republican terrorists, when, on 22 June Sir Henry unveiled the war memorial at Euston Station. Afterwards he returned home in full dress uniform to 26 Eaton Place, where Reginald Dunn and Joseph O'Sullivan, both ex-servicemen, were waiting for him. Sir Henry drew his dress sword, the only weapon he had to defend himself with but he was powerless against his assassins' bullets. As the two killers were chased down Ebury Street, not an easy feat for O'Sullivan as he had a wooden leg, they seized a cab, then a Victoria (a two-seat, four-wheeled carriage), firing as they fled at their pursuer, they injured two policemen. They were seized by the ever increasing crowd and it was only swift police intervention that prevented them being lynched. Sir Henry was buried in the crypt at St Paul's Cathedral. Dunn and O'Sullivan were hanged on 10 August 1922.

Frederick Herbert Charles Field, 1936

This thirty-two-year-old Royal Air Force deserter twice confessed to the murder of two different women, on each occasion withdrawing the confession at his trial. On 2 October 1931, Nora Upchurch, a twenty-year-old prostitute, was found by some workmen, strangled in the basement of 173–9 Shaftesbury Avenue, an empty shop backing onto New Compton Street. One of the men, Frederick Field, the last person known to have visited the premises prior to discovery of the body, came under suspicion due to a statement he made regarding a key to the premises, which he claimed to have given to a man who had a gold tooth and was wearing plus fours. However, insufficient evidence meant no charges were brought against anyone and at the inquest the coroner's jury brought in a verdict of murder by person or persons unknown.

Then in July 1933, Field sold his story to the newspapers claiming that he had murdered Nora Upchurch. He was arrested, but his story was not consistent with the facts, as he claimed he had strangled her with his bare hands, when in fact the victim's own belt had been used as a ligature. He was nevertheless put on trial at the Old Bailey and, having previously retracted his confession, the judge directed the jury to acquit. Field then decided to join the Royal Air Force but he eventually deserted. When in 1936 he was arrested for desertion from the armed services, he immediately confessed to the murder of Beatrice Sutton, a middle-aged prostitute, found strangled in her flat at Elmhurst Mansions, Elmhurst Road, Clapham, on 4 April 1936. On this occasion the police made sure that the statement he had given them contained incontrovertible evidence, concerning what was in the flat and exactly how the victim had died. Despite once again attempting to evade justice by withdrawing his confession, the jury found him guilty of murder and he was hanged on 30 June 1936.

George Brain, 1938

Thirty-year-old prostitute Rose Muriel Atkins, commonly known as 'Irish Rose', was murdered on the night of 13 July 1938. She had been stabbed with a cobbler's knife, beaten over the head with a starting handle and afterwards run over with a motor vehicle, which left tyre marks on her body – found in Somerset Road, Wimbledon the following morning, close to the All England Lawn Tennis Club. The tyre marks left on her legs were identified as coming only from certain models of either Austin or Morris motor-cars.

Twenty-seven-year-old van driver George Brain was employed by a wholesale boot suppliers and repairers in St Pancras. He lived with his parents in Paradise Road, Richmond. Irish Rose was reported as being seen getting into a green van at about 11.30pm the previous night. When, two days later, Brain's employers reported to the police that both their green Morris Eight van and Brain had gone missing having first embezzled £30 from them, a possible link was established. The van was soon traced to one of Brain's workmate's garages. There were bloodstains in the van and a bloodstained knife was found in the garage. The tyres also matched the tyre marks on the victim's legs. After Brain's photograph was published he was spotted by a school-boy at Sheerness on the Isle of Sheppey and arrested on 25 July. He claimed that Rose Atkins had tried to blackmail him threatening to reveal to his employers that he was using the firm's van for pleasure. He said he had lost his nerve and hit her with the starting handle but had then suffered a blackout and had no recollection of subsequent events. Tried at the Old Bailey, it took the jury just fifteen minutes to find Brain guilty. He was hanged on 1 November 1938.

Gordon Cummins, 1942

Twenty-eight-year-old, 5ft 7ins tall, multiple murderer Gordon Cummins horribly mutilated and killed four women in six days after picking up his unsuspecting victims in West End pubs and clubs in wartime London. Born in New Earswick, North Yorkshire, Cummins was well educated but not industrious. He moved to London and before World War Two and worked in a laboratory. In 1936, he married a theatre producer's secretary. He was called up in 1941 and joined the RAF, training for the air-crew. In 1942, he was billeted in St John's Wood, where his colleagues nicknamed him 'The Duke' on account of his phoney Oxford accent. On Saturday 8 February 1942, Cummins left his RAF billet and went to see his wife, from whom he borrowed money. He then went to the West End.

The following morning the body of forty-two-year-old pharmacist, Miss Evelyn Margaret Hamilton, was discovered in the doorway of a brick air-raid shelter in Montagu Place, W1. She had been strangled and her handbag, containing the sum of £80, had vanished. Cummins repeated the pattern of taking money and small items of little value from his victims.

On 10 February, an ex-actress and Windmill Theatre showgirl, turned prostitute, thirty-five-year-old Nita Ward (real name Mrs Evelyn Oatley), was found almost naked and dead on the bed, in her flat at 153 Wardour Street, W1. She had first been strangled, then her throat cut and the lower part of her body crudely torn open with a tin opener. On Thursday 13 February, another prostitute, forty-three-year-old Margaret Florence Lowe (known as Pearl), was found murdered in her flat, Flat 4, 9–10 Gosfield Street, W1. She had been strangled on her divan bed with one of her silk stockings and her body cut and disfigured by a razor and a knife, which had been left nearby. In the kitchen was a half-empty bottle of stout, a crucial piece of evidence, as the bottle had Cummins' fingerprints on it from his left hand; and it had been established that the murderer was left-handed, by the pressure exerted during strangulation, evident by the bruising on the neck of his victims.

Chief Inspector Greeno, Detective Inspector Higgins and Home Office pathologist Sir Bernard Spilsbury were attending the crime scene, when news came of yet another murder. Thirty-two-year-old Mrs Doris Jouannet (also known as Doris Robson), of 187 Sussex Gardens, Paddington, the wife of an elderly hotel manager, a naturalised Frenchman, who at the time of the murder was on duty at a West End hotel. Mrs Jouannet led a double life, working as a prostitute when her husband was at work. She has been killed in the early hours of that morning and had been strangled by a scarf, which was still wrapped round her neck and her body slashed several times with a razor blade. Later that evening, Cummins picked up Mrs Greta Heywood near Piccadilly and had a drink with her at the Trocadero Hotel. When Cummins became what Mrs Heywood described as 'unpleasantly forward', she decided to leave. Cummins followed her and eventually caught up with her in Alban's Street, where he forced her into a doorway and tried to strangle her. She passed out and fortunately, before death overcame her, Cummins was disturbed by a delivery boy taking some bottles to the nearby Captain's Cabin. Cummins panicked and fled, leaving his gas mask behind. It had his service number printed on the case. Cummins tried to murder again that night, picking up a prostitute named Mrs Mulcahy. He tried to strangle her, but she freed herself and screamed. Cummins fled, leaving behind his RAF webbing belt.

Through the serial number on the gas mask case, Cummins' involvement in the four murders was quickly established and items belonging to his victims were found amongst his possessions. His trial began at the Old Bailey on Monday 27 April 1942, before Mr Justice Asquith; and with overwhelming and conclusive evidence against him, it ended the next day. The jury took just thirty-five minutes to find him guilty. He was executed on 25 June 1942.

Cummins is believed to have committed at least one other murder. Police suspect that he strangled nineteen-year-old prostitute, Maple Church, in October 1941, as the pattern of bruising corresponded with that of his other victims, indicating that the killer was left-handed. The killer had also rifled her handbag.

Harry Dobkin, 1942

Wartime fire-watcher Harry Dobkin, working in Kennington for a firm of solicitors, had in his youth been obliged to undergo a marriage arranged by a matchmaker, at Bethnal Green Synagogue in 1920. Rachel Dubinski was not to be the wife of his dreams and after three days the newlyweds parted forever but not before a baby had been conceived. A son was born nine months later and Harry, having supported him into adulthood, was now expected to continue supporting Rachel through a £1 a week maintenance order, which he resented. On 17 July 1942, demolition workers were clearing the site of a Baptist church near the Oval Kennington in St Oswald's Place that had been bombed in 1940. In the cellar beneath what had once been the vestry they prised up a large slab of stone and revealed a human skeleton indicating foul play, not just another bomb victim. The remains were examined by Professor Keith Simpson and identified through dental records as being Rachel Dobkin, who had been reported missing by her sister Polly on 12 April 1941. Sufficient flesh remained in the neck to show strangulation as the cause of death. Rachel had gone to meet her husband on 11 April 1941 to discuss the late payment of her maintenance. Harry Dobkin was arrested and charged with murder. His trial commenced at the Old Bailey on 17 November 1942. He was found guilty and hanged on 27 January 1943.

John George Haigh, 1949

John George Haigh committed a series of murders, which became known as the Acid Bath Murders. Born in 1909, at Stamford, Lincolnshire, he was the son of an electrical engineer. Grammar-school educated, Haigh worked in a second-hand car showroom, as an electrician in a cinema and as a salesman. He served several prison sentences, one when he was twenty-five, when he received fifteen months for obtaining money by false pretences. Then having set up under a false name as a solicitor, he defrauded his clients of over £30,000, to which he was sentenced to four years' imprisonment. Released on licence in 1940, he took to stealing from evacuated houses. In 1941 he was caught and sentenced to twenty-one months' hard labour. When he was released in the autumn of 1943 he went to work for an engineering firm in Crawley, Surrey, having by his own stealth managed to evade conscription.

In 1944, Haigh, who styled himself as a businessman and inventor, lived at the Onslow Court Hotel, Kensington and rented the basement of nearby 79 Gloucester Road, which he used as a workshop, where he had a sideline business repairing one-armed bandits and pin-ball machines. Dapper in both manner and appearance, Haigh endeared himself to the mostly elderly, well-to-do female residents at the hotel. Haigh ordered several carboys of sulphuric acid and a 40-gallon tank, which were delivered to his workshop. On 9 September 1944, he killed an acquaintance, twenty-one-year-old Donald McSwan there, by hitting him over the head, then dissolved his body in acid. The following year he killed McSwan's parents after first luring them to his workshop on the pretext that their son, who was on the run for evading conscription, wanted to meet them. He likewise disposed of their bodies in acid. The forged power of attorney of the McSwan's property, which included four houses, netted Haigh a small fortune.

For greater secrecy Haigh gave his basement workshop up and rented premises in a more secluded location, situated behind Hurstlea Products in Giles Yard, Crawley. In 1947 he befriended Dr Archibald Lewis and his wife Rosalie, after he had expressed an interest in purchasing their house, situated at 22 Ladbroke Square. He later lured them to his 'factory' in Crawley and shot them both, before destroying their bodies in acid. Again Haigh gained financially from these killings. He managed to fend off enquiries from the Lewises' family and business associates by forging letters. By 1949, the meticulously well-mannered Haigh had all the accoutrements of a successful businessman, including Savile Row suits and an Alvis motor-car. One of the long-term residents at the Onslow Court Hotel was sixty-nine-year-old, Mrs Olive Durand-Deacon, a well-off widow. According to Haigh, she approached him about an idea she had for producing artificial fingernails. He was running short of money and had already been approached about his bill at the hotel (£5 15s 6d a week plus 10% service charges), which now amounted to almost £50. Mrs Durand-Deacon wore expensive jewellery and clothes, a ready source of money. He agreed to help with her enterprise and he arranged to meet her outside the Army and Navy Stores in Victoria Street at 2.30pm on 18 February. She was never seen alive again.

The next day, Haigh, asked another resident, Mrs Lane, about Mrs Durand-Deacon's whereabouts, as she had not turned up for her appointment with him. Later, to satisfy her, Haigh drove Mrs Lane to Chelsea police station to report Mrs Durand-Deacon missing. It later transpired that Haigh had driven Mrs Duran-Deacon to Crawley, shot her, then over a two-day period dissolved her body in sulphuric acid. When he reported her missing, his glib manner aroused police suspicion and on finding he had a record they went to Crawley to investigate. They found Mrs Durand-Deacon's false teeth and there were traces of blood in the workshop; and Home Office Pathologist Dr Keith Simpson found a human gallstone in the gravel outside. Fragments of a left foot were also found, which when reconstructed and cast in plaster fitted Mrs Durand-Deacon's shoes exactly. Her plastic handbag (now ubiquitous but a very unusual item at the time) and several other items linking Haigh to her were found.

John Haigh was under the mistaken impression that without a body he could not be convicted of murder. When he realised otherwise he caved in and confessed to eight murders in total, three of which are believed to have been fictitious. He didn't do himself any favours when he asked police what chance they felt anyone had of being released from Broadmoor. They realised his invention to add further weight to his later claim that he drank his victims' blood in an attempt to prove his insanity.

Haigh was tried for only the murder of Mrs Durand-Deacon. The trial opened at Lewes Assizes on 18 July 1949, before Mr Justice Humphreys. It lasted less than two days. Dr Yellowlees, an early exponent of forensic psychiatry, was the only one of nine doctors who examined Haigh to speak in his defence. Dr Yellowlees later wrote about the 'sadly overrated Haigh case', describing Haigh as 'medically mad' but not 'McNaghten mad', referring to the McNaghten Rules, used since 1843 as the accepted definition of insanity in law. On the second day, the jury retired to consider their verdict at 4.23pm and returned to the court at 4.40pm with a guilty outcome. John Haigh was hanged on 10 August 1949, seventeen days after his fortieth birthday.

Derek Bentley, 1953

This highly controversial case involved two youths and the murder of a policeman. The fatal shot was fired by sixteen-year-old Christopher Craig, on 2 November 1952, during an attempted burglary at a London warehouse, but he escaped hanging on account of his age, although his nineteen-year-old accomplice Derek Bentley offered no violence, he suffered the ultimate penalty. Someone spotted the two youths entering the warehouse premises and called the police. Realising they had been rumbled, Craig and Bentley went onto the flat roof and hid behind a lift housing. As a detective climbed onto the roof Craig began shouting abuse at him, but Bentley immediately surrendered. It was at this point that Bentley allegedly called out 'Let him have it,

Chris'. Craig immediately fired the gun and the bullet grazed the officer's shoulder. When confronted on the rooftop by Police Constable Miles, Craig shot him in the head. Having run out of ammunition Craig ran to the edge of the roof and jumped off, falling thirty feet and fracturing his spine and left wrist in the process.

During their trial at the Old Bailey, before Lord Chief Justice Lord Goddard, it was clear that despite having fired the fatal shot he could not be hanged on account of his age. Much was made of Bentley's calling out 'Let him have it, Chris', being interpreted as both an incitement to commit murder and a request for Craig to hand over the weapon. Illiterate and with learning difficulties, Bentley did not fare well under questioning and cross-examination. It took the jury just seventy-five minutes to find both youths guilty of murder. Craig was sentenced to be detained at Her Majesty's Pleasure and Bentley was given the death sentence. Despite a huge public outcry and appeals from his family, an appeal failed and Bentley was hanged on 28 January 1953.

This case was instrumental in the argument leading to the abolition of the death penalty. Over many years Bentley's father and his sister, Iris, campaigned for a free pardon. Mr Bentley died in 1974. It was not until 29 July 1993 that Derek Bentley was granted a royal pardon in respect of the 'sentence of death passed upon him and carried out'. In 1996 Derek Bentley's remains were removed from the precincts of Wandsworth Prison and reburied in a family grave. However, the royal pardon did not fully exonerate him of the crime of murder for which he had been convicted. On 30 July 1998 the Court of Appeal quashed his conviction for murder.

Between 1878 and 1961, 135 executions took place at Wandsworth, with the exception of three executions for treason, those being of Duncan Scott-Ford, in 1942, August Sangret, in 1943 and John Amery, in 1945, all the other executions were for murder. The final executions at Wandsworth took place in 1961, when Victor John Terry was hanged on 25 May and Henryk Niemasz suffered the same fate on 8 September.

All hangings in Great Britain were suspended for five years in 1965. The gallows and condemned suite at Wandsworth were located in E wing and was the only gallows to be kept in full working order in an English prison after the abolition of the death penalty for the crime of murder on 18 December 1969. The gallows were serviced every six-months until 1992 and remained in situ in E wing until 1993, when they were dismantled. Wandsworth's gallows are presently an exhibit at the Galleries of Justice in Nottingham.

Although capital punishment was abolished for the crime of murder in 1969 in Great Britain, it was not abolished for that crime in Northern Ireland until 25 July 1973.

The death penalty remained on the statute books for certain other crimes, which were gradually removed over the years, until 1998, when amongst the few capital crimes remaining were piracy with violence and treason. In 1998, all capital crimes having been removed from the statute books in Great Britain and Northern Ireland, the death penalty was finally abolished. Today, Wandsworth Prison is designated an adult male Category B Local prison. It contains eight wings on two units, accommodating 1,665 prisoners.

CHAPTER 9

Other Prisons North of the River Thames

Millbank

Situated in Millbank, Pimlico, with its entrance facing the River Thames, Millbank Prison, originally constructed as the National Penitentiary, occupied the site of today's Tate Gallery (Tate Britain). It was built in the shape of a six-pointed star, each point being in the shape of a pentagon, and in the centre of each pentagon was a tower, from where the warders could observe the prisoners. This star-shaped structure was set within an outer octagonal wall. At the centre of the site was a circular chapel, surrounded by the governor's house, various offices and laundries, which in turn were surrounded by six pentagons of cell blocks, with five courtyards incorporated into the design; which in plan form is not only ingenious in the intricacy of its structure but also exceedingly beautiful from a purely aesthetic point of view. The two pentagons to the north-west, situated furthest from the entrance, housed female prisoners, the remaining four pentagons were used for male prisoners.

The site of the prison was purchased in 1799 on behalf of the Crown by the philanthropist Jeremy Bentham, with the intention of erecting his Panopticon prison there but the plan was abandoned in 1812. An architectural competition was held with forty-three architects entering for the prize of designing the new Penitentiary. The competition was won by William Williams, drawing master at the Royal Military College, Sandhurst. Williams' design was completed in 1821 having been overseen by three successive working architects. Construction costs of about £500,000, more than twice exceeded the original estimate.

Millbank contained 1,000 cells, with three miles of corridors within its walls. Disregarding the aesthetics, which in principal were very fine, the simple fact was that the building did not work as a prison and was an abysmal failure. The network of corridors proved so difficult to navigate, that even the warders got lost. The air system worked well for ventilation but its design enabled prisoners to communicate with each other between cells. The running costs of Millbank turned out to be so high, at £16,000 per annum, that the authorities soon decided such costs were unsupportable. The problems encountered at Millbank resulted in a new National Penitentiary being built, which manifested itself in the form of Pentonville, in 1842.

Millbank's status was downgraded by Act of Parliament in 1843 and it became a holding depot for convicts awaiting transportation. When large-scale transportation ended in 1850, eventually dwindling to no transportation at all in 1867, Millbank's role turned to that of an ordinary local prison. In 1870 it became a military prison. When this closed in 1890, this startling building stood empty for two years until its demolition in 1892.

The Fleet Prison
The Fleet Prison, built in 1197, situated off today's Farringdon Road, just outside the city walls, was the first building in London to be specifically designed as a gaol. It is arguably the best known of London's debtor prisons. During its long lifetime its buildings were destroyed three times, first in the Peasants' Revolt in 1381, then in the Great Fire of London, in September 1666; and also in the Gordon Riots in 1780.

The Fleet Prison contained around 300 debtors and their families. It was not unusual for inmates to beg from their cell windows or from the 'grille' facing the street on the Farringdon side of the prison, in order to pay for their keep. It was a prison for those convicted under the Star Chamber and the Court of Chancery. The Fleet Prison like others in London was a profit-making enterprise. Nothing was free in the Fleet, excepting perhaps some of the harsh punishments that were frequently dished out to prisoners unable to pay their dues. There were fees for turning keys, fees for putting on irons and fees for taking them off again. Even visitors had to pay fees. The Fleet Prison charged the highest fees in the whole of England. Prisoners with a trade might continue to work and earn while being held captive at the Fleet, but most were reduced to begging. Inmates did not necessarily have to live within the prison itself; some took lodgings nearby. So long as they paid the Keeper for loss of earnings, that was considered perfectly acceptable. The area in which prisoners could exercise this privilege was known as the 'Liberty of the Fleet'.

Within the Liberty of the Fleet came a loophole enabling those who were of a mind to obtain a 'quickie wedding'. Ministers and some- times bogus ministers conducted these marriages in taverns and houses. Couples wishing to marry in secrecy or in haste flocked to the area. When sailors were on leave, there could be as many as 300 weddings a week. Many thousands of such weddings took place, before the Marriage Act of 1753 put an end to them.

On 27 February 1729, the recently formed Gaols Committee visited the Fleet Prison. They were appalled at the condition the prisoners were living in and the ill-treatment they received. Amongst other wretched inmates, they found the baronet Sir William Rich, in irons. Unable to pay the prison fee, Sir William had been burned with a red-hot poker, hit with a stick, and kept in a dungeon for ten days for having wounded the warden with a shoemaker's knife. Further investigations into the goings on at the Fleet resulted in the Keeper, Thomas Bambridge and his predecessor John Huggins, being accused of extortion and murder; and they were committed to Newgate. Both were eventually acquitted, but a special Act of Parliament was passed to dismiss Bambridge from his post. Attitudes towards debtors were gradually changing. Other prisons opened and conditions at the Fleet had badly deteriorated. After serving as a prison for over 700 years the Fleet Prison was closed in 1842, sold to the Corporation of the City of London in 1844, who demolished it in 1846.

Ludgate Prison

Three prisons bore the name Ludgate on three separate sites, stretching over more than 500 years. The original Roman Ludgate formed one of the gates to the city and stood on what is today called Ludgate Hill; believed by some to have allowed access to what was at one time an important burial ground situated in the vicinity of Fleet Street. One tradition which has passed down the centuries is that Ludgate was built by (some describe him as mythical) King Lud, who by tradition rebuilt the city walls and laid out the streets. He was supposed to have reigned during the century of the Roman invasion *c.*66BC, and to lie buried close to the city gate that bore his name; and by tradition it was from King Lud that the name for the hill, the gate and the prison was derived. However, it has been suggested 'lud' is more likely derived from the word 'lode', which means an open drain or ditch for draining one course of water into a larger course.

The 'Lud Gate' was rebuilt *c.*1215, and images of King Lud and his sons adorned the gate from 1260. As had become the custom at London's gates, Ludgate housed a small prison for petty offenders, formed out of rooms above the entrance *c.*1377 and enlarged in 1464. Ludgate took the same petty offenders and debtors who were confined in the compters and other London gaols, but being the place where freemen of the city, merchants, and the well connected were incarcerated, Ludgate was by far the most comfortable place in which to be imprisoned. This was highlighted in 1419 when the citizens of London complained that Ludgate was so comfortable that the inmates 'were more willing to keep abode there than to pay their debts'.

Since as early as 1382, during the reign of Richard II, when the Court of Aldermen had chosen Newgate as a place of incarceration for serious criminals, Ludgate was chosen to incarcerate London's citizens for 'debts, trespasses, accounts and contempts', for members of the clergy and for freemen of the city. The window of one of the rooms in Ludgate afforded prisoners the opportunity to beg from passers-by. As was customary in all of London's debtors' prisons the gaolers extorted money from the inmates for lodging and food and for turning the key on entry or discharge. In 1431, during repairs and renovations at Ludgate, all its prisoners were temporarily transferred to Bread Street Compter.

One of Ludgate's prisoners, incarcerated for debt as a boy, rose to great heights,. His name was Stephen Forster. The story goes that in 1463 during the reign of Edward IV, Ludgate was enlarged by that 'Well disposed, blessed, and devout woman, the widow of Stephen Forster, fishmonger, Mayor of London in 1454'. According to tradition, the young Forster was imprisoned in Ludgate for debt. Being one day obliged to be at the begging grate, a rich widow asked him how much would release him. He said, 'twenty pounds'. She paid it and took him into her service, when by his indefatigable application to business, he so gained her affections that she married him; and he earned such great riches by commerce that she concurred with him to make his former prison more commodious, and to endow a new chapel. Stephen Forster's arms – three arrow heads – were emblazoned above the prison entrance. The enlargement of the prison to the south side formed a quadrant some 38ft long and 28ft wide. There were prisoners' rooms above it, with a leaden roof, where the debtors could walk, and both lodging and water were free of charge. On a wall in the chapel was placed a brass plate which bore the inscription:

> *Devout souls that pass this way,*
> *For Stephen Forster, late Lord Mayor, heartily pray,*
> *And Dame Agnes, his spouse, to God consecrate,*
> *That of pity this house made for Londoners in Lud Gate;*
> *So that for lodging and water prisoners may nought pay,*
> *As their keepers shall all answer at dreadful doomsday.*

Ludgate was rebuilt in 1586. The gatehouse had a statue of King Lud, facing towards the city and St Paul's and another of Elizabeth I, facing west towards Westminster and Whitehall. Virtually the whole of Ludgate was destroyed by the Great Fire on Tuesday 4 September 1666. The gaolers having deserted the prison, its occupants broke out, as did similarly the prisoners at nearby Newgate. The statue of Good Queen Bess, turned yellow in the heat of the flames but remained intact, prompting the poet John Crouch to pen the lines:

> *Though fancy makes not Pictures live, or love.*
> *Yet Pictures fancy'd may be fancy move:*
> *Me-thinks the Queen on hite-hall cast her Eye;*
> *An Arrow could not more directly flye.*
> *But when she saw her Palace safe, her fears*
> *Vanish, one Eye drops smiles, the other tears.*

Ludgate having been damaged in the Great Fire beyond repair was rebuilt forming a new prison and city gate built in the vicinity of the old Ludgate. During a redevelopment programme in the year of George III's accession in 1760, when the city walls and gates were demolished to ease obstruction and allow the free flow of traffic, Ludgate was taken down and its materials sold for £148. Its prisoners were moved to a specially prepared section of the London Workhouse, in Bishopsgate Street. Intended to have provided only a temporary solution to housing Ludgate's prisoners, the facility was still in use until 1794, when a small building and yard adjacent to Giltspur Street Comptor, was given the name Ludgate, probably to preserve the tradition and retain the special status that Ludgate was the place of incarceration for freemen of the city of London. Being partly encircled by Giltspur Street Comptor, Ludgate was little more than an annexe and was eventually absorbed into the compter. In 1813, work began on the construction of what was to become the last of the city's debtors' prisons. The Mayor and Corporation of the City of London being well aware of the ancient tradition of keeping freemen apart from lesser prisoners, when Whitecross Street opened in 1815, and the name Ludgate was revived for a wing in which to house freemen.

The City of London Compters
The word 'compter' is derived from 'counter', the keeping and counting of official records. The City of London Compters fell under control of the sheriffs. The compters were gaols for petty offenders

and debtors, deemed more important than the lock-ups but less significant than London's larger prisons. Although they fell under the direct jurisdiction of the sheriffs they were seldom administered by them directly but rented out to keepers.

Bread Street Compter

Bread Street Compter was built in the early fifteenth century. Records do not show or describe what it appeared like but it probably took the form of a converted town house. During the rebuilding of Newgate in 1425 some of the prisoners were brought to Bread Street, and likewise in 1431, when Ludgate was being repaired, all its prisoners were temporarily transferred to Bread Street. During its latter years the prisoners at Bread Street had the misfortune to be in the charge of a brutal and disreputable keeper. Richard Husband, dealt harshly with the prisoners, extracting from them whatever he could to his own advantage. As complaints mounted against him it became necessary for the mayor to intervene. Such was the strength of feeling against Husband that in 1550 the mayor sent him to Newgate to be kept in irons, as punishment for his mistreatment of those placed in his care. Released after a few days and reinstated at Bread Street, Husband was soon up to his old tricks, and even extended the cheating of his prisoners to offering a safe haven to rogues and disreputable women, providing them with lodgings for fourpence a night. However, because he effectively was renting Bread Street Compter from the sheriff and had valid title to the building, he could not be ejected from it. Possibly because of this situation the City of London authorities closed Bread Street Compter in 1555 and transferred its prisoners to the newly built Wood Street Compter.

Poultry Compter

Like Bread Street Compter, records do no show when Poultry Compter was actually built, but it was probably formed out of a town house and may have its foundation in the fourteenth century. It stood in the city on the north side of Poultry. In 1425 it became a temporary home to some of Newgate's inmates, while it was being rebuilt under Sir Richard Whittington's bequest.

Thomas Dekker, a prisoner at Poultry Compter in 1598, wrote:

> ... jailers hoarsely and harshly bawling for prisoners to their bed, and prisoners reviling and cursing jailers for making such a hellish din. Then to hear some in their chambers singing and dancing, being half drunk; others breaking open doors to get more drink

to be whole drunk. Some roaring for tobacco; others raging and
bidding hell's plage on all tobacco ...

In 1801 the prison had a reduced capacity because of its dilapidated
state, which prompted one commentator to remark:

... The rooms were out of repair, but the debtors kept their floors
clean ... All the other parts of this close and crowded prison are in
so ruinous and insecure a state, that, if it was not shored up in many
places, it would tumble down.

In 1802, Poultry Compter's condition had deteriorated even further
and it became necessary to move the prisoners temporarily to the
compter in Giltspur Street. Some renovations having been successfully undertaken, the prisoners returned. However, conditions at
Poultry Compter continued to deteriorate and in 1812, such was its
condition that it was deemed beyond reasonable repair. The prisoners
were removed to Whitecross Street Prison and Poultry Compter was
demolished.

Wood Street Compter
Wood Street Compter was built in 1555 as a replacement for Bread
Street Compter. Built to hold seventy debtors and offenders arrested
in the City of London, prior to their removal to Newgate. It soon
gained a reputation for ruthless exploitation and neglect of prisoners.
    In 1616, William Fennor, a poet and actor, was arrested for minor
offences and, commensurate with the level of the offences was taken
to Wood Street Compter. He was so enraged by what he saw at Wood
Street and the treatment he himself received, that in 1717 he
published an account of his observations.
    Regarding the matter of fees, Fennor wrote:

For what extreme extortion is it when a gentleman is brought in by
the watch for some misdemeanour committed, that he must pay at
least an angell [sic] before he be discharged; he must pay twelvepence for turning the key at the – side dore [sic] two shillings to
the chamberlaine, twelvepence for his garnish for wine, tenpence
for his dinner, whether he stay or no, and when he come to be discharged at the booke, it will cost at least three shillings and sixpence
more, besides sixpence for the bookkeepers paines, and sixpence for
the porter ... And if a gentleman stay there but one night, he must
pay for his garnish sixteen pence, besides a groate for his lodging,

and so much for his sheetes ... When a gentleman is upon his discharge, and hath given satisfaction for his executions, they must have fees for irons, three halfpence in the pound, besides the other fees, so that if a man were in for a thousand or fifteen hundred pound execution, they will if a man is so madde have so many three halfpence.

Regarding the matter of gaolers at Wood Street Compter, Fennor observed:

... men that, having run through their trades as they have their estates, at last are forced to take upon themselves this most base and odious kind of life; which they no sooner have obtained but are as proud of it as a lousy prisoner of a fresh suit, or a beggarly rhymer of twelvepenny dole when he oweth ninepence for ale. They are men that have no quality in them but one, and that is to ask money, and, like lawyers, without their fees they will do nothing. They imitate ravens, kites and crows that feed upon the corruption, stinking garbage, and guts of any carrion ... so these feed upon the follies and vices of the age ...

Commenting on prisoners pursuing their trades within the compter:

... here you shall see a cobbler mending old shows, and singing as merrily as if he were under a stall abroad; not far from him you shall see a tailor sit cross-legged (like a witch) on his cushion ... you may behold a saddler empanelling all his wits together how to patch this Scotchpaddle handsomely, or mend the old gentlewoman's cropper that was almost burst in pieces. You may have a physician here, that for a bottle of sack will undertake to give you as goode a medicine for melancholy as any doctor will for five pounds. Besides, if you desire to be removed before a judge, you shall have a tinker-like attorney not far distant from you, that in stopping up one hole in a broken cause, will make twenty before he hath made an end, and at last will leave you in prison as bare of money as he himself is of honesty.

And on conditions in The Hole:

In this place a man shall not look about him but some poor soul or other lies groaning and labouring under the burthen of some dangerous disease; the child weeping over his dying father, the mother over her sick child; one friend over another, who can no sooner rise from him, but he is ready to stumble over another in as miserable a plight as him he but newly took his leave of. So that if a man come thither he at first will think himself in some churchyard that hath been fattened with some great plague, for they lie together like so many graves.

Destroyed in the Great Fire of London in 1666, Wood Street Compter was rebuilt on the same site. It was closed in 1897 and its prisoners transferred to Giltspur Street Compter.

Giltspur Street Compter

Giltspur was designed by the notable architect George Dance and opened in 1791, to hold debtors and minor offenders. It became a busy prison with upwards of 6,000 committals annually. Built to accommodate 203 prisoners, sometimes as many as 250 prisoners were being held there, of which between thirty and forty would be debtors. Unlike the other compters, Giltspur Street's regime seems to have been humane and easy going. Few punishments were meted out, records showing on average only twenty punishments in any one year, although escapes were frequent.

Prisoners were divided into four classes: Debtors, Felons, Misdemeanours and Assaults. There were nine prison years. At Giltspur Street strict classes were not adhered to, it being deemed prudent to allocate accommodation according to the space available at any given time.

When Giltspur Street Compter was demolished in 1855 the prisoners were moved to Whitecross Street Prison.

Bridewell

King Henry VIII's Bridewell Palace, situated in Bridge Street, Blackfriars, where the River Fleet flowed into the River Thames, and named after a famous well in the vicinity of St Bride's Church, was completed in 1520. Built on the site of the medieval St Bride's Inn, at a cost of £39,000, Bridewell's function as a royal palace was short lived, as in 1553 Edward VI gave the palace to the City of London for the housing of homeless children and for the punishment of 'disorderly women'. When the city took full possession of Bridewell Palace in 1556, its buildings were converted for use as Bridewell Prison and Hospital. It opened its doors to take its first prisoners on 16 December that year. On that first day a woman was firstly whipped at Bridewell, then pilloried in Cheapside for having abandoned her baby.

The Bridewell became the first house of correction in England and a major charitable institution into the bargain. Following the dissolution of the monasteries, the poor had no means of support saving charity. Life in London was particularly harsh for the destitute, as many came from outside the capital seeking work, swelling the ranks of the poor and needy. Bridewell, as a house of correction, was a training institute for destitute youths but, soon took on the role of a workhouse and place of punishment for vagrants, beggars, paupers and petty offenders. The name 'Bridewell' was subsequently adopted by other prisons in London and elsewhere, and today the name usually refers to the city's main detention facility.

Bridewell Hospital was established to provide both a home and training for deserving children. The apprentices from the Bridewell were considered more desirable than parish apprentices, as on success-ful completion of their apprenticeship they were given the freedom of the City of London and a charitable contribution known as Lock's Gift (being the substantial sum of £10), towards setting up as an independent master. In the late seventeenth century, there were around 100 apprentices at the hospital, the trades they were taught included glovemaking, shoemaking and weaving.

Most of the Bridewell was destroyed in the Great Fire of London in September 1666. Some of its buildings were repaired, but most were completely rebuilt. The wide range of offences punishable at the Bridewell resulted in large numbers of offenders passing through its doors. The highest number of offenders punished in the Bridewell was in the year 1784, when 2,956 were committed. In 1800 there were 1,989 commitments.

The provision of medical facilities at Bridewell was far in advance of any other London prison. There was a surgeon, physician and infirmaries for the sick. Prisoners were regularly checked for disease. Following a visit to Bridewell by prison reformer John Howard in 1789, he passed very favourable comments on the facilities he found there:

Each sex has a workroom and a night-room. They lie in boxes, with a little straw on the floor ... There are many excellent regulations in this establishment. The prisoners have a liberal allowance, suit-able employment, and some proper instruction; but the visitor laments that they are not separated ... no other prison in London has any straw or bedding ... There are, very properly, solitary cells for the Bridewell boys, in which one was confined and employed beating hemp.

Bridewell continued to serve London as a prison until its closure in 1855, when its remaining prisoners were transferred to Holloway. Most of the buildings were demolished in 1863.

Tothill Fields

Westminster Bridewell as the prison at Tothill Fields was originally known when it was constructed in 1618, at the northern end of the present day Rochester Row, was built to house petty offenders and vagrants; it remained in operation until 1834, when a new prison, erected on the north side of Francis Street opened, and the old prison was knocked down in 1836. The prison at Tothill Fields went through a series of name changes, being variously called Tothill Fields Bridewell, Tothill Fields Prison and Westminster House of Correction.

As a house of correction, the purpose at Tothill Fields was to compulsorily put to work able-bodied but indolent paupers. The prison was enlarged in 1655 and during the reign of Queen Anne (1702–14) its role was extended to include the incarceration of criminals.

In April 1779, Reverend James Hackman was committed to Tothill Fields Bridewell by magistrate Sir John Fielding, for the murder of Miss Martha Raey at the Theatre Royal, Covent Garden. (see pages 50–4), prior to his pre-trial transfer to Newgate.

The new prison, opened in 1834, as a replacement for the original Westminster Bridewell and had a ground plan passed on the shape of the ace of clubs. Each 'leaf' effectively formed a separate prison, with a courtyard in the centre and an exercise yard beside each cell block. It contained 549 cells, accommodating as many as 900 prisoners. One of the most high profile prisoners to be held at Tothill Fields was François Benjamin Courvoisier, a valet who murdered his employer, Lord William Russell.

What is today's Dunraven Street, running parallel with Park Lane and lying between North Row and Wood Mews, Mayfair, was, in 1840, Norfolk Street. It was there, at No. 114, a small but elegant three-storied house, that Lord William Russell, a seventy-three-year-old widower, lived with his staff of three servants: a cook, maid and valet, François Benjamin Courvoisier who was Swiss. Lord William was by all accounts, an irascible, tetchy, somewhat peevish old gentleman, a younger son of the Duke of Bedford and uncle of the then Secretary of State for the Colonies.

On the morning of 6 May 1840, the housemaid, on coming down-stairs from her quarters on the top floor, found the principal rooms in disarray. In the dining room, furniture had been turned upside down, the drawers of the escritoire were opened and had been rifled, there was a bundle lying on the floor, as though thieves had been inter-rupted. It appeared that a burglary had taken place. She summoned the cook and they called Courvoisier, who, much to their surprise came from his room already dressed. This was unusual in itself, because he was habitually late in the morning. Together they went upstairs to their master's bedroom. While Courvoisier opened the shutters, the housemaid saw that Lord William was lying dead on his bloodstained bed.

Help soon arrived and, despite the general mayhem elsewhere in the house, it was first assumed that Lord William had committed suicide. His throat had been cut from ear to ear, a towel had been placed over his face and this was soaked with blood, which also covered the pillows and bedding. However, it soon became apparent that this was no suicide, when it was found that some silver and other valuable items were missing. Suspicion was aroused by the bundle in the dining room, which contained small items of plate and jewellery that a thief would normally have put into his pocket, leading those investigating the crime that the scene had been staged, but fortunately for them, not with any degree of expertise. In this the police were not wrong.

In his Lordship's bedroom several items were missing, including money. The futile efforts of the real murderer to throw suspicion on burglars had been amply proved to the satisfaction of the police, who were convinced the culprit was from within the household. Courvoisier was taken into custody and the cook and maid placed under surveillance. Three days later a search of the butler's pantry provided further circumstantial evidence against the valet and Courvoisier was committed for trial. He was first held in Tothill Fields Prison. A subscription was raised from foreign servants in London, to provide funds for his defence.

Courvoisier was transferred to Newgate shortly before his trial which opened at the Old Bailey on 18 June. He pleaded not guilty. Madame Piolaine, a Frenchwoman, gave evidence. She had, unbeknown to Courviosier, already been taken to Tothill Fields and identified him. Louis Piolaine and his wife's cousin, Joseph Vincent, ran a small hotel, the Dieppe, in Leicester Place. Several years before the murder, Courvoisier had worked there for about a month. Six weeks before the murder Courvoisier had called on Madame Piolaine and a few days later returned with a brown paper parcel which he asked her to look after for him. When her husband read about the murder case the parcel was opened and it was found to contain items of silver belonging to Lord William Russell. The jury had no difficulty in deciding upon a guilty verdict and Courvoisier was sentenced to death. After he had been taken to Newgate following sentencing, he admitted that he had been justly convicted.

Courvoisier was only prevented from suicide by the vigilance of his captors and he said he intended to open a vein with a bit of sharpened stick, which had been taken away from him when his mattress was changed. The execution took place outside Newgate on 6 July 1840. The hangman was William Calcraft.

The common practice of allowing mothers to be imprisoned with their babies or small children and debtors to be allowed to have their families with them, was not always without its complications. Life within the walls of a prison inevitably meant that little innocents were sometimes mixing with, and often being influenced or indoctrinated by some seriously flawed individuals. Some children were imprisoned because of their own crimes, often illiterate and with very little learning of their own, they fell vulnerable pray to the unprincipled old lags incarcerated with them at Tothill Fields and other penal institutions, who further schooled them in every nefarious and illegal vice imaginable. In 1845, it was decided that Tothill Fields would hold only males under the age of seventeen and women.

The regime at Tothill Fields was reasonably tolerable. The most serious punishment, whipping, was used considerably less than it was in many of London's other prisons. Between 1851–55 the punishment was only inflicted twice. In 1861 the oldest boy at Tothill Fields was eighteen years old, he had lied about his age to get in. There were boys being kept there as young as six, and one boy was only five, having stolen 5s 9d from a till (this being his second offence). However, the majority of inmates were each between fourteen and sixteen. Tothill Fields was closed in 1884. Since 1895, Westminster Cathedral has stood on its foundations.

Whitecross Street Prison
The last of the debtor's prisons to be built in the City of London was erected by the Corporation of London in 1815, on Whitecross Street (which runs from Old Street to Chiswell Street), to accommodate 490 debtors. It operated along similar lines to London's other debtors' prisons. As Poultry Compter had become so dilapidated its debtors were transferred to Whitecross Street as soon as it opened.

Times were changing as were attitudes towards debtors. When the Bankruptcy Act passed the seals in 1869, outlawing the imprisonment of debtors, Whitecross Street's function became redundant. Its prisoners were set free, although a few had been incarcerated for such a long time that they found it difficult to adjust to the outside world. One account stated that a prisoner who had been imprisoned at Whitecross Street for twenty-seven years, having no home to go to, returned to the prison on the day following his release, seeking shelter. The prison was demolished in 1870.

Wormwood Scrubs
In 1874, the Head of the Prison Department, General Sir Edmund Du Cane of the Royal Engineers, inspired by the building of Sing Sing prison in the USA, came up with a plan to build a prison on land at Wormwood Scrubs (known locally as The Scrubs), a 200-acre area of open land, located in the north-eastern corner of the present day London Borough of Hammersmith and Fulham. Wormwood Scrubs Prison was built using entirely convict labour between 1875 and 1891. General Sir Edmund Du Cane was himself the architect. The bricks for the prison were manufactured on site. The prison accommodation took the form of four parallel blocks, the complex being entered through an imposing twin-towered gatehouse, each tower incorporating a portrait of prison reformers John Howard and Elizabeth Fry. The 13ft by 10ft cells were arranged in galleries and had individual ventilation. With a capacity of 1,000 inmates, the prison originally held both men and women serving short-term sentences.

Prisoner's received their meals in their cells. Male prisoners were set to work on cranks and treadmills. Some picked oakum, others made shoes and the sewing of sacks and mail bags was undertaken by some of the inmates. Many of the women serving sentences at Wormwood Scrubs were held with their young children, some even gave birth in the prison. Babies were kept in a nursery. Their mothers were allowed to spend part of each day with them and walk with them round the yard.

From 1902, after Newgate was demolished and Holloway Prison became a women-only prison, Wormwood Scrubs has held only men, some for serious offences. In 1904, one block at Wormwood Scrubs was turned over for use as an allocation centre, in which young offenders were assessed before being sent to Borstal. The Borstal system was a recent innovation, having been introduced following a meeting in 1895 when the subject of a new type of institution for the incarceration of youths was mooted. The reasoning behind this was that by separating them from hardened criminals and offering them training in useful skills, the individuals concerned would not be corrupted by their elders and would be less likely to re-offend. The name was derived from the village of Borstal, in Kent, where the first such institution was opened.

During World War Two the prisoners were moved to other prisons and the entire complex of buildings was taken over by the War Department for use as secure office space. MI5 and M18 operated from Wormwood Scrubs for the remainder of the war.

In 1994, a new hospital wing opened and in 1996 two of the original four wings were refurbished to modern standards and the building of a fifth wing completed.

Today, Her Majesty's Prison Wormwood Scrubs is an adult male category B prison, for prisoners over the age of twenty-one, sentenced or on remand from local courts. It has a capacity of 1,277. Each cell is equipped with integral sanitation and a television.

The prison contains five main wings and several smaller dedicated units:

A wing, used for remand and sentenced prisoners.

B wing, used for remand and sentenced prisoners.

C wing, used for prisoners on an Intensive Drug Treatment System, offering support for offenders with substance misuse needs.

D wing, has single cell accommodation for workforce prisoners (those prisoners working in the prison kitchens, gardens and prison grounds) and Difficult to Manage Programme prisoners, as well as those prisoners unable to share accommodation.

E wing, has single cell accommodation, used primarily as a resettlement of prisoners unit.

The Super enhanced wing, is used for prisoners considered to be trustworthy and who have key roles within the establishment, such as peer support or educational support programmes.

The Conibeere Unit, is used for prisoners with substance misuse problems, requiring a stabilisation regime.

On 10 March 2009 the prison was listed as a Grade II building of historic and architectural interest.

CHAPTER 10

Other Prisons South of the River Thames

King's Bench Prison and House of Correction

The first King's Bench Prison was built in Southwark during the fourteenth century in Angel Place, to the east of what is now Borough High Street, to hold prisoners of the Court of the King's Bench, in which cases of defamation, bankruptcy and other misdemeanours were heard.

The Court of the King's Bench sat in Westminster from the thirteenth until the nineteenth centuries. This first prison was burned down in 1381 by Wat Tyler's mob during the Peasants' Revolt, rebuilt and again burned down in 1450, rebuilt again. Before the Bankruptcy Act of 1869, which abolished debtors' prisons, men and women were imprisoned at the whim of their creditors, sometimes for decades, until their debts could be discharged, the King's Bench Prison principally served the purpose of a debtor's prison. During the early Tudor period new buildings were constructed, enclosed behind a high brick wall. These buildings survived until 1761, although by this time the prisoners had been transferred to the new King's Bench Prison. This had been built in St George's Fields on a 4-acre site, on the corner of the present Borough Road and Borough High Street, at a cost of £7,800, and opened in 1758.

This new larger prison had 224 rooms and a courtyard surrounded by a high wall. The prison was burned down during the Gordon Riots of 1780 (see page 53) and quickly rebuilt. The prison was described by one commentator in 1828, as 'the most desirable place of in-carceration in England'. For those able to afford it, inmates enjoyed the prison's taproom (where plentiful supplies of beer were readily available), wine room and market, which included chandlers' and butchers' shops. For a small fee prisoners were allowed to leave the prison for a few days. On payment of a larger fee, prisoners were allowed to live in the 'Liberties or Rules of the King's Bench', which included the inns and taverns surrounding St George's Fields. The

King's Bench Prison held many wealthy men and women, as well as members of the upper classes. In 1815, Lord Cochrane was found guilty of Stock Exchange frauds and imprisoned here. Like many other debtors' prisons, the poorer prisoners generally lived in filthy, overcrowded wards. They often survived by begging at the prison gate, but many succumbed to gaol fever, which was rife.

In 1842 the prison was renamed the Queen's Prison and received prisoners from the Marshalsea and Fleet prisons. Following the abolition of imprisonment for debt in 1869, the prison ended its life as a military prison, known as the Southwark Convict Prison. It was demolished in 1880.

Horsemonger Lane Gaol
Horsemonger Lane Gaol was built to replace the old Surrey County Gaol, a Tudor gaol fashioned out of the White Lion Inn, which stood nearby on Borough High Street. Built as the Surrey County Gaol to accommodate 400 prisoners and originally known as the New Gaol, Horsemonger Lane Gaol was constructed between 1791–98 to a design by George Gwilt the Elder, architect to the county of Surrey, who had also designed the adjacent Sessions House. Behind the impressive gatehouse lay four wings, three for petty criminals and one for debtors. As Surrey's principal prison it was also the county's principal place of execution. Executions took place either outside the gaol itself, or on the roof of the gatehouse. One-hundred and thirty-one men and four women were executed there between 1800 and 1877. Among the most high profile criminals to be executed there were:

Colonel Despard and his Six Associates, 1803
Colonel Edward Marcus Despard, Irish by birth, had served in the Army in Honduras. On his return to England, aggrieved at his treatment by the military, he became involved with various radical groups. He subsequently became involved in a conspiracy to kill the king, overthrow the government and seize the Tower. Government spies uncovered the conspiracy and in November 1802, Despard, along with over thirty soldiers and labourers were arrested at the Oakley Arms in Lambeth and examined by magistrates at Union Hall in the Borough. The ensuing trial resulted in Despard and nine others being found guilty of treason and being sentenced to death.

Three men were recommended for mercy and reprieved, but Despard, John Francis and John Wood (both soldiers), Thomas

Broughton and John MacNamara (both carpenters), shoemaker John Wratton and slater Arthur Graham, were executed at Horsemonger Lane, above the gatehouse, along with Colonel Despard on 21 February 1803, by William Brunskill. As traitors the seven men should have been hanged, drawn and quartered but the authorities generally regarded this form of punishment as unpalatable, so it was modified to decapitation after death.

On the morning of the execution soldiers were stationed around the gaol and in neighbouring roads. The scaffold had been erected on the roof of the gatehouse and a block on which the traitors were to be beheaded had been placed near the scaffold, along with copious amounts of sawdust to soak up the blood. All seven men were hanged together. Colonel Despard's body was cut down first, carried to the block and beheaded by a masked man, who then took the head by the hair, held it up so the large crowd got a good view of it, then hollered the words, 'This is the head of a traitor, Edward Marcus Despard.' The other bodies were similarly cut down and beheaded, the heads being held up to the crowds as the masked man proclaimed, 'This is the head of another traitor', along with the dead man's name.

The Mannings, 1849

Maria de Roux was born in Switzerland. She came to England to work as a lady's maid and shortly had an affair with fifty-year-old Irishman Patrick O'Connor, a London docks exciseman and money lender, who had built up a considerable fortune. After she met twenty-eight-year-old Frederick Manning, a guard on the Great Western Railway, who was the same age as herself, she married him in May 1847, although she kept in touch with O'Connor. After Manning was dismissed on suspicion of being involved in two robberies on trains, their financial difficulties began.

Having moved to 3 Minver Place, Bermondsey, the Mannings invited O'Connor to dine with them on 8 August 1849. They murdered him and buried his body beneath a large flagstone in the kitchen. They then went to his lodgings and stole money and some share certificates. Not long after, police had visited them to find out if they knew anything about O'Connor's whereabouts, the couple absconded in different directions; he to Jersey, she to Edinburgh. When police returned to Minver Place again they made a search and discovered O'Connor's body buried in quicklime. He had been shot through the head and hit with a blunt instrument. The couple had not covered their tracks very well and were quickly apprehended and taken to Horsemonger

Lane Gaol. At their trial at the Old Bailey it was revealed that Maria Manning had shot O'Connor and her husband had finished him off with a crowbar.

The Mannings were hanged on 13 November 1848 before a crowd of 50,000. The black bombazine dress Maria Manning wore at her execution created such an unfavourable impression that sales of the material were severely reduced for a considerable time afterwards.

Catherine Wilson, 1862

Catherine Wilson has the distinction of being the last woman to be hanged in public in London. She was found guilty of the murder of Mrs Maria Soames in Alfred Street, Bloomsbury, who she was nursing. Mrs Soames died on 17 October 1856, having been poisoned with large doses of colchicum, but it was not until Wilson attempted and failed to kill Mrs Sarah Carnell in February 1862 that an investigation was held into Mrs Soames' death. Following a trial at the Old Bailey for attempted murder, which resulted in Catherine Wilson's acquittal, she was immediately rearrested and charged with the murder of Maria Soames. Evidence suggested that Wilson had murdered several other patients by poisoning them, all for financial gain; but she would not confess to anything. Found guilty of murder, she was hanged on 20 October 1862.

Louis Bourdier, 1867

Louis Bourdier, a thirty-two-year-old Frenchman, a currier by trade, murdered thirty-three-year-old Mary Anne Snow (with whom he cohabited and had three children), on Tuesday 10 September 1867, at 3 Milstead Terrace, Old Kent Road, slitting her throat. She had threatened to leave him and he couldn't bear to part from her. Mary lived for some time after she had been attacked and was quite sensible when a doctor arrived, but died about two minutes afterwards from the 6-inch gash to her throat, which was between one and two inches deep in places and had severed veins and arteries on both sides of her neck. Found guilty of murder, Bourdier was hanged on 15 October 1867 by William Calcraft.

By 1859 the gaol was no longer named Horsemonger Lane Gaol but was now Surrey County Gaol, as Horsemonger Lane itself had been renamed Union Road (today called Harper Road). The gaol closed in 1878 and demolished in 1880. Thereafter, executions were carried out at Wandsworth. Today the site of Horsemonger Lane Gaol is a public park, Newington Gardens.

The Compters of Borough and Southwark

The Borough Compter, also known as Southwark Compter, was built in the sixteenth century within the walls of the old parish church of St Margaret's, which also housed an Assize court. This first compter was mostly used to incarcerate Southwark's petty offenders and debtors and survived until 1676 when it was destroyed by fire. A temporary compter was fashioned out of one of the buildings of the Marshalsea Prison, serving Southwark until it was replaced by a third compter, built in Mill Lane, Bermondsey, in 1687. Destroyed during the Gordon Riots of 1780, a fourth compter was built on the same site, surviving until 1848, when the building was converted to a female prison. This closed in 1852 and the building was demolished in 1855.

White Lion Prison, Southwark

This small prison for the County of Surrey, informally known as the 'Borough Gaol' existed from the sixteenth century and was situated in Borough High Street, close to the Marshalsea and King's Bench Prisons. Converted from the ancient White Lion Inn during Tudor times, it was replaced by Surrey County Gaol, initially referred to as the New Gaol but more usually known as Horsemonger Lane Gaol, constructed between 1791–99. When the King's Bench Prison was rebuilt between 1755–58, on a new site near the original prison, part of the buildings that once formed part of the medieval White Lion Inn were incorporated into the fabric.

Brixton Prison

Brixton was built in 1820 and opened as the Surrey House of Correction, with a capacity for 175 prisoners. It soon gained a reputation for being one of the worst prisons in London, and was noted for its small cells and poor living conditions. Almost from the outset, the prison was functioning over its capacity and overcrowding was a major problem, compounding its reputation for the severity of the regime there. Rarely fewer than 200 prisoners were being held at Brixton, but on occasions in excess of 400 were being crammed into what had rapidly become one of London's unhealthiest prisons. In 1821, Brixton became the first prison in London to install a tread-wheel, to be worked by prisoners who had been sentenced to hard labour.

Conditions for women were particularly harsh, with newly arrived female prisoners being required to spend four months in solitary confinement. Following this period and a female's introduction into the general prison population, she would be required to maintain a 'condition of silent association'.

The prison was gradually expanded to ease the problem of over-crowding but conditions at Brixton remained grim. In 1851 the Surrey magistrates closed Brixton and transferred prisoners to the newly built Wandsworth House of Correction. In 1853 Brixton House of Correction was purchased by the government to use as a prison for female convicts, principally as a correctional facility for women who opted for imprisonment rather than for penal transportation to Australia, although others preferred the comparative liberty offered by transportation rather than serving a long sentence in the grim austerity of a London prison.

Brixton became the first prison exclusively intended to hold women. The original treadwheel had been replaced by a treadmill. This in turn was superseded by a laundry once Brixton was turned over to women prisoners only, in which the women were put to work to launder not only their own linen and other items of washing, but also that brought in from other prisons. A nursery was opened for prisoners' children under the age of four years. And from 1860 prisoners were allowed to keep their children with them until the end of their sentence.

In 1882 Brixton became a military prison and remained in use for that purpose until 1898, when it became the trial and remand prison for London and the Home Counties, a function it still serves to this day, its primary purpose being to serve the local magistrates' courts, in addition to inner London crown courts. Conditions at Brixton remained notoriously unpleasant. When prisoners are locked in their cells in the evenings, the vacated communal areas are overrun with vermin.

More modern facilities have gradually been introduced over the years. There is a Learning Skills Centre, where inmates can pursue education courses, such as Information Technology, English, Mathematics and various art courses. There is also a gymnasium, where more physically inclined inmates can participate in accredited programmes. Today, Brixton is the oldest of London's prisons that still receives prisoners.

Fulham Prison
It seemed like radical ideas at the time in the nineteenth century, when prison reformers mooted the plan to reform criminals and prepare them for their return to society, rather than merely punishing them simply by leaving them incarcerated in a prison cell. In 1856, a

reformatory was opened in Fulham, with accommodation for 180 females, with the intention of training the inmates, taken there from various prisons as they were approaching the end of their sentences and teaching them the necessary skills to enable them to find work as domestic servants. Inmates were quick to take advantage of the comparatively relaxed rules and atmosphere and it was not long before the regime there had become more prison like. The buildings had also taken on the appearance of a normal prison, surrounded by a high wall and entered through a gateway topped with spikes. The authorities soon realised the experiment had failed. The facility was expanded to accommodate 400 adult females and renamed Fulham Prison in 1871. Fulham Prison closed in 1888.

Belmarsh Prison

Located in Thamesmead in the London Borough of Greenwich, occupying 60 acres, and built on part of the site of the former Royal Arsenal in Woolwich, Belmarsh Prison is categorised an adult male Category A prison.

Belmarsh Prison opened on 2 April 1991, adjacent to Woolwich Crown Court, with an operational capacity of 933. Belmarsh serves a dual role, serving the Central Criminal Court and Magistrates' Courts in south-east London, in addition to holding high security prisoners on remand or awaiting trial.

There are four residential house blocks:

House block one, holds prisoners serving on year or over.

House block two, holds prisoners with one year or less to serve.

House block three, holds induction prisoners, remand and also the vulnerable prisoners overflow.

House block four, holds vulnerable prisoners, drug-free spur and remand prisoners.

In addition to these four blocks, Belmarsh also contains a high security unit, holding high and exceptional risk category A prisoners.

Accommodation comprises a mixture of multi-occupancy cells, accounting for roughly 60% of capacity, the other 40% being given over to single-cell occupancy.

Belmarsh West Prison

At the time of writing (2011) London's newest prison is under construction in south-east London. Belmarsh West, is being built to the designs of architects Capita Symonds as a Category B local prison to accommodate 900 male prisoners. The new prison, due to be completed during the first half of 2012, will be centred around a 600-cell four-storey house block as well as including associated buildings to provide education, rehabilitation and support facilities.

CHAPTER 11

Ecclesiastical Prisons

Lambeth Palace

Lambeth Palace, situated on the south bank of the River Thames, across from the Palace of Westminster, has served as the official residence of the Archbishop of Canterbury since the twelfth century. In keeping with the tradition of many of England's ecclesiastical palaces, such as at the nearby Bishop of Winchester's palace, in Southwark (see The Clink, below), clerical offenders were imprisoned at Lambeth. Perhaps not surprisingly, during the Reformation, many Catholics were held there. At the outbreak of the Civil War it was used as a prison for the holding of Royalists and remained in use for that purpose until Charles II was restored to the throne in 1660. A tower built within the palace's precincts in 1435, became known as the 'Lollards' Tower', spurned by the legend that Lollards (considered to hold extremely dangerous views, and inspired by the teachings of John Wycliffe, desiring a bible in English, as opposed to Latin, amongst other 'radical' ideas for the time), treated as heretics by the church, were imprisoned there shortly after the tower was built. On 12 January 1414, thirty-nine Lollards were burned at St Giles' Fields. One 'suspected' Lollard sympathiser, Sir John Oldcastle (on whom Shakespeare based his character Sir John Falstaff), was arrested in 1413 but escaped. Having been recaptured in 1417, he died a most horrible death, being executed at St Giles' Fields, suspended in chains and roasted over a fire.

The Clink

The church of St Mary Overie (meaning over the water), which has its origins in the seventh century, was rebuilt in 1106 and destroyed by fire. Its rebuilding commenced in 1220 and continued for almost 200 years; and was to become the first major Gothic church in London. Known as St Saviours from 1539, and since 1905 as Southwark Cathedral, this was once a favourite place of sanctuary for those fleeing across London Bridge to escape the city's justice, gaining the entire area a reputation for licentiousness and villainy, which spread throughout Southwark and along Bankside (the area which today lies between Blackfriars and Southwark Bridge). Ownership of various lands in the vicinity was split, amongst others, between the Archbishop of Canterbury and the Cluniac Order, who inhabited the nearby priory at Bermondsey.

One of the most important landowners was the Bishop of Winchester, who had his residence there. Construction commenced on Winchester Palace (also known as Winchester House) in 1107 and continued until 1144, it was built as the Bishop of Winchester's London residence; and occupied by successive bishops from 1109 to 1626. Built during a time when bishops were often statesmen as well as clergymen, Winchester Palace was conveniently situated for the royal court at Westminster. Henry VIII reputedly met his fifth wife Catherine Howard at Winchester Palace in 1540.

Built to form part of Winchester Palace, between the River Thames, the common sewer and the bishop's fish ponds, was the bishop's lock up or prison. A prison had come under the jurisdiction of the Bishop of Winchester since as early as 860, probably in the form of a single cell in a priest's college. In medieval times it was usual for bishops to have cells in their palaces in which to hold those who offended against ecclesiastical law. The new building included two prisons, one for men and one for women. Prisoners were held securely in the dungeons which formed part of the cellars of the palace. The dungeons were highly inhospitable places with various types of irons to hold prisoners in some discomfort, manacles, chains and fetters. What grew to become one of the most notorious prisons in London's history, particularly feared for its dampness and squalid condition, became known from early in its existence as the 'Clink Prison'. The origins of the name are unknown but it is generally believed to be onomatopoeic, being derived from the striking of metal, the clinking and clanking of the prison's doors as they were locked and bolted, or the sound of the chains worn by the prisoners. The use of the phrase to be 'in the clink' passed into common English usage to mean 'be in prison'. As lords of the manor, the bishops held jurisdiction over offenders against the laws of the manor and those causing a breach of the peace. By 1180 much of the land in the vicinity was owned outright by The Clink and became known as 'The Liberty of the Clink'.

By the reign of Elizabeth I, thanks to its brothels, theatres and bear pits the area in the vicinity of Winchester Palace had become one of the most nefarious in the whole of London. For centuries before this, many of the brothels on old Bankside operated on land owned by the Bishop of Winchester and contributed a substantial income to the estate, as they were licensed and supervised by the bishop. The brothels were known as 'stewes', the prostitutes plying their trade there within the 'Liberty of the Bishop of Winchester' or 'The Liberty of The Clink', were nicknamed 'Winchester Geese'.

In 1450, The Clink was burned down and the prisoners set free by rioters during protests against the Statute of Labourers. The rioters raided Winchester Palace and murdered several clerics. Following these events Winchester Palace was rebuilt and enlarged and The Clink rose again. As well as the usual offenders debtors were also imprisoned there.

Life for prisoners in The Clink could be very harsh, particularly those without money to pay the gaolers to alleviate some of the inconveniences of being incarcerated there. Not untypically, the gaolers at The Clink were very poorly paid and it was necessary to resort to various and sometimes ingenious means in order to supplement their income. The gaolers extorted money from prisoners on their admission and release for turning the key (on entry or discharge), a practice from which 'turnkey' is derived. Prostitution became a feature within The Clink itself, with a portion of the proceeds being returned to the keeper of the prison. The hiring out of rooms within the prison provided another source of income. The hiring of various items to prisoners ranging from furniture, such as beds (otherwise some straw, and not always in a sanitary condition is at best all a prisoner was likely to receive), bedding, candles, fuel for heating and various foodstuffs. The gaolers also accepted payment for fitting lighter irons and for those willing or able to pay a higher fee, their complete removal. The unscrupulous activities even extended to imprisoned madams being allowed to administer the running of their brothels, for a suitable financial consideration; prisoners being allowed outside the prison to beg on payment of a fee; the poorest prisoners being obliged to beg at the grates which led up to the street level, often resorting to selling the clothes off their back in order to obtain coins to pay for food. Torture was also a feature at The Clink and a pillory and ducking stool were also located outside the prison.

During the reign of Henry VII, The Clink became a Royal Prison and during the following reign one particular Bishop of Winchester, Stephen Gardiner (*c.*1483–1555), appointed bishop in 1531, rebuilt The Clink in three buildings next to Winchester Palace. However, this did not result in an improvement in the conditions in which the unfortunate prisoners were kept. The 'Common' side of The Clink (poor side) became renowned for its filthy, unsavoury beds, which were described as being full of vermin. Some unfortunate wretches incarcerated there were naked and wracked with disease. One fearsome rat-infested dungeon, known as the 'Hole', was where many prisoners were simply left to die. Many died of gaol fever. The opportunistic, hypocritical sycophant Bishop Gardiner had a reputation for spending an inordinately high proportion of his time with his whores, and it was widely spoken about on Bankside that he had been 'bitten' by some of his Winchester Geese, which in colloquial parlance meant he had caught venereal disease. Having been sent to Rome to further Henry VIII's divorce from Catherine of Aragon, he supported the royal supremacy in his *De vera obedientia* (1535), and was instrumental in Thomas Cromwell's (Earl of Essex (*c*.1485–1540)) downfall; he himself imprisoned and deprived of his offices during the reign of Edward VI; released and restored by Mary I in 1553, whereupon he became an arch-persecutor of protestants. The Clink held many of them, including some high profile prisoners, such as John Hooper (1495–1555) Anglican Bishop of Gloucester and Worcester, who was taken from The Clink to be burned at the stake in Gloucester in February 1555, he being a martyr during the Marian Persecutions; as was John Bradford (1510–1555) held prisoner in The Clink prior to his martyrdom at Smithfield on 1 July 1555.

During the reign of Elizabeth I many Catholics were incarcerated in The Clink, along with dissenting Protestants and debtors. When the bishop's powers were suppressed in 1642 Winchester Palace was converted to a prison for Civil War Royalists. In 1649 the former bishop's palace was sold to a property developer and converted for various uses from shops to dye houses. Although the Clink continued to be used as a prison, mostly for debtors, it became severely decayed. Records show that in 1732 only two prisoners were recorded as being held there, The Clink being of little use as a prison because of its dilapidated condition. The Clink continued to deteriorate until it was of no further use as a prison. In 1745 a house in Bankside was used as a replacement and in 1776 was again taking in debtors. This was burned down during the Gordon Riots of 1780 and never rebuilt, so the history of The Clink came to an end.

A museum known as The Clink Museum is located on part of or close to the actual site of The Clink adjacent to the ruins of Winchester Palace.

Ely Place

The bishop's palace known as Ely Place was built towards the end of the twelfth century between Holborn and the city walls, to serve as the London residence for the Bishops of Ely. An early mention of it is in 1286, when the bishop was John de Kirkby. In keeping with other such palaces elsewhere in London, Ely Place contained a prison for holding clerical offenders. In 1643 Ely Place itself became a prison by order of the Long Parliament and the Serjeant-at Arms was appointed Keeper. When the bishops again took up residence there, the original prison like many other prisons, such as The Clink Prison, took in debtors. An eighteenth century commentator included this prison on his list of the harshest prisons in England. He wrote:

> In the Bishop of Ely's prison, prisoners unable to pay for 'easement of irons' were chained to the floor on their backs, with a spiked collar around the neck and heavy iron bars over the legs, until they somehow found the money.

Ely Place remained the London residence of the bishops of Ely until 1772, when it was sold to the Crown and Edmund Keene Bishop of Ely, commissioned a new Ely Place, constructed in Dover Street, Mayfair, to the designs of architect Robert Taylor. Taylor also designed the cul-de-sac of fine houses, with its distinctive beadle's gatehouse, built on the site of the original Ely Place.

CHAPTER 12

Miscellaneous and Notable Small Prisons and Lock-ups

Sponging (or Spunging) Houses

Sponging houses existed throughout London for centuries. Although they held debtors, they were not prisons as such but were used as a stop-gap between a debtor being arrested and his or her eventual incarceration (or satisfactory settlement of his debts) in one of London's many debtors' prisons. They were usually private homes, often the bailiff's own home. When a person got into debt, or indeed simply refused to pay for items or services they had received, their creditor would lay a complaint concerning that particular individual's indebtedness with the sheriff. Accordingly, the sheriff would instruct his bailiff to take the debtor in charge and the debtor would then be taken to a sponging house; where it was hoped the necessity of his or her removal to a debtors' prison could be alleviated by the debtor making an arrangement of some kind with his creditors.

The name for a 'sponging house' is derived from an actual sponge, based on the simple fact that a sponge when squeezed, readily gave up what it had absorbed. To coin-a-phrase, it goes without saying the individuals taken to yields its contents. The debtors delivered to London's sponging houses were certainly 'squeezed' to see what ready money could be got out of them. Indeed, the squeezing did not only exercise considerable effort on behalf of the creditors, but a debtor was also squeezed for the benefit of the Keeper of the sponging house, as he was required to pay rent for his lodgings and food whilst staying there, which were invariably levied at an extortionately high price. However, should a debtor not be able to settle matters to the satisfaction of his creditors, he was taken before a court and committed to a debtors' prison.

The Tun, Cornhill

From 1283 until 1401, a small house of correction stood in Cornhill. Known as 'The Tun', it was used to incarcerate street walkers and lewd women. It was built adjacent to an ancient well, the site of which today is marked by an iron pump, erected in 1799.

The Savoy

The original medieval Savoy Palace, home of John of Gaunt, Duke of Lancaster, which fronted the River Thames, was almost completely destroyed during the Peasant's Revolt in 1381. Rebuilt in the sixteenth century, the former palace became a hospital, then served various other purposes including being used as an army barracks. In 1695, the Savoy's building was adapted or rebuilt to serve as a military prison, for the incarceration of military offenders and deserters. This prison survived until 1793. Today the Savoy Theatre and Savoy Hotel stands on its site.

Neptune Street Prison

In 1688, James II ordered that there should be a court house with a prison for the Liberties of the Tower of London, which the Tower itself, the land on Tower Hill and, from the seventeenth century onward, the small area of the Minories, Old Artillery Ground and Well Close. A court house and prison was duly erected in Well Close at the corner of Neptune Street, officially the gaol of the Tower Royalty. The Liberties of the Tower of London were outside the jurisdiction of the City of London and the County of Middlesex. To the governance of the Tower was granted the authority for the maintenance of law and order, to try by appointed magistrates, sitting with the governor of the Tower, before whom were brought all persons within the Tower Liberties accused of treason and felony as well as minor offences. Adjacent to the Court House, and interconnecting with it, was a public house known as the Cock and Neptune, the landlord of which acted as gaoler to the court when the Justices were sitting. In the nineteenth century G R Sims wrote:

> ... The prison, which was in Neptune Street, was originally one in which poor debtors were confined for indefinite periods ...

John Howard, the philanthropist, visited the prison in 1777 and noted there were very few prisoners to be seen there. By 1792, the prison was still in use but was described as 'ruinous'. However, it continued to serve the Liberties of the Tower of London well into the next century and was still in use when the Duke of Wellington was Governor of the Tower (1826–52). However, later in the century, the old prison subsequently became a lodging house.

Watch Houses and Round Houses

Queen Mary I (reigned 1553–58) ordered cages and stocks to be erected in every parish in London. These were used to hold drunks or those breaching the peace, especially at night, before they could be taken before magistrates the following morning. Amongst the cages were those at London Bridge and Willesden.

Many of the wealthier parishes constructed large brick round houses or watch houses, although some already had a watch house within the parish boundaries. Watch houses, many of which contained temporary holding facilities, had been situated throughout London since the reign of Edward I (1272–1307). The watch used to patrol the streets and keep the peace. Later watch houses included St Marylebone Watch House, established in 1753 and Hampstead Watch House, established in 1829. Among the most well-known round houses were St Anns' Round House, Soho, where Jack Sheppard was imprisoned following his arrest in May 1724 for attempting to steal a man's watch in Leicester Fields. Sheppard had also been held in St Giles' Round House some years earlier, having been informed on by his brother, Thomas, who was incarcerated in Newgate for trying to sell some stolen goods. However, young Jack did not remain a prisoner there for long, as he soon made his escape through the roof.

St Martin's Roundhouse, was arguably the most notorious of London's round houses. Located opposite the church of St Martin's in the Fields, Savage, Merchant and Gregory were taken there for the night following the stabbing of James Sinclair in Robinson's Coffee House, on 27 November 1727 (see pages 39–41), it was also the scene of an outrage in July 1742. Some constables, having been drinking heavily, became over-zealous regarding their authority and took it upon themselves to arrest as many citizens as they could, and took a large number of women in charge. Into one room they crammed twenty-five women, with little air (through inadequate ventilation for so many souls) and no water. On the following morning, four women were discovered to have died and two more passed away later. Once news got out, the fury of the mob knew no bounds and the entire building was torn down the next day. William Baird, the Keeper of St Martin's Roundhouse, was convicted of murder and transported to America.

The Lock up at Cannon Hall, Hampstead

Cannon Hall, the magnificent Queen Anne mansion, situated in Hampstead, once housed a magistrates' court in part of the stable block. Within the perimeter wall of the hall in Cannon Lane, in about

1730, was built a lock up. This parish lock-up contained a dark, single cell. It was used for about a hundred years, until the newly formed Hampstead Police Force opened its Watch House in Holly Mount, in 1829, which contained its own holding facilities.

The Hulks

The Hulks were former naval ships no longer considered either useful, being too worn-out to be used in combat, or ships which were no longer seaworthy, converted for use as prison ships, moored in the vicinity of Woolwich and Plumstead Marshes. They came about following the American War of Independence when transportation of prisoners to America ended. To ease the severe overcrowding in prisons, the creation of temporary prisons in hulks was considered the best practical solution.

The first hulk, the *Justitia*, an old Indiaman, was anchored near Woolwich in 1776. Convicts were put to hard labour on shore. Conditions on board the hulks were harsh. The food was hopelessly inadequate and sanitary conditions bordering on perilous. What occurred on the *Justita* was not untypical of life for prisoners in the hulks. In the first eighteen months, of the 632 convicts taken on board, 176 of them died. By 1841, there were eleven hulks moored in the River Thames. When transportation to Australia and other colonies began, convicts awaiting transportation were temporarily held in the hulks. The hulks remained in use until 1859.

Sources and Further Reading

London Metropolitan Archives Selective List:
Newgate Prison CLA/035
Calendars of Indictments CLA/047/LJ/10, MJ/C/J,OB/C/J
Visiting Justices Minutes 1814-77 CLA/035/02/050–052
Wood Street Compter CLA/028/02/001–003
Compter CLA/032/01/037
Giltspur Street Compter CLA/029
Southwark Compter (Borough) CLA 031
Miscellaneous records relating to prisons and compters CLA/032
Bridewell Hospital CLC/275
Ludgate Prison CLA/033
Whitecross Street Prison CLA/034
Middlesex Prisons MJ/SB/B
New Prison Clerkenwell MA/G/CLE
Middlesex House of Correction Cold Bath Fields MA/G/CBF
Holloway Prison CLA/003
Wandsworth Prison ACC/3444
Wormwood Scrubs LMA/4417

Birkenhead, Earl of, *Strafford*, Hutchinson & Co, London, 1938
Burghclere, Lady, *Strafford* (2 vols), Macmillan & Co, London, 1931
Byrne, Richard, *Prisons and Punishments of London*, Harrap, London, 1989
Clamp, John, *Holloway Prison. The Place and People*, David & Charles, Newton Abbot, 1974
Crew, Albert, *London Prisons of Today and Yesterday*, Ivor Nicholson & Watson Ltd, London, 1933
Herber, Mark, *Criminal London*, Phillimore, Stroud, 2002
Howse, Geoffrey, *Foul Deed & Suspicious Death in London's East End*, Wharncliffe Books, Barnsley, 2005
Howse, Geoffrey, *Foul Deeds & Suspicious Deaths in London's West End*, Wharncliffe Books, Barnsley, 2006

Howse, Geoffrey, *The A to Z of London Murders*, Wharncliffe Books, Barnsley, 2007

Irving H B, *Trial of Franz Müller*, William Hodge & Co, 1911

Laing, D (Ed), *Baillie's Letter and Journals 1637–62*

Rice-Davies, Mandy (with Shirley Flack), *Mandy*, Michael Joseph, London, 1980

Wade, C E, *John Pym*, Sir Isaac Pitman & Sons, London, 1912

Wedgewood, C V, *Strafford 1593–1641*, Jonathan Cape, London, 1935

Young, Filson, *Trial of Bywaters And Thompson*, William Hodge & Co Ltd, 1923

Young, Filson, *Trial of The Seddons*, William Hodge & Co Ltd, 1914

Index